WE LIVED HERE:
STORIES OF SEATTLE'S CENTRAL AREA

WE LIVED HERE:
STORIES OF SEATTLE'S CENTRAL AREA

Interviews by Madeline Crowley

FALL 2019

CHIN MUSIC
PRESS

SEATTLE

Publisher:
Chin Music Press
1501 Pike Place #329
Seattle, WA 98101

www.chinmusicpress.com

ISBN: 9781634059787
Library of Congress Cataloging-in-Publication data is available upon request.
First [1] edition
Cover and page design by Kimberly Kent
Cover photos: Madeline Crowley, Aaron Dixon, Jack Dunn, Dee Goto.

Printed in the USA

Table of Contents:

To my parents and my husband,
without whom this book would not exist.

INTRODUCTION

Due to my ebullient dog, I knew nearly every neighbor over the many blocks in every direction in my Central Area Seattle neighborhood. Often, those who stopped to chat were retired, many of them Black folks whose family had come here during the Great Migration north to work during the World War II war effort. Some were in family homes dating back nearly eighty years. Usually, they'd generously share warm, vivid tales of the neighborhood as it was: packed with nightclubs, filled with kids playing on streets, fueled with music. But they'd also talk about the difficulties they faced as the neighborhood changed and how that change has brought a pall of quiet.

As I listened to those memories, I began to discern how the history of this fascinating and unique area was one largely unknown but to those who'd lived here. Larger Seattle seemed generally ignorant of the Central Area's history—despite the fact that the neighborhood nurtured Ray Charles, Quincy Jones, Jimi Hendrix, and very briefly Bruce Lee. Not to mention that the first Black FBI agent in Washington state had grown up on the same turf as radicals of every stripe. Many neighbors reminisced about the healthy and well-respected Black Panther Party as well as the neighborhood police officers and firemen.

In 2012, the entire neighborhood rallied together in grief and shock—momentarily—in the aftermath of the tragic shooting of Justin Ferrari. Then very quickly, among some vocal parties, conversation about the community became reductively and hurtfully 'us-them.' I overheard some wildly non-factual information being shared and realized there was a compelling need to collect and share local stories, to convey the complexity of the actual history here in our shared community. I set out to do interviews to capture a history that was fast disappearing with the sale or removal of every house in the Central Area.

As I began to record and capture their stories, I tried to create a balance of interviews—differing occupations, politics, religions, ancestries and races—despite the fact that interesting people often demurred from participation. I was posting the interviews on a blog, 'People from the Central Area and Their Stories,' and for this and many other reasons, I could understand why some wouldn't want to participate.

This project isn't the work of journalism or of analysis; it is the work of listening. Sadly, that is a far rarer experience than it was twenty years ago and rarer than it should be in our global digital culture. Many people, especially our elders, are hungry to be listened to for even a half hour. A great deal of the experiences that shape the emotional core of someone, of lived experience—

particularly the bitter things in life—are held, or carried, silently. That information is sometimes not shared even with spouses, or family, and especially their children. Sometimes the very best and sometimes the worst that a person has experienced isn't fully known by even those closest to them.

It wouldn't be an exaggeration to say that all the memories entrusted to me have schooled me; I have had over fifty-six teachers (as not every interview has been made public). Many of those people told their stories with their hearts wide open—and I've found an open heart can inspire love. And so nearly fifty-six times, I experienced a very specific type of love—the love of one heart opening to another. There is a kind of magic in sympathy or empathy—in listening without judgment to someone's truth, as they felt it to be.

Memory isn't Fact nor absolute Truth; it's memory, it's selective, it's self-reinforcing and it's malleable. Still, in every case, it's how that person made sense of the events of their lives. In most cases after listening to them speak, then transcribing and editing their words, I was changed—perhaps in my outlook, perhaps in my knowledge, perhaps in my understanding but after nearly every interview I was different than before the interview.

Since these interviews were conducted—by the time this book went to press—quite a number of those interviewed are no longer in our community and more than ten percent are lost to us. It's not surprising when a preponderance of the people were in their eighties, but it is lucky that their accounts of their lives are preserved for us, for our city, for their communities and their families in these pages.

This project, begun in 2012 and published years later, has been a graduate school in so many things– learning to interview, to preserve documentation, to transcribe, to learn the basics of photography, lighting, and photo editing as well as photo restoration. I worked with Seattle University to find interns, manage their projects and encountered some very special people who chose to do some transcription. And as significantly, some of the grants or awards I gratefully received included aspects that also helped me develop new skills, like having to speak in public. All of that too has enlarged me and my capabilities. I am deeply grateful for all I've learned from doing this, to the people of the Central Area past and present, to the generosity of King County and the City of Seattle and to so many of its organizations. I'm deeply grateful for every bit of this experience.

—Madeline Crowley

12TH AVE TO 23RD AVE

BETWEEN

MADISON & YESLER WAY

Aaron Dixon has survived bullets, betrayals and intrigues while fighting for social justice with the Black Panther Party. Despite all that, he retains an almost otherworldly calm, charm and warmth that draws people to him.

"Whenever I meet any of my friends from childhood we all agree we were really lucky to be growing up in Seattle and particularly in Madrona. It was like a cocoon. We were almost protected from what was going on in the outside world. It was a really special place and a special time."

YOU MENTIONED IN YOUR BOOK, *MY PEOPLE ARE RISING*, THAT YOUR EARLY CHILDHOOD WAS IN CHICAGO. WHAT WAS YOUR NEIGHBORHOOD LIKE IN CHICAGO?

The south side of Chicago, it was all Black, Black every day, all day. Everywhere you went, there was nothing but Black people. Policemen, all the businesses, everything was all Black.

WAS THE DIVERSITY A SHOCK WHEN YOU FIRST MOVED TO THE CENTRAL DISTRICT?

Well, it was different. We had also lived in Champaign, Illinois, in Burch Village. My mother says it wasn't a housing project, but it was. It was a housing project. It was all Black, everyone in Burch Village was Black. The only White people we saw were our teachers and the milkman and the breadman who came by to deliver.

I wouldn't say it was a shock when we first came here and saw such diversity, because we were so young. When you're little, you just take everything in. For my parents this neighborhood was the perfect environment, especially for my father.

WHAT WERE YOUR FIRST IMPRESSIONS OF MADRONA WHEN YOU WERE SMALL?

I remember first being impressed with how big the trees and houses were. I was happy that the Madrona Playground was right across the street from our house. When you're young and you move into someplace new, though, your biggest issue is trying to fit in with the kids in the neighborhood. That took a little time. It didn't take much time, though. Very quickly we felt we were privileged to live on top of this big hill in this nice neighborhood.

WHAT ABOUT THE OTHER KIDS IN THE NEIGHBORHOOD?

I mentioned this in my book. Like kids anywhere, when you're new you have to fight to fit in; it's how you learn how to fit in. One impression that stuck out was there was so many different types of nationalities in the area: Filipino, Chinese, Japanese, White kids. But on the other side of 34th Avenue, it was all White. It wasn't long before we had friends of all ethnicities. And White friends too. We had experiences with families of different ethnicities as we grew up, that made it a really special place to grow up.

DID YOU HAVE A RELATIVELY HAPPY CHILDHOOD HERE?

I did. It was happy. Whenever I meet any of my friends from childhood, we all agree we were really lucky to be growing up in Seattle and particularly in Madrona. It was like a cocoon. We were almost protected from what was going on in the outside world. It was a really special place and a special time.

I'VE HEARD THE NEIGHBORHOOD NOW IS COMPARATIVELY SEDATE. WHEN YOU WERE GROWING UP IN THE SIXTIES AND SEVENTIES, IS IT TRUE THAT THE COMMUNITY HAD MORE PARTIES AND MORE KIDS PLAYING IN THE STREETS?

That was the time of the baby boom generation; there were just so many other kids around. There were kids everywhere. Seattle had to build all these schools in this area: Madrona, Leschi, Mt. Baker. There were so many more kids in the neighborhood than there are today.

WAS THE STYLE OF CHILD-REARING BACK THEN, 'GET OUT OF THE HOUSE AND GO PLAY OUTSIDE?'

It was. There was no hanging in the house. There was no lying around watching TV. We didn't even know the word 'boring.' It was a different time. There weren't any video games. There was nothing like that. Every year, every spring, we built our own go-karts. We used the parts from our Christmas presents like the wheels from skates. We made bows and arrows; we made stilts, skateboards and slingshots. Lots of kids had BB guns; there was no problem having a BB gun back then. Some kids had .22s. We just found so many things to do in the park across the street. We'd play Ping-Pong on rainy days. You just couldn't be in the house; your parents weren't going to put up with that. There was so much to do.

WAS THE DIVERSITY OF THE NEIGHBORHOOD COMMON AT THAT TIME OR WAS SEATTLE UNUSUAL IN THAT RESPECT?

No, Los Angeles, Oakland were also mixed. Blacks and Asians lived together at that time. Richard Aoki, who became the field marshal of the Black Panther Party, he lived in a Black neighborhood.

PERHAPS THAT'S A WEST COAST THING?

Yes, that is definitely a West Coast thing. We're closer geographically to Asia so you naturally have more Japanese here than you do on the East Coast, and Chinese, too.

WHEN DID YOU BECOME FRIENDS WITH GUY KUROSE? (LATER A PEACE ACTIVIST AND KARATE BLACK BELT.)

My younger brothers both went to Madrona Elementary and I finished my last year at Coleman Elementary School. My brother Elmer had a Japanese friend named Hugo who was Guy's older brother. I knew Hugo before I knew Guy. I got to know Guy in junior high.

IT'S INTERESTING THAT THERE WERE JAPANESE PEOPLE WHO WERE INVOLVED IN THE PANTHER PARTY, BUT WERE THERE ALSO CHINESE PEOPLE?

No, but there were Chinese people we'd gone to school with who were activists involved in other organizations, like Michael Woo, Director of Got Green, the activist group fighting poverty and global warming.

13

DO YOU THINK THE JAPANESE INVOLVEMENT AND SUPPORT OF THE BLACK PANTHER PARTY HAD TO DO WITH INTERNMENT?

I don't know. Maybe so. The internment issue did affect older Japanese people. They really came out and supported the Panthers with donations and in lots of other ways. At the time, I didn't know why they supported us. It was puzzling to me but it would make sense if it had been because of their experience of internment.

HOW DID YOUR FAMILY REACT WHEN YOU JOINED THE BLACK PANTHERS?

My parents were supportive of that decision. Yet, they did tell me earlier, 'No, you shouldn't join the Marines.' They did say that. I was a college student so they understood I would make my (own) decisions. Also, I think they had a sense of this change in the culture that was beginning to take place, as well as all the events of the Sixties, especially the assassinations. They already had a political consciousness and political awareness so they could see the how the Civil Rights Movement moved into the Black Power Movement. We just became part of that movement.

WERE THEY TERRIFIED FOR YOU, HAVING HAD THAT HISTORICAL KNOWLEDGE OF WHAT HAD HAPPENED IN THE PAST TO THOSE WHO STOOD UP TO MAINSTREAM AUTHORITY?

I don't know if they were terrified. I think it was probably similar to sending your child off to war, you're worried about them, you want them to come home, but if they're fighting for a just cause you accept that this is what they have to do. They never expressed any fear to us (kids), even though they got calls in the middle of the night making threats on our lives, they never told us until much later. They kept that to themselves.

IT SOUNDS LIKE A SIGNIFICANT REASON THE BLACK PANTHER PARTY IN SEATTLE WASN'T SMASHED AS IT WAS IN OTHER PLACES WAS BECAUSE IT HAD BROAD, LOCAL SUPPORT. DUE TO THE QUALITIES THAT YOU AND YOUR BROTHER ELMER HAD, THE PARTY YOU BUILT HERE WAS VIEWED AS A PART OF THE LARGER COMMUNITY. DO YOU REMEMBER OTHER INSTANCES OF SUPPORT FROM THE NEIGHBORHOOD?

14

We used to do fundraising events; we'd sell soul-food dinners. All the neighborhood women would get together to cook these dinners, and we'd deliver them to people. The people supported us by buying the food for the dinners while others bought the dinners. Also, there was a huge music scene in this neighborhood. There were a lot of bands and a lot of musicians in this neighborhood. Elmer was in a couple of bands too. The musicians were always willing to support us by playing fundraisers. We had one at Garfield Park. We never had a problem getting two or three bands to participate.

There was other significant support though; I mention this in the book. There was a man, an undertaker at a funeral parlor on 12th Avenue. He called and told us to come over because he had something for us. Inside, there was a line of caskets but one of them was filled with rifles. He went out of his way to get these rifles for the party. They were old weapons but they were weapons nonetheless. That meant a lot to us.

Then, there was the old Black man who worked for the Justice Department. He went way out of his way to warn us they planned to eliminate us.

There were so many different types of support. Mr. Melonson lived four houses down from us. He worked at Boeing and was originally from Texas. He had a big family, seven kids. All his kids went to Catholic School. He was very conservative and strict with his kids. When we joined the party, he told his kids not to associate with us. One night, there was an incident. It was probably a set-up by informants who infiltrated the party. We were all walking along together and suddenly they shot at some police officers. Then, they disappeared. I found myself alone. I had to hide so I ran into Mr. Melonson's backyard, but I had forgotten he had these ten-foot tall bushes and a fence so there was no way out. I heard the policemen getting out of their cars and then coming up the front stairs. I pulled my gun out, I thought, 'This is it.' Then, Mr. Melonson came out onto the back porch and silently waved me inside. After I was hidden inside, the police came in the backyard looking for me. Mr. Melonson saved my life.

Then, I also go into this in the book in more detail, but Seattle Mayor Wes Uhlman also prevented the ATF (Federal Bureau of Alcohol, Tobacco and Firearms), who had days prior launched deadly assaults on other branches of the Black Panther Party, from coming in and launching an assault on the Black Panther Headquarters here. He told them if they attempted to raid our office, he'd send the Police in our defense. I remain grateful for that.

JUMPING BACK TO THE EARLIER MENTION OF BEING CATHOLIC. THIS HAS COME UP IN OTHER CONVERSATIONS I'VE HAD ABOUT THE NEIGHBORHOOD. PEOPLE WILL TALK ABOUT BLACK CATHOLICS EXPRESSING A SENSE OF SUPERIORITY OVER OTHER BLACKS. IS THERE A SOCIO-ECONOMIC DIFFERENCE?

There is. It's probably even more so now. Catholic school costs money. When I was a kid, I wanted to go to Catholic school or to the military academy. We felt like they were getting a better education than we were. And they were getting to wear those uniforms. Later, I did put my daughter into St. Therese when she was in middle school. A lot of people from a higher social-economic category had their kids in Catholic schools. I think that now there's an even bigger difference between families who can afford that and families who can't.

WHAT DO YOU SEE AS THE BIGGEST CHANGES IN THE NEIGHBORHOOD SINCE YOU WERE YOUNG?

Well, the lack of kids in the area. There used to be kids of all ages out playing in the street. Sometimes, when I go to the Madrona Park I see only young kids with their parents. When we were kids playing at the park, there were no parents there. That was a place for kids. Parents would send their kids over to the park to be with other kids.

Also, people are definitely not as friendly as they used to be. People aren't friendly; they're not open. When you walk down the street, no one says, "Hi." They don't acknowledge you; they don't nod at you and recognize your existence. When I was growing up here, we knew everybody in the neighborhood, White, Black, pink, red, it didn't matter. Everybody knew everybody. Everybody was friendly to everybody. This area was a community.

Doug Chin is a serious, accomplished man with a winning, deadpan sense of humor. His family was one of the first Chinese American families to settle in the Central Area. He is an author and historian and was an activist in the 1970s. Doug will tell you what you need to hear, in no uncertain terms.

'*We never used to call it the Central Area; if you asked me where I lived, I'd say near Providence, or pretty close to Garfield. Everybody knew Providence Hospital. When I came back in in the 1970s from the Bay Area, they called it the ghetto and now they call it the Central Area. Since I had lived here in the 1940s, it was like, 'What are you talking about, man?' The neighborhood kept being called different things.*"

Doug on the 1940s Central Area:

In the 1940s, when I was around six or seven years old, we'd play kick-the-can down the road until sometimes midnight. We'd play in the street, me and my brothers and the White kids across the street, and the Black kids from next door, we'd play together all the time. Especially summertime, we'd play mostly in the streets but sometimes we'd go to Leschi and stuff. We didn't have this elaborate playground equipment in the parks.

My family lived on 19th and Fir for a couple of years, sharing the house with another family. Then, my parents got a house on 17th, between Jefferson and Alder, and right across the street was a synagogue. In my early years there were a lot of synagogues in that area, four or five within a few blocks.

When I was young, I remember Jewish people walking to synagogue on Saturdays. Also, the Sisters of Providence would walk around the neighborhood in their habits so when they appeared everybody had to be polite. The Sisters lived over on 18th and Marion; that house still stands. They were the Sisters of Providence of Providence Hospital. They also taught the Chinese ladies English.

As the years progressed, more and more Blacks moved in. The Central Area was in transition; when I was born it was predominantly White working class. By the mid-forties it started to change; almost daily I'd see a White family moving out of the neighborhood. And people of color were moving in. When I left to join the army in 1960 it was still pretty mixed. Well over fifty percent Asian, a lot of Japanese and African Americans. As it changed, it became more and more Black and Japanese.

DOUG ON THE 1950S CENTRAL AREA:

It was a pretty interesting neighborhood. I was growing up and playing basketball; I was quick. If I'd gone to another school, I would have made the team. I couldn't make Garfield's team because they were too good.

I might be small but I used to be athletic. I used to play ball all the time. The guys wanted to play sports like basketball, football and baseball. There were pick-up games in the parks. Most of the guys playing sports were Japanese and African American, with some Chinese. They established a Boys Club on Spruce and 19th in 1954, and we used to hang out there all the time to play sports. You'd hang out there after school then go home and eat, then go back and play some more.

Sometimes we'd go steal stuff like Coca Cola from the plant on 14th between Spruce and Cherry. They used to make Coke there, the trucks would be there, and we'd lift the fence up and crawl under and grab a whole case. Those bottles are heavy. We'd get the whole thing and then realize what the hell are we going to do with all this? We'd run down the street at nighttime. It was a fun time in those days. We had some good times.

We used to hang out at that Buddhist Temple on Main Street and play basketball inside. Every Saturday they'd show samurai movies—for free. We were all there. Lots of people would go there; on Saturday nights that place was packed.

In the Fifties, race relations were really good, especially if you played ball. There was a Stern's Grocery Store on 19th and Spruce and everybody used to go there to buy their meat. In those days there were a lot of small stores and the supermarkets were just starting to appear, so you'd go to the grocery store and then the bakery on 14th and Alder. We'd get bread and donuts and stuff. It was where the Juvenile Detention is now. They had the best bread; everybody would go there to get bread. Wonder Bread used to be there too on Jackson Street. It was pretty good. The area was definitely not like it is now.

We used to never call it the Central Area; if you asked me where I lived, I'd say near Providence, or pretty close to Garfield. Everybody knew Providence Hospital. When I came back in the 1970s from the Bay Area, they called it the ghetto and now they call it the Central Area. Since I had lived here in the 1940s, it was like, what are you talking about, man? The neighborhood kept being called different things.

DOUG ON THE 1960S CENTRAL AREA:

A lot of things centered around Garfield High School; that was the big institution, everybody knew Garfield because it was good at sports. There was a music scene too. The big hit was Ron Holden, *Love You So*. He wrote it in prison and when he got out he recorded it. His dad, Oscar and his brother, Dave, are famous musicians too. Jimi Hendrix went to school when I was there but I don't remember that. My next door neighbor said, 'Don't you remember he used to come over to our house,' but I don't remember. I don't remember the guy.

And the Japanese had this group, the Skyliners; they used to play here and in Las Vegas. The former music instructor at Washington Junior High was the band leader. We had some other groups, Charles Woodbury, and they had a rock-and-roll scene. I never went, but a lot of my Black friends went to Birdland on Madison. Ray Charles used to play there. Madison was hopping; people were excited about going out to Birdland.

I have to say that in the mid-sixties my family actually moved; a lot of the Chinese and Japanese families moved because there was too much racial tension between the Blacks and, well, everybody. They were really angry. People told me they were walking on 23rd Avenue and they'd get rocks thrown at them.

DOUG ON BEING PART OF FIRST CHINESE AMERICAN FAMILY IN THE CENTRAL AREA:

I need to give you some background. My great aunt's husband and her family, the Dong Family, used to be the head of Chong Wa. This was the Chinese umbrella organization, consisting of tongs and family associations. My great uncle, Mr. Dong, was also the head of a trading company and a curio shop on 2nd and Seneca. That land was later sold to the Washington Mutual Bank. He was a big-time merchant. He was one of the very first Chinese Americans to move into the Central Area.

My mother was born in Norfolk, Virginia, but she went back to Guangdong Province in China. She came back to America in 1937 because my dad was here. My father came in the second decade of the 1900s, and he came to work as a houseboy for my Great Uncle Dong. He was able to come despite the Chinese Exclusion Act because he came as a student. The act didn't allow laborers, so you had to be a student, merchant or a diplomat. He went back to China, so to come back to the US he had to come as a merchant for my grand-uncle's business. My father worked at the curio shop.

Later, my dad was a waiter. He saved money and probably inherited from my aunt when she died, so he opened a Chinese restaurant on Capitol Hill. We used to work there when I was in junior high and high school in the mid 1950s. Sometimes my friends would come up there to eat.

I just knew we weren't living in Magnolia or Broadmoor but we thought, 'It is what it is.' We knew we weren't well off. We weren't impoverished or homeless. We heard about places like Laurelhurst, but it was like hearing about Hollywood. No one we knew went there or lived there. But it (the Central Area) was never thought of as, 'Oh, it's so dirty and there are vacant houses.' You just accepted that there were a few houses that weren't well maintained. It wasn't so bad that houses were getting condemned. Some people took care of their yard; some people didn't.

DID GROWING UP IN THIS NEIGHBORHOOD PREPARE YOU FOR GOING INTO THE SERVICE?

I think knowing people from different races helped not only in the Army but in employment. You know how to relate to people. You're not surprised if someone does this or that because you've seen other cultures; that's a benefit. I worked in government most of my life, doing community relations, working with people with different backgrounds.

IS THERE ANYTHING YOU MISS FROM THE OLD NEIGHBORHOOD?

Growing up here you learned appreciation for racial relations, civil rights and appreciation for different cultures. You also learned about how people from different income levels face different challenges. When I was a kid, you went to the dentist only if your teeth were falling out; you only went to the doctor when you were pretty damn sick. You realize (that people experience) different things because of the environment they lived in. It was a good experience, to see and live through different situations. Then, you compare that to the American Dream and you see what it is and what it can be. I say this, though, I don't think the poverty that I lived around was as bad as it was in other areas in the US.

WHAT DO YOU THINK OF HOW IT'S CHANGED?

Physically, it's better now. The houses are renovated and there's new construction. It looks better nowadays, I hate to admit it, but it looks better than it did in the 1950s and Sixties because then there was a lot of blight. With gentrification my perception is that a lot of African Americans have moved out and some of Asians are moving back into the area, as well as White folks moving down from Capitol Hill, as the Central Area is more affordable.

Bob Santos sparkled with energy, charisma and depth—that very energy allowed him to accomplish real change in Seattle—and he was such fun. Growing up in the Central Area of the 1940s, with its multi-ethnic communities, laid the foundation for him to become an enormously effective community leader.

> '*But the kids of those immigrants, we accepted each other. That's why Seattle became a little bit more liberal in the mix of races than did other neighborhoods in other cities. In San Francisco and Los Angeles you had a separate Chinatown, a separate Japantown and a separate Manilatown. Here it was the same area; everyone was together. So, it was natural for the kids of immigrants growing up together to interface with other kids. That made Seattle become, then, a leader in that kind of (intercultural) Civil Rights Movement.*"

Bob on his life in the Central Area:

I was born in 1934 in Seattle's International District (the ID). My dad was professional prizefighter and my parents lived in the ID in the early 1930s. Then, my mother passed away in 1935. My dad couldn't take care of my older brother and me. He was a widower and his fighting career caused him to slowly lose his eyesight due to boxing injuries. Eventually an aunt, my father's sister, took us in. They lived in the Central Area on 14th and Spruce and later on 14th and Columbia.

When my father completely lost his eyesight in 1945, I became his seeing-eye dog, so I would come down from the Central Area to the NP Hotel in the ID to take care of him. I lived in the Central Area and went to school there. I was running back and forth between the two neighborhoods so I could take care of Dad.

I hung out with kids in the Central Area, mostly at the playground at the old Maryknoll School. That was a missionary school; the Sisters came in the 1920s on a mission to convert Asian Americans, Japanese nationals and Japanese Americans to the Catholic faith. They established the church and school between 16th and 17th Avenues. Ninety percent of us were Japanese and the rest were kids from the neighborhood. I attended Maryknoll Elementary for kindergarten and first grade.

I was in first grade in 1942, when our neighbor's kids, the Japanese kids, were rounded up and taken to concentration camps. First to Puyallup and then Idaho. After that, the school became much more like a community center. The church still operated during the war but the school closed. The Filipino community grew around that church. Initially, it was Japanese and then it became Filipino during the war years.

There were a couple of German families in the church too: the Dodenhoff family and the Schmidt family. We always asked those kids, 'How come you aren't in jail? We're at war with Hitler.' And no one could give us a reason.

When you're a second grader, you start to understand that there's a color thing involved. Our German neighbors, the Dodenhoff family, had a pile of kids. And the Schmidt family in the apartment behind us, they weren't sent to concentration camps. They were White. And the Japanese kids were considered yellow. We got the idea that there was something different about *us*. At that time, we didn't realize it was racism or discrimination, we just knew something, somehow was different. We could hardly wait for the Japanese kids to come back because then they'd get picked on instead of us. It wasn't until later that we understood that it was racism that extended from the administration of Roosevelt to the Supreme Court and all the way down.

Despite the neighbor kids being sent away, my experience growing up was exciting. Growing up in the Central Area there were the Black families, especially the Bown family. Millie Bown Russell was a leader in the Civil Rights Movement and her sister, Patty Bown, was a jazz pianist who had to leave Seattle to become famous in New York. Wherever she played the celebrities would hang out.

We were sponsoring dances at the Maryknoll Hall, and a kid named Quincy Jones had a band called Bumps Blackwell Orchestra that would play at our dances. Later on, he attended Seattle University. He started writing and arranging music there; that's when he changed from being a trumpet player to a writer and arranger. One of the first concerts I had ever been to in my life was his concert playing the old standard tunes but arranged by Quincy. It was really innovative rhythms.

None of us knew that he'd become the superstar that he is but even so, we always bragged about him in the neighborhood as a trumpet player. The Black families, especially the Black Catholic families and the Filipino families, we really bonded. The Bown family and the Maxi family and the

Kola family all sent their kids to Immaculate. We became the neighborhood kids. The guys were sort of the hoods. We had dances. There were two older Filipino American kids, Dorothy Ligo and her future husband, Fred Cordova, they started the Filipino Youth Association (FYA) which later merged with the CYO (The Catholic Youth Organization). We had our own youth group and we used to meet at the old Maryknoll School.

We held dances and had basketball teams. When the Japanese kids came back in 1945 from their concentration camps we had athletic leagues: Japanese kids, Filipino kids, Chinese kids. We formed a basketball league and played at the old Buddhist Temple on 14th and Main. During the war, of course, that was converted into a military depot for the Coast Guard. It was very sacrilegious at that time but war is war. During the old days, growing up, we used to play basketball in the Buddhists' auditorium gym. When the Coast Guard took over, we used to hang out at the Collins Playfield at 16th and Main; that was our athletic hang out.

WHERE WAS MANILATOWN?

Right in the center of Chinatown on Maynard and King to Weller, along 5th and 6th Avenues. This was the area where all the Filipino immigrants lived in the SRO (single room occupancy) buildings. Our businesses were on those streets, so we encroached upon Chinatown, but still had our own individual Manilatown.

Right there, when the war started, my uncle Rudy and a Japanese gentleman owned a gambling hall and a casino. It was in the basement of the Freedman Apartments on Maynard Avenue between King and Weller streets. The casino was in the basement. It was very large, probably the largest casino in the city of Seattle. You know, illegal stuff, payoffs and the like. The Chinatown core was famous not only for paying off cops but even the King County Attorney's Office. Everybody was on the take until the late, late Sixties and Seventies. Then came in an Assistant Chief Eugene Corr, really a cool guy; he reformed the area. Uncle Rudy and Danny Woo were indicted for illegal gambling.

As a young adult, I was beginning to get involved in the Civil Rights Movement, so they both had me testify at their trials saying that these guys were leading Asians in the Chinese and Filipino communities. So, that was pretty cool. I don't think anybody got any jail time. It was a reality, gambling was a big deal down here.

I READ THAT THE GAMBLING AND THE MUSIC MEANT THERE WERE BIG CROWDS OF ALL TYPES OF PEOPLE DANCING AND MIXING WHILE IN THE REST OF SEATTLE CLUBS WERE ALL WHITE.

The gambling halls were Asian and the music was African American. That's when Jackson Street became the jazz capital of the West Coast. We had military bases nearby: Fort Lewis, Fort Lawton, the Naval Base on Pier 91 and the Naval Yard at Bremerton. So, all the African American soldiers would come to Seattle. All these nightclubs on Jackson started to cater to the military guys because they had a lot of money to spend. So jazz was born. I remember walking from the NP Hotel up Jackson Street to my aunt's house. It would take me two hours to get home because wherever there was music playing I would stop and sit on the stairway to listen. I knew all the bouncers, they all knew me as the little kid down the street. I'd sit there for hours listening to the jazz. There were a couple of record shops on 12th and Jackson and whenever I could scrape up money, I'd buy the new jazz records coming out from here. I'd scrape up money to attend the Norman Grant's Traveling Jazz concerts; it was exciting times, especially after the Japanese came back because then our youth groups held very successful dances at the Maryknoll and then that became kind of a center of the youth movement, the Jitterbug movement with the teenagers.

I HEARD THAT THE FILIPINO COMMUNITY LOVED DANCING.

The Filipino community in the mid-Sixties had their weekly dances at Washington Hall. My aunt and uncle lived a block north on Spruce Street. Every Saturday night my gang of friends would go to Washington Hall for the dances. They always charged the men at the door.

You have to understand that because of the restrictive immigration laws passed for Asians, there were immigration quotas. So, there were several thousand more single Filipino men than Filipino women here. Especially so in spring and summer when Filipino men would come here before and after going to Alaska to work in the salmon fisheries and canneries. They'd come back loaded with money, so the Filipino community would have dances Friday, Saturday and sometimes even Sunday night.

Those years, before and after the war, being a young adult was really wonderful. The White kids, the Filipino kids, the Japanese and a few Chinese kids and the Black kids, we all grew up together. Our group was some of the first, in my experience, at least that I can remember, where there was intermarriage, Japanese and Filipino, Chinese kids and White, Black and Japanese…

25

B
O
B

S
A
N
T
O
S

So, WHILE THE REST OF THE NATION STILL HAD MISCEGENATION LAWS, PEOPLE HERE WERE INTERMARRYING AND WERE INTERCULTURAL LONG BEFORE THAT WAS EVEN DREAMED OF IN THE REST OF THE COUNTRY?

That's right. And a lot of that happened in the International District and Central Area because of the restrictive covenants about who could buy property.

The immigrants from China, Japan and the Philippines were restricted to this area, were forced to live together, forced to do business together; they kept our cultures and our languages alive. A few of the leaders from the Japanese, Filipino and Chinese community interfaced but most of the people just lived in the same area. But the kids of those immigrants, we accepted each other. That's why Seattle became a little bit more liberal in the mix of races than did other neighborhoods in other cities. In San Francisco and Los Angeles you had separate a Chinatown, a separate Japantown and a separate Manilatown. Here it was the same area, everyone was together. So, it was natural that the kids of immigrants growing up together for us to interface with other kids. That made Seattle become, then, a leader in that kind of (intercultural) Civil Rights Movement.

As our kids grew up and then met the kids of these staunch White families, their grandkids are meeting and mixing and even with gay kids. These staunch older people are starting to realize this is what's going to happen, so deal with it. They're the ones that are key in these changes in the law because they're voting to support these changes.

I READ ABOUT YOU WORKING WITH BERNIE WHITEBEAR WHO WAS NATIVE AMERICAN AND FILIPINO AND THAT THAT TYPE OF INTERMARRIAGE WASN'T RARE. CAN YOU TALK ABOUT THAT?

That was the case in my family. When my grandfather emigrated from the Philippines he landed in Canada, a place called Nanaimo, probably the only Filipino there for a thousand years. He was running away from something because we never knew his real name. He took the name of Nicol, Cornelio Nichol. In the last eight years my wife and I went to Nanaimo to check it out. It's beautiful, it's north of Victoria BC. The main street in Nanaimo is Nicol Street, so grandpa took that name. He married a woman who was half French Canadian from Quebec and half Alaska native from Cape Fox Island, so we have native in our family.

Returning, though to the subject of the Central Area, the Maryknoll missionaries left the church in the mid-Sixties. The mission sold that property to the Archdiocese, and they renamed the complex the St. Peter Claver Center. The center hired me as executive director of CARITAS, a tutoring social service agency centered at St. Peters. So, as a young man, I went back to my roots at our old church and our old hangout as it became the St. Peter Claver Center. And that building became one of the centers of the Civil Rights Movement in Seattle.

The first people who rented out space were the Black Panthers for their breakfast program, Elmer and Aaron Dixon. Also, there was a group of Indians from Montana who had left the reservation and met at St. Peter Claver Center. It was also the meeting place for a group of elder Catholic women called the Marion Club. When it was time for me to invoice these groups, I told Father Macintyre and the Archdiocese, 'They're doing the Lord's work.'. People in the Civil Rights Movement learned they had a place at St. Peter Claver Center where they could meet, where 'Uncle Bob' will let us meet for free. So, that's where all the meetings were, and it was all centralized in the Central Area, 14th-16th-17th and Jefferson. Tyree Scott would meet there. Now, because the Black Panther Party Breakfast Program got there so early, at six a.m., to get the food ready for the kids by seven. At the same time, Tyree Scott and the United Construction Workers would meet there to plan the shutdown of construction sites where no Black workers were employed. Activities started at six a.m., so who had to open up? Me.

Then groups that wouldn't naturally communicate—like a union-based organization and young people who were perceived to be radicals—were in the same space. I would imagine there was time for conversation so there would have been an awareness…

I would sit in all these meetings. I wouldn't go to the Black Panther Party meetings; their meetings were held at Elmer's Mom's house, so I didn't go to those. CAMP (Central Area Motivation Program) with Larry Gossett, had meetings there. Also, when Bernie Whitebear and the Indians were planning an occupation of Fort Lawton, I was there. That's actually where I first met Bernie, in 1970.

A lot of the Chicanos with Roberto Maestas were attending meetings that were held by the United Farmworkers. The United Farmworkers sent up two women, Nancy and Sara Welch, and Fred Ross Jr. I gave them space at St. Peter Claver Center in old classrooms so their meetings to plan boycotts of Safeway were there. And that's where I met Roberto Maestas. That's where I met Clara Frasier. She was the employee in City Light who was trying to infiltrate women into the workforce for City

Light. Women climbing the telephone poles and all that. She led that fight. She was a really outstanding speaker and she really rallied women, organized women, working-class women, White women, Asian women, Black women. She founded Radical Women and she also formed the Socialist Party Movement. They would meet at St. Peter Claver Center, too, so you had all these crazy people.

There there were still nuns living in the convent on the other side of the Church. One day, Bernie and his young folks were rallying about the occupation and the strategy of what to do with the property if they were to get it. They were doing a Native American ceremony where they do the blessing with the burning of sage, chanting and the drums. One of the nuns runs into my office and says, 'The kids, they're starting to smoke sage.' I tell her, 'It's OK, sister.'

AS I'VE BEEN MEETING ACTIVISTS AND HEAR ABOUT SUCCESSFUL SOCIAL JUSTICE MOVEMENTS IN THE 1960S AND SEVENTIES AND THEN I THINK ABOUT WHERE WE ARE TODAY, WHAT CHANGED? WHY WAS THERE THIS FERVOR AND ACTION THEN? THERE ARE A LOT OF THE SAME PROBLEMS TODAY, BUT THERE DOESN'T SEEM TO BE A FEELING THAT PEOPLE CAN DO SOMETHING ABOUT IT.

Organizing demonstrations was easy, everyone wanted to march for civil rights, against the (Vietnam) war, people even wanted to go to jail. It was a badge of honor. In particular, in our community as we started to join Tyree Scott and Larry Gossett and the Indians and the Latinos in their quest for justice, our community was developing leaders. I started at CARITAS and then moved to Inter-Im (the International District Improvement Association). We had all these young people. We'd make one phone call and the next day two hundred young people would show up. We were fighting against the Kingdome. We were fighting to preserve this neighborhood. Every week there was a street action. That's fine, but what happens after the street action? The mayor will say, 'OK, let's sit down and talk about your needs and how can we help.'

IT SOUNDS LIKE THAT DEEP VALUE OF TEACHING AND INVOLVING THE YOUNG KEPT THIS COMMUNITY VIABLE.

In the early 1970s, Ben Woo was an architect and a leader in the old-timers' Chinese community and the Asian community. He said, 'Hey, Bob. Let's take a trip down the West Coast and see what's happening in similar communities.' We went to LA and looked at Little Tokyo. It had become a really commercial area because money from Japan came in and built new hotels that displaced the old-timers. They were also pushed out by the newer, higher-tech businesses. We looked at the old Chinatown in LA and that was completely wiped out. The new Chinatown was built, and the businesses went to the new one. The worst one was in San Francisco. The old Manilatown on Kearney Street, ten blocks of Manilatown was all wiped out when they built the new Financial Center. When the very last surviving building was to be destroyed, the community came out and protested to preserve it.

We looked at that and thought, why did they wait till the last building? They should have been pro-testing at the first building. Here in Seattle in the 1970s, the same thing was happening; investors from Hong Kong and Japan were looking at the International District. We not only had demonstrations about encroachment, against stadiums, we also wanted to preserve the area for those that built it.

WHAT WAS YOUR HAPPIEST MEMORY OF THE CENTRAL AREA?

At Maryknoll Kindergarten, I fell in love with a girl named Pauline. In first grade I'd go around with my dad to the gambling halls down in the ID. Since my dad had been a boxer, he was a hero not only to the Asian community but also in the Seattle sports scene. After he retired from boxing, he'd go to all his favorite places: the restaurants, the barbershops, the gambling halls, the haberdashery shops, and he'd bring me along. At the gambling halls, if these guys were winning, I'd get a nickel, a dime or a quarter. We'd go from spot to spot. If my dad forgot a place, I'd tell him we had to go there. I got all this change together.

In the first grade, Pauline was sitting up by the teacher. We had wooden desks with two people facing each other, so I paid my way up to sit next to Pauline. I remember I had to pay a couple of folks off to sit next to Pauline. That was the happiest day of my life. Of course, one day we went to school and Pauline and all the other Japanese kids had been hauled off to concentration camps. And only the Filipino kids were left. That was the saddest day of my life.

DeCharlene Williams, 21st Ave & East Madison

DeCharlene Williams long tended the Central Area Chamber of Commerce, kept track of local history and published her own books on the neighborhood. She was larger than life in a tiny frame; realistic and outrageous; a spitfire—a pistol; complex and deeply caring. She is very much missed.

"It's called lineage. To leave something behind, a lot of people don't think like that, but I do…"

DeCharlene on her life in Seattle's Central Area:

My name is DeCharlene Williams. I'm located at East Madison and have been here since April 1968 when they were killing Martin Luther King. I'm still standing because the Lord Jesus Christ is my savior. He has guided me and put me on this path, protected me, wanted me to stay right here and be a voice for this community.

I want people to know that we had organized crime here in this area through crooked policemen, crooked mayors and crooked city councils. The only person who tried to help us was a man called Sam Smith, a councilman, now deceased. I want you to know what happened to the Black businesses, the ones that wanted to do right were forced to do wrong or were pushed out of existence.

Our community was redlined (real estate covenants). Black people were pushed out of existence, hard working Black people were killed for their property. This has been going on ever since 1968 when I moved onto this corner of Madison Street. I have been here a long time; I built this community. I've been on this corner for forty-five years so I have been here for the good, the bad and the ugly.

When I bought this building in 1968 (real estate people generally) wouldn't sell to women. I was able to buy this building from Washington Metro Savings and Loan. I bought the building from a Black man, Mr. Henderson, who knew Mr. Grose (the first large property owner settling and platting this area, a respected Black pioneer and businessman). The developers drove him crazy, but he didn't tell me all that when he sold to me. See, when I bought this place I was only twenty-three years old. Then, I found about all the trouble that was going on here.

In the years I first bought this building was when Mayor Braman was in office (1964-1969). He was a crook and a gangster. He had crooked police who blackmailed all the Black people and made them pay him off. He sent his cronies to press you to buy advertising space in the newspaper, to make me pay for an Ad every week. I fought that by getting a group of people together to run Mayor Braman out. And it worked. We ran Mayor Braman out and his policemen went to jail.

His administration used crooked cops and they'd have people break in your house and steal stuff. These people would break into your house while you're at work, we called it 'snatch and grab.' You'd come back from work and there would be no TV, they'd take all your valuables. They kept a house right near here where they were putting all the (stolen) stuff.

At that time, I was young and very hot-tempered. I didn't take anything from anybody. They broke in my store and stole all the clothes I had in here. At that time, I was opening Seattle up for fashion modeling. Sandy Hill, Kathleen Wise and Lynn Sampson had a show on King 5 TV and they put me on the air. I'd go to New York, buy the latest evening wear, and then bring them to the show with my models. I called it, 'Junk Jewelry and Bitches Dresses.' I used to also wear hats so people called me the Hat Lady.

If you look at *The Facts Newspaper*, I write a column there every week. Next to my column is an old picture of me when I was about twenty-five years old with the hat. It was my signature, that hat.

So, anyway, I was telling you when the police was stealing stuff, every six weeks I bring it in (stock for the store) and they take it. I bring it in and they take it. I found out that there was a house over here full of stolen goods through a lady who sent me a note through the post office. So, I gave guns to all my fashion models. I went over there, kicked the door in. Collared me a couple of people, took my shit out of there and took it back over to my store. Then, the police was acting scared. I told them, 'Hell, I'm not scared.'

SO, WHO WAS IN THE HOUSE?

The criminals.

I THOUGHT YOU MEANT THE POLICE WERE…

That was the house (kept) for the police. They (the criminals) were giving the stuff to the police.

SO, THE POLICE WERE FENCING IT?

That's right. The police take what they want then they fence it. Also, all the businesses around here, the cocktail lounges had to pay them.

PROTECTION MONEY?

That's right. Another thing they had going then was Coffee Royales. Coffee Royales is coffee with whiskey in it. And they (the police) had Jimmy's Café; a place up there called Promenade, his daddy was a criminal too. He was a crook; he would pay the government off so he was selling Coffee Royales. See, he didn't have a liquor license. So he served liquor like that.

SO HE HAD A LICENSE FOR A COFFEE SHOP BUT IT WAS REALLY A BAR?

That's right. That's what I'm trying to tell you. Then lots of people would go in there. I was going to beauty school near there. I found out what they were doing so I stopped going there. I started eating at this woman's place, a Japanese/Chinese kitchen, called Momma's Kitchen. It was little place with fried rice. When I stopped going to his place, the owner of Jimmy's Café started cussing me out when I walked past. He was mad because I was Black but I wasn't utilizing his business. I told him, 'Hell, no. Because you're a criminal.' I wasn't but seventeen at the time. I told him, 'You're selling whiskey in there. I'm not going in there with that whiskey business.'

All these years, I've been able to keep tabs on what's been going on because I keep reports on all the businesses in this area for the Chamber of Commerce. I keep track of everything (about local businesses) in here so we don't lose track of the history. This report is from 1992 (pulls out a chamber report) when we had the first Black chief of the Fire Department, Claude Harris. The Black community fought for him and we haven't had a Black chief since.

These reports documented how they excluded Black people from certain jobs. If you got a job that was worth anything then it was always the most hazardous work, where you might get hurt or killed. (The thinking was) better them than me, so Black people here have gone through a lot.

You see, Washington state, including Seattle, is a racist place. A lot of people don't want to own up to that but it's so racist it is not even funny. The establishment here has always been able to block people out but I always work around them. I'm watching the establishment at all times so I know what they do and how they do it.

Back in the 1990s through 2000 the police were still up to the same things. They got rid of Deano's and Oscar's (both notorious nightclubs) by implicating them with drugs. One time, the police sent some girls in my store with some 'hot' curling irons. When I say 'hot,' I mean stolen. So, I asked, 'Why would I want to buy your stolen curlers?' The girls said they bought them at the store. One girl said, 'I can't twist 'em myself and I can't get my money back at Bartells because I've already used them.' I told them, 'You take those curlers and get your ass out of here. Those curlers didn't come from Bartells, they came from a beauty supply store. You don't have a license to sell me anything; you're not a vendor, so get the hell out of my shop. You're making me mad, so you get out of here while you're still walking.' And so the girls left. I opened the door to look and they were across the street handing the curlers back to the police. And I yelled, 'Hey!' so they'd know I saw them. They were trying to implicate me in buying stolen goods.

Do you think the girls were trying to let you know?

Hell, no! The police sent them in here. What the police do is send criminals into your place to try and get you to buy stolen goods. They tell the criminals it'll take time off their sentence; they put them up to it. I told them don't ever come back in here again. Then these people from the streets used to chop holes in my roof every six weeks. So, I put some hot (electrified) barbed wire up here. I have a switch where I turn it on at night. I put a sign up that said, 'See owner before going on the roof.' Then, the police call me and ask me about the sign, I told them it was to keep people from chopping holes in my roof. And the policeman said, 'You're not supposed to put a booby trap on the roof. I understand you've got some wires attached.' I said, 'Damn right, I do.' He told me, 'You can't have a booby trap on your roof.' So, I told him, 'Well, you're not supposed to have people cutting holes in my roof either.'

Another time, they (the police) had this one guy working for them. It was 1976. That guy worked for the police but I didn't know that (plainclothes). I went into the Post-Intelligencer and shot three times. They put me in jail. He was after me and he was going to kill me.

So, can you explain that a little bit more? You went into the offices of the Seattle Post-Intelligencer and you shot a gun? Did you shoot in the floor? Or in the air?

I shot three warning shots…bam, bam, bam!

Were you shooting in the air? You weren't aiming at anybody? Weren't you worried about hitting someone?

No. I'm from Texas. I'm a shooter. I know how to shoot.

So, you're saying, if you were aiming at someone, you would have hit them?

People who know me know that about me.

In a newspaper article I found on this, they said you were drunk.

The newspaper thought I was drunk but I wasn't. I don't drink. They gave me a breathalyzer. I was acquitted. Anyway, that guy ran me down there from the freeway…

Who did?

That one man (plainclothes) who was working for the police. Then this other man, a wonderful man, a (uniformed) policeman came to arrest me (at the Post Intelligencer). The thing is I had dreamed about him the night before, that all this was going to happen to me. When it started, it was like I had already been through it. I had started off from work, this man (plainclothes) from the police started chasing me, but it was all like I had been there before…

SO, IF I'M FOLLOWING YOU, THE MAN WHO CHASED YOU WORKED FOR THE POLICE DEPARTMENT? SO YOU SOUGHT TO BE PROTECTED, AND YOU WENT TO THE POST-INTELLIGENCER?

Yes. I was running down there because I had to get help and protection. Before all this I had called the police and told them people were threatening me. And they told me I had to bring a cut in.

YOU HAD TO BE INJURED?

They said, 'Bring the cut in, there's nothing they can do till I show them a cut.' I said, 'I'm not going to let anybody cut me. If they come at me with that, I'm going to shoot.' I said, 'We're not going to have any cuts on me.' So, then that morning that man ran me down there.

WHEN YOU SAY HE RAN YOU DOWN THERE, DOES THAT MEAN HE PUT YOU IN HIS POLICE CAR?

No, he was chasing me in my car. I was watching him, mirroring him; you know how you mirror people? Look in the mirror and he's behind you. So I ran into the Post-Intelligencer for help. And I shot three times in there. They put me in jail, arrested me and bailed me out.

SO A GOOD POLICE OFFICER HELPED YOU?

It's in my book, *Black Success: Get out of the Ghetto*, and I wrote about him (the good police officer). I wrote a book on all this. I'm going to publish it too.

WHAT WAS THE NAME OF THE GOOD POLICE OFFICER?

He had a German name. He lived in Bellevue. He was off-duty but he said something told him to go toward the Post-Intelligencer. He saw me; he reached his hand out and said he had seen me in a dream. He was a born-again Christian with a curly Afro. He reached his hand out and I went to him. He asked, 'What's going on? You're in trouble. I saw you in a dream.' I told him, 'I saw you too.' This is how I know the Lord is real.

This man (the good officer) put me in this police car and said, 'I'm going to protect you, stay right with me. They're trying to snatch you away. I'll find out about you. I'm going to arrest you and put

35

you under my custody.' So, he took me downtown, put me in a cell and then he came back and said, 'How come you didn't tell me that you were that woman? The one on Madison, you own that building. You're the most prominent Black businesswoman in the city. Your name is DeCharlene. Why didn't you tell me that? Then I would have known what this was all about.'

Around that time, the City Administration was stealing property in the Mt. Baker neighborhood to make the new freeway. The major players had bought up a lot of property; ordinary people were forced out of their homes. A lady who was working for me lost her home over there, Jean Audrey. People said that the mayor was behind it.

So, this policeman (the good officer) told me this and the police helped me. There were good and bad police. There was another good cop, Detective Roy Burt. He helped me a lot.

There were property grabs also happening in Ballard. They were taking property for the Burke-Gilman trail. There's a woman named Suzie Burke, I met her from being on the Task Force and learned about how all this worked. I also found out about it from a man named Jim Kimball who helped me, he was with the Rosenberg Insurance Company. He's a White man. He found out how the same thing was happening in Ballard. He was running for office; he's a wonderful man.

So, from his point of view, you were a target because you were a landowner, a Black businesswoman on an important street?

They had plans for Madison all the time. I never knew that. He was the one that told me that. That was on May 14th 1976. The person who was behind it was my husband. I was trying to get rid of him, trying to get a divorce from him. He was a gambler and I didn't know it. He was involved with the Black Family (Chicago gang) but I didn't know that at that time.

Was that connected to the Black Panthers?

The Black Panthers are different; that's a community. They were good people, people trying to help others. They ran drug dealers out of the area. They helped found the Carolyn Downs Clinic. I was talking about the Black (Mafia) Family; they are gangsters. They're underground; they come out of Chicago. My ex-husband had lived in Chicago. He was trying to deal my property off.

WAS THIS A COMMUNITY PROPERTY STATE THEN?

It wasn't community property. It was my property because I owned it, I bought it before I met him. I never commingled my property. I never put his name on it. I was married to him but it was mine. So, I had to pay to get rid of him from the value of a house we lived in. I had another house that was rented out. He didn't want the bills, he wanted this building so he could sell it to the developers downtown.

Later, in 1983, I formed the Chamber of Commerce here to help Black people to open their eyes, to show them they have to plan their businesses; to show them not to do crooked business. You see, once you start buying and selling hot goods, that makes you a criminal. You got to make a business plan and then you stay in business.

IT DOES SEEM LIKE THE CRIMINAL ENTERPRISES HERE ARE DISORGANIZED.

But they think they're organized. They're doing what someone tells them to do. It's all connected. When I was on the Task Force in 1985, I tried to tell the mayor the Crips and Bloods were coming into Seattle. I was in California on a buying trip and I overheard people saying in a restaurant, 'Seattle was open.' I guess God wanted me to hear that and little old me, I'm sitting in the back behind the high rollers, picking up all their gossip and hearing them talk.

WAS THAT BEING RUNNING OUT OF LOS ANGELES?

It's run out of everywhere. You don't know who's running it. It was a White man who gave them a half-million dollars and told them to come up here and take this city over. They wanted properties. It was all about properties and land. They buy low and sell high. They want to get you out of your place.

THEY MAKE IT UNINHABITABLE?

That's right. They make it awful for you to live. Look at me, I bring it (goods) in and they take it out. They break out all my windows, boom, boom, boom. Then, they said, 'Well, who is this woman she won't budge?' I replaced the windows and they said it must be hard on her pocketbook. Next, they sent criminals chopping holes in the roof. Finally, the Fire Department tells me they won't suck the

37

water off my floors any more, not unless I pay. I realize then what I have to do; I'll fix it. So I started running through the neighborhood with a .38. Bang, bang! Now, they knew, here I come. Suddenly, they're gone. See? It's just gangsterism in the area.

So, then you used your gun to scare the gangsters away?

Shoot up the place, and I did. That's what happened. If you look at these books different people wrote, they'll tell you about me and you'll see that's really what happened. And then the gangsters, they stopped.

Weren't you worried about stray bullets?

I did what I had to to survive. I like to be feminine. I'm a feminine woman. I like to be decent. I like the Lord. But I don't let people mess with me. What has been hard is…I grew up too off the same Tobacco Road all these people did. It's been hard.

I worked my way up. I had three jobs to get this place, to have my own business. Nobody gave it to me. When I was coming along, they had the SBA (Small Business Administration) but they wouldn't help Blacks. That's what people got to understand. I worked for my success and I'm not letting people just walk in and take it. That's how I am. The gangsters used to send people in here and they broke all my glass doors out so I had these wood ones made and put in.

And in the end who's behind it is White folks, White people, developers. All this building around here today, they want my property because they want to build a high rise here. Right now, they've got plans for this; I'm in their way. They're waiting for me to die. I'm seventy years old so they figure I should be dead. That's how people plan stuff.

Right now, I'm going through some stressful times with all the building of high-rise buildings in this area. This pushes families out. Developers don't want families here.

DO YOU MEAN THAT DEVELOPERS PLAN TO PUSH THE WORKING CLASS OUT?

Yes, it is the same thing here. At the University of Washington (Urban Planners) make the maps; the maps are already drawn. They draw the future. It's already thought out and planned. It's already on the maps. But they lose sight of the history and what's actually lived here.

This development is going to make two classes: the rich and the poor, we're seeing the redistribution of wealth all over the globe. They don't want people to know.

Ultimately, I found out it wasn't just about me and my property; it was about this whole area. It was about the plans for this area, the plans for this area is to have high density and they don't want family homes here. It's not for families, they're not building for the people that live here now, the people of today; they're building for the people that are coming after us in thirty years. And still people don't understand what's going on; they stand there looking stupid. And the developers who are taking everything from our community—it's not for us; it's not our day. It's for the people who'll come next. Just visualize you're driving in your car and you look in the mirror, what do you see?

WHAT'S BEHIND YOU?

It's not us. It's the people who are coming behind us. The people today are carrying the folks to come. Does that make sense to you?

IT DOES.

And so you understand what's going on. And a lot of these people don't understand what's going on. The White folks, White people think they're doing something smart by booting all the Negroes out, the Black people out but they're knifing their own self, shooting their own self in the foot. Because they aren't realizing there are plans for density; it's about greed. It's about money. Nothing for the people. It is the government taking over your lands. They have a small group of people, millionaires and billionaires, and those people are in the fight now.

39

Michelle Purnell-Hepburn has spent her life in financial institutions, learning at her father's knee and then working at the Liberty Bank as a teenager. Her family had an outsized impact on the Central Area through the Liberty Bank, the first African American owned and community-supported bank in Seattle. She radiates competence, kindness and grace while inspiring admiration and aspiration.

"Here we come, these few people wanting to start a minority-owned bank. I just think the powers that be were not quite prepared for that at that time."

WHERE DID YOUR FAMILY LIVE IN THE CENTRAL AREA?

My family lived on the outskirts, on Lake Washington, in what is now the Mount Baker neighborhood. That's where I grew up. We had been the first (African American) family north of the bridge on Lake Washington. Unfortunately that house is gone due to the new I-90.

It's hard to see your neighborhood destroyed that way.

YOUR PARENTS CONTRIBUTED TO AN IMPORTANT PART OF CENTRAL AREA HISTORY. THEY WERE PART OF THE LIBERTY BANK.

Well, the Liberty Bank of Seattle was a dream of my father. He wanted African Americans to have the ability to create their own destiny. Liberty Bank, though, was really an offshoot of an existing financial institution already in the Central Area called Sentinel Credit Union. This was much like Salal Credit Union but much smaller. That had began, I believe, in the late 1940s, maybe the Fifties, and the original membership were the Masons.

These were the Prince Hall Masons who met in the Central Area just off of Cherry Street. On the corner was *The Facts Newspaper*. Fitzgerald Beaver was the proprietor there. One block east was the Masonic Hall, which I believe is condos now, across the street was the (then Phyllis Wheatley) YWCA. That corner of the Central District was where the Sentinel Credit Union started. I started working there when I was very small, embossing and stamping pamphlets. There was a stamp and you had to be very precise with it. I got my start there.

I have to admit that my father and his Masonic brothers, their dreams were bigger than a credit union. They wanted a financial institution. A bank. My father, my mother and seven to eight other community leaders founded the Liberty Bank. The initial meetings, the gathering of signatures and the issuing of and the tracking of stock, that was all done in our basement.

The charter was applied for more than once and was denied. Eventually, the charter it was approved and the bank opened in late May 1960.

CAN YOU EXPLAIN WHAT THE SITUATION WAS FOR THE AFRICAN AMERICAN COMMUNITY WITHOUT HAVING THEIR OWN BANK? WHAT DID THAT MEAN FOR THE AVERAGE PERSON?

For the average person that meant you had to go to the big banks, the SeaFirst Bank or the People's Bank or Seattle Trust. Then, you basically had to prove your worth, to prove that you had collateral, to prove that you maintained your home, and show that you had a business plan. I'm using terms that are used now that weren't used then.

WHAT HAPPENED TO THOSE WHO WERE NOT ABLE TO ACCESS BANKING SERVICES?

Without access to banking services you are forced to operate by the cash on hand in order to run your entire business. Or you're finding credit through loan sharking which is charging you a ridiculous rate.

NOW, I HADN'T THOUGHT ABOUT THAT, THERE MUST HAVE BEEN THEN AN UNOFFICIAL ECONOMY. IF YOU CAN'T GET LOANS FROM BANKS?

You borrow from friends, from family or from others.

AND THERE WAS AN ACTIVE NIGHTCLUB SCENE IN THE AREA...

There was.

YOU MENTIONED EARLIER THAT YOU HAD FAMILY HERE BEFORE YOUR PARENTS ARRIVED?

My paternal grandparents arrived here in 1941. My paternal grandfather arrived here in the 1930s. There's a family story that one of our family was here even earlier, though I can't prove it.

My grandfather either wired or wrote a letter to my father telling him that the streets out here were paved with gold. That meant that you could come here and you could make a name for yourself. You could own property. You could have a business. The racial divide was not as wide here, which is why my parents moved out here.

There's a reason why they're so many African Americans from the South, from Louisiana, in the Central District because that's what was the track. Our track was from the Tennessee area, then to Chicago and then out to Washington, to Seattle, to the Central Area. My maternal grandparents came out after my parents.

So there was this move, this great migration of people to this new place. All in all, the ability to make a home and make a community in a place where there wasn't a huge African American community is absolutely amazing. They had to come to know who was in charge, who were the big power players. They had to learn who were the movers and shakers in the larger community and in the African American community.

But by the 1960s, this amazing group of individuals who founded this financial institution wanted something more. Dare I say they wanted legitimacy. That's not the right word, they wanted the African American community to be recognized. They pooled their resources, which is basically what a credit union is, and if they pooled their resources, we could get on with each other and we wouldn't need these other institutions (that were reluctant to serve ethnic and non-White businesses).

The original board members were: Dr. James Jackson (who had his practice on Union); Dr. Robert Joiner (who had his practice on Madison, and he actually delivered me as well); Mr. Holbrooke Garrett; my mother, Mardine Purnell, was Secretary of the Board; Mr. Tokuda (who had a drugstore in the Central Area on 34th). That was the only drugstore I ever went to until I moved away. They were wonderful people. In my father's later years, they would deliver to him when he couldn't make the trip because we'd been customers for so long. I was so sorry to hear Kip, his son, had passed on.

The board also was: Rev. Samuel Berry McKinney (Pastor Emeritus of Mt. Zion); Phillip I. Burton was the first president (he lived on Day and 32nd); and Mr. Jack Richlen. So these were people we saw all of the time. The ribbon-cutting ceremony was an amazing day. Mayor Braman and Governor Evans attended and it was such a proud day for the community. Such a proud day! I do have pictures of the first day, of the ribbon-cutting. It was an exciting time. It was a time of change. Liberty Bank was opened less than two months after Martin Luther King was killed and a few days before Bobby Kennedy was killed.

WHEN YOU READ ABOUT THE TUMULT THEN, TO HAVE LEADERS KILLED, INVESTIGATIONS TO BE UNCLEAR...

The country was still reeling from President John F. Kennedy being killed. It was a scary time. There was such uncertainty. There were all kinds of threats on the bank. We had threats on our family. Yet, my father and my mother and the directors felt this is what the community needs.

The ribbon-cutting was late May 1968 and my dad became President in 1971, I believe. This meant having someone who had really strong skills, banking skills, for our fledgling bank and so my dad left Sentinel Credit Union to take on the presidency. My mom remained on the board. And where my dad went, I went. I had odd jobs from the time I was little, and I became a teller at the bank when I was in college.

YOU MUST HAVE ALWAYS BEEN REALLY DETAIL-ORIENTED.

I had two really detail-oriented parents. My mother was an IRS auditor and my dad worked as a civil engineer for the Navy and the Credit Union. Being detail-oriented was part of my DNA.

So when the bank opened, and after, my parents were extremely protective of me, given the issues. Just people saying or doing stupid things. I think on some level there were some community members, some customers that needed charge offs. You had people who had loans and couldn't pay it back. There's still all of that, but even with that, it is still such a point of pride. Especially for the

43

stockholders, they owned a piece of history. You should talk to Dr. Rev. Samuel Berry McKinney; he and Mr. Richlen are the only surviving board members. Dr. McKinney also knew Dr. Martin Luther King. He's a wonderful man.

MR. WILLIAM G. LOWE TOLD ME THAT AT THE TIME OF THE ASSASSINATION OF DR. REVEREND KING THERE REALLY WAS A BIG SHIFT IN THE AFRICAN AMERICAN COMMUNITY. THERE WERE PEOPLE WHO BELIEVED IN EVERYTHING DR. KING EMBODIED AND THERE WERE ALSO PEOPLE WHO WERE YOUNGER AND ANGRY.

There was a loss of hope. And the Voting Rights Act and the Civil Rights Act, those were symbols of hope, a hope that would not have even been a gleam in my grandparent's eyes. Even after the Civil Rights Act, I think some of the divisions between the younger and the older were based on the fact that the older were the ones who had lived all their lives before the Voting Rights Act. They were the migration, they were there in the South where every other day there was a lynching; that just was what it was. So, to tell them to forget that; it's not possible. When you live in a time when survival is preeminent, that focus doesn't just disappear when the situation changes. That becomes hardwired.

SO, WHEN THE BANK FOUND ITS FOOTING, CAN YOU THINK OF A STORY THAT SHOWS HOW THE BANK WAS ABLE TO FUNCTION IN AND FOR THE COMMUNITY?

I would say that the Liberty Bank was run very much like a credit union, and that's how it functioned for the community. What I mean by that is my dad knew everybody. He had been a Mason. He had lived in the Central Area. My mom was in Eastern Star and in various community clubs. We just knew a lot of people and they'd bring friends into the bank to introduce them to us. So, they would now be known.

There were all sorts of businesses. My favorite businesses were Lloyd's Heating Oil and Mr. Hill's Barbecue. The bank had small business loans, all sorts of consumer checking accounts. Also, people just came into the bank, especially if my dad was there and his door was open, to talk about what was going on in the community, what was going on nationally; it was a hub for the community. People were excited when we put in a walk-up and then a drive-through. That was a really big deal. Many of our customers had businesses down the street. Judge Stokes had

44

law offices across the street. We were part of the daily fabric of the community. Miss Helen had her restaurant; Mr. Greenlee's law offices were right next door to the bank, and they lived across the street from our house. There was an incredible sense of belonging.

I GUESS, THEN, WHATEVER YOU DID SOMEBODY WHO KNEW YOU SAW YOU DO IT.

That is so true, because again the African American community was small in comparison with the total size of Seattle. We all did help raise 'me.' You're right, if you did something it was going to get back to your parents. I remember once my sister was walking between 23rd and the Mt. Zion Church. Someone called my parents to say, 'Your daughter is on Madison Street.' And she was just walking to school.

IT'S A KIND OF LOVE…I DO THINK ACCOUNTABILITY IS ABSOLUTELY ESSENTIAL FOR YOU TO BECOME WHO YOU CAN BE.

It kept me out of trouble. It kept my sister out of trouble, and my nieces. I'm very grateful that my parents were very strict. In that strictness, that's why I get to do what I do today. I didn't veer off the path very far. There was a sense of belonging.

People felt if they walked into Liberty Bank they were going to get a fair deal. I think, though, some people thought we were always going to say 'yes.'

SO, WHAT DOES IT MEAN TO BE ABLE TO ACCESS CREDIT WHEN YOU HAVE A SMALL BUSINESS?

Oh, it's everything. Businesses run on credit, businesses run on being able to cover to pay expenses to stretch receivables if that's what needs to be done. You can do that with a line of credit. A line of credit is a measure of trust that the financial institution will be there for you, and you are going to do your part to pay back that financial institution. It is the relationship of trust. And trust is huge in the African American community. Trust is huge. It's huge, period, but in the African American community or any disenfranchised community, it's even bigger.

45

Can I hear more about how trust is important in banking?

I look at you and based on who you are, what you've done, the assets you have, and the plans that you have for your business or your life, I am deciding to give you money because I trust that you're going to pay me back. But then I'm actually willing to look at you, to listen to you, to hear your hopes and your goals because you want to buy a house, or start a business or whatever it is that you want to do.

The laws that we have now about non-discrimination, those weren't there then; so people could literally say, 'We don't lend to (people like) you,' before you even opened your mouth, before they even knew what your business was worth. Just because of what you looked like, just because you happened to have more melanin than someone else. The mainstream banks wouldn't give you a chance. Yet, with someone else, an all-American boy, they would give him a chance.

Do you think that's changed?

No, not really. I think generally we are afraid of what we don't know, so depending on how you were raised, depending on how old you are…If you were raised in a community that was integrated, probably there was very little of that.

Still, I know that two of my friends—one is a commissioner and one is a judge—were just in Nordstrom on their lunch hour, so they probably were dressed very much like a judge and a commissioner. They were profiled. They were followed in the store. This is a judge and a King County commissioner! All they're doing is looking at clothing—clothing they can afford. They called it out and were told it wasn't the case that they were being profiled.

Unfortunately, it happens every day. There's a wonderful woman, she and her husband have two lovely children of mixed race. Their children are gorgeous. On Queen Anne Hill last week someone said, 'Those are such beautiful children you're taking care of.' She replied, 'Thank you, they're mine.' She was asked, 'Both of them?' She was just like (shakes her head)…sometimes you may think it but you don't say it. Are they yours? Who else would they be? Do you also say that to a Caucasian who's adopted an Asian child? When you are in a small community and you're not in the majority, it takes resilience.

THAT'S WHY I THINK THIS PROJECT IS IMPORTANT. IT SHOWS HOW DIVERSITY IS A STRENGTH OF A COMMUNITY AND BY EXTENSION THAT'S TRUE FOR THE COUNTRY.

What that entails, though, is a belief in abundance rather than scarcity. If you want something that's fine, because there is plenty to go around. When you believe that there is enough, when the belief in scarcity begins to change, there's more opportunity for all of us. There really is plenty for all of us. That's the belief system I grew up with. If I work hard enough, if I put my ducks in a row like anyone else, I'm not better than, not less than. I do my part.

They've done studies with people and people do tend to feel comfortable with people who look like them. They're starting to study that in different cultures.

However, if you allow your children from a very early age to be just children, then they figure out that all people are similar. I think that to be born and raised in Washington there were some real perks in racial diversity and coming together. There were some real boundaries and some real drawbacks as well, not growing up in a community that was as far as the eye could see everybody looked like me. People my age who had that experience, they have a very different connection to their community than I do.

YOU MENTIONED THERE WAS A MOVEMENT OF PEOPLE OUT OF THE CENTRAL AREA IN THE 1970s. I'VE HEARD THAT THE BLACK MIDDLE CLASS MOVED OUT. IS THAT YOUR VIEW?

I would say so, yes. As people realized that you could afford to move to Madison Park or Seward Park or Mt. Baker or wherever, as they believed that times had changed enough that if you did move and wanted to pursue the American Dream, you weren't going to be killed. My parents had lived on Lake Washington Boulevard, they moved in 1954 out of the Central Area proper and to the Mt. Baker area. It was like, 'We can!' Now, in no way did we anticipate that it was going to hurt the community at all because where we banked and where we shopped was still in the Central Area. Some were able to afford more and unfortunately we saw the grass was greener somewhere else instead of making it greener in the Central Area. Some of us did, but not all of us.

WHAT HAPPENED? IT WASN'T JUST BLACK FLIGHT, THERE WAS ASIAN FLIGHT, WHITE FLIGHT?

There was all kinds of flight at that time.

THERE HAD TO BE SOMETHING HAPPENING IN THE NEIGHBORHOOD TOO. THERE HAD TO ALSO BE AN IMPETUS TO MOVE. WAS SOMETHING PUSHING PEOPLE OUT?

I don't know. Reverend McKinney would know. You should talk to him because that started before my time.

My oldest friend, since from when I was three years old, lived on 31st. We lived on Lake Washington Boulevard about four blocks away. We went to Epiphany Day School together. Her father was a judge and when he and his wife decided they could afford to move, they went to Seward Park.

My parent's flight was earlier. It was when they could afford a view in 1954. When the bridge came, they had to move but they would have been happy to spend the rest of their days on Lake Washington Boulevard.

They were the first in their family to have paid for their house. That was huge. And it was a huge blow when they were forced out. Then they moved to the southern end of the lake. People say, 'Oh, you've got this big house,' but they don't understand—we were happy where we were. It was a middle class house that they had painstakingly remodeled. It was their house; it was where they planned to spend the rest of their days. What happened later wasn't because of White flight, it was because of the bridge.

YOU CAN PUT SO MUCH LOVE INTO A HOUSE. THAT MUST HAVE BEEN HARD.

Especially for an African American man, like my father, who moved here so he could own property. And own it lock, stock and barrel.

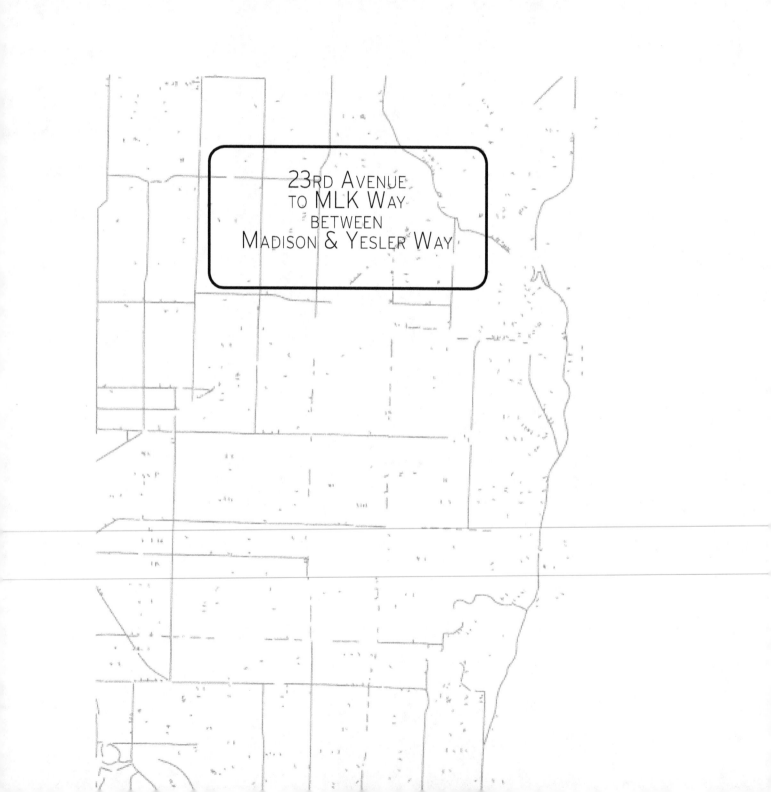

23rd Avenue
to MLK Way
between
Madison & Yesler Way

Linda Emery Lee Cadwell was a teacher before her retirement. Hers is a great love story interspersed with tragedy in two very different chapters. She is welcoming, bright and feminine with untold reserves of strength. She is the widow of Bruce Lee and the mother of two children with him, Brandon and Shannon Lee.

> "*There are a lot of people out there who have suffered and been able to go on. It either shatters your heart into a million pieces and destroys you or it opens your heart and keeps them right there in your heart. And it opens you to all the suffering of people all over the world.*"

Were you born in the Central Area?

I was actually born in Everett, just a short ways away. My parents were from that area. When I was five years old, my father passed away from a sudden heart attack, very early, at forty. Then my mother, sister and I moved to Seattle. So from the age of five on, I lived in Seattle.

Neither my older sister nor I stayed in Seattle after high school, pretty much. Still, I loved growing up in Seattle; it was a good place for us. I grew up in Montlake, then when I was in high school, or maybe junior high, we moved to Capitol Hill to 11th Street. That house is very near Seattle Prep, so I consider that where I grew up.

How was your experience in junior high? It is such a fraught time.

I had a good time in junior high and high school. I had a lot of friends. I didn't get into any of the problems that are so prevalent today—like bullying. I just had a nice group of friends so I enjoyed my experience. I got along with almost everybody.

There were a lot of changes after those years. I graduated in 1963. I know a lot changed after that in coordination with the Civil Rights Movement. Changes really needed to happen, but we didn't know about that when we were in junior high and high school.

A LOT OF PEOPLE HAVE REMARKED THAT WHEN THEY WENT INTO THE LARGER WORLD THEY REALIZED HOW UNIQUE THEIR EXPERIENCE OF RACE AND CLASS HAD BEEN AT GARFIELD HIGH. WAS THAT YOUR EXPERIENCE?

Oh, yes. After graduating, I came to know about the outside world that I had no idea of when I was in high school because Garfield was very racially mixed. It was about forty percent Black and about twenty percent Asian and about twenty percent Caucasian. I had friends among every race. Many of my girlfriends and guy friends were Asian. We're still friends. I also had a number of Black friends, mainly from being a cheerleader and an orchestra member, and both groups were mixed.

After graduating, I learned that my Asian friends were redlined and could not purchase homes in certain areas. I had no idea that kind of thing went on because we all got along so well in high school. Then, the big bad world showed me a lot of different pictures.

Actually, we were very lucky to go to high school at that time, because whether it was on the surface or deeper, and I choose to think it was deeper friendships because I still have friends from all different races from high school, it (those friendships) was real for us at the time. But it wasn't real for the whole world or outside the doors of the high school.

SOME PEOPLE HAVE DESCRIBED IT AS A KIND OF BUBBLE BECAUSE WHEN THEY DID ENCOUNTERED THE OUTSIDE WORLD, THE SHATTERING OF A SEEMING IDYLL WAS A BIT VIOLENT.

That was very well put because, certainly, with the Civil Rights Movement we came to understand there were all these tensions outside that weren't happening inside the school as far as my experience…Maybe our Black or Asian friends had different experiences but we certainly were friendly and we all did things together.

BESIDES REDLINING WERE THERE OTHER THINGS THAT SHOCKED YOU ABOUT RACIAL RELATIONS OUTSIDE THE GARFIELD DOORS?

There were things I didn't know until well after high school, for instance, the poverty of some classmates and difficult family situations. I didn't really realize the extent of class distinctions between kids that came from wealthy families.

NOW, IT SOUNDS LIKE WITH FRIENDSHIP THERE WAS NO BARRIER, BUT CARVER GAYTON TOLD ME THAT THE GARFIELD ADMINISTRATION TALKED TO HIS CLASS ABOUT MAINTAINING BARRIERS AROUND INTERRACIAL DATING ESPECIALLY BLACK AND WHITE.

I suppose there were as far as dating. I don't know if anybody ever told me you're not supposed to date a Black guy; that probably never came up because that kind of was taboo…it was understood from parents and families. However, I certainly ended up marrying an Asian person, so… I didn't really go by the rules. I had a great many Asian friends, girls and boys, in school. In fact my first sort-of boyfriend, you know, back in those days we didn't really pair off that much, everybody kind of did everything together, my first sort-of boyfriend was half Japanese. When my mother found out that I liked him, that's when I found that that was taboo. She did not like that at all.

DID THAT PRESENT AN ISSUE BETWEEN YOU AND HER?

Well, yes. It was an issue. I got the word; that was not expected in our family. And then what happened, a couple of years later, I marry a Chinese. That was not welcome in my family either because they didn't know Bruce at that time.

You know, Bruce Lee has a history at Garfield High as well. He was friends with Mr. Wilson who was the philosophy teacher. I don't know how their friendship came about but anyway Mr. Wilson used to invite Bruce Lee to come to his classroom to give lectures on Chinese philosophy. That's how he became integrated with a lot of students at Garfield—he became a person who some of us congregated with.

HOW DO YOU THINK THE LECTURES AND INTERACTIONS DREW PEOPLE TO HIM?

Bruce was a very animated speaker and just a few years older than the students he was lecturing. He also interspersed his talks with Gung Fu movements as they related to Chinese philosophy so he was very popular. Also a number of the class members became students of Gung Fu outside of class and then I started taking Gung Fu lessons.

LINDA **WHAT INTERESTED YOU ABOUT GUNG FU?**

I liked the physical aspects of Gung Fu plus I had many Asian friends taking it and I had spent a lot of time in Chinatown.

EMERY **WHAT DID YOU LEARN IN GUNG FU THAT'S STAYED WITH YOU?**

LEE Some of the self-defense moves have stayed with me although, knock-on-wood, I have not had to use them. Over time, I began to see the relationship between the physical movements and the philosophical aspects that related to real life.

CADWELL Anyway, from taking Gung Fu, one thing led to another. As far as my family was concerned, (sighs) I'm not very proud of this but I just didn't tell my mother that I had this special friend, Bruce Lee, who was Chinese. When we did get married, we were planning to elope and tell them later (laughs). We didn't realize that if you take out a marriage license, it's published in the newspaper in the Vital Statistics part of the newspaper. I don't know if they still do that, but whoever reads that? Only my old maiden auntie…

IT WAS PROBABLY NEXT TO THE OBITUARIES.

(laughs) Yes! She calls up my mother and says, 'There's a Linda Emery who's going to marry a Bruce Lee, what do you know about that?' Oh, everything hit the fan! It was serious in my family. They called up a family council, my aunt and uncles and everyone came. Bruce was sitting there on the hot seat. They tried to talk us out of it and all of that and (laughs). Anyway, we went ahead with it; that was the best thing in my life (laughs).

There was one aunt and uncle; they were very religious, Christian. They told us that this was against God's wishes and the Bible and all that. They literally disowned me for all the time that I was married to Bruce. In fact, after Bruce passed away, the next time I saw that uncle, he put his arms around me and said, 'Welcome back to the family' (laughs ruefully). I didn't have those kinds of thoughts, of course, so that was really…I didn't think there was anything wrong with being with someone who wasn't of my race. It never occurred to me. It never occurred to Bruce either.

People asked me did you ever suffer discrimination…you know, I can understand my mother's feeling because she was worried that her daughter would suffer from this decision, suffer discrimination and be looked down upon and all that. We never did suffer any discrimination, really. I always think you are treated by a person in the way you present yourself to that person.

Bruce was never a person to be meek (laughs) or bow down to anybody else, so he was always treated as an equal and we were too. The only time I was ever looked at sideways was when we lived in Hong Kong (laughs) and of course some Chinese people would look at me and wonder, 'Hmm, why'd he marry her?'

How were you treated by neighbors and acquaintances in Hong Kong?

I was well-treated by Bruce's friends and family mainly because Bruce was so well-loved. I got a lot of stares and unflattering remarks from strangers.

Were your University of Washington friends and acquaintances supportive? Did you feel pressure to elope only because of family?

The pressure we experienced was solely from my family members. My friends all loved Bruce and wanted the best for us.

I think when you look back at World War II where Japan was the aggressor, all Asian people were treated that way by Americans because there were leftover hostile feelings by Americans at Asians. By the time I married Bruce in 1964 there were people of that World War II generation who thought that was an evil thing to do. Those feelings die hard.

As much as we like to think we are free-thinking people of our own creation we are shaped indelibly by the times we live in.

Look at the times we live in now—who we think is bad just because of where they're from and what they believe in.

55

LINDA

WELL, INTERRACIAL MARRIAGE HAS GONE FROM TABOO TO VIRTUALLY OF NO CONSEQUENCE.

I didn't realize that in 1964, in fourteen states, it was against the law in to marry interracially. Of course, that is all gone now.

EMERY LEE

SO YOU WERE AN OUTLAW AND YOU DIDN'T EVEN KNOW IT?

Yeah, really! My cousin married a Black fellow a little later. I always remind her I laid the path for this in the family. They're still married forty-five years later. They live in Boise.

CADWELL

BOISE IS KIND OF A HOMOGENEOUS PLACE.

It is, but it's getting better, much more acceptance of all kinds of people. My children grew up in a metropolitan center with a Chinese father so they were used to interacting with many types of people, which they liked. I do too. That does get a little boring here, in that way, without much diversity.

AFTER IT WAS DISCOVERED YOU WERE GETTING MARRIED, DID YOUR MOTHER COME TO THE WEDDING?

Yes, my mother, grandmother and Taky Kimura (who is from Seattle). That was it. Then we left and moved to Oakland immediately, as that was the plan from before we got found out! My mother was very sad.

It didn't really take long for her to get to know Bruce. He was a very charming fellow (laughs) and she came to love him dearly and my son and daughter as well. The other members of the family who thought it was against God's law did not get to know him. My aunt and uncle who lived here in Boise were so generous and outgoing. He was the total opposite of the other uncle, who was his brother. He was so welcoming and said, 'Bruce is welcome in this family any time.' He was the head of the YMCA so that was his philosophy. Then when his daughter went to marry a Black man, he told me he had to swallow hard and remember what his philosophy was and then welcome him to the family too.

It was so funny that those two brothers were from the same family and had such totally opposite opinions.

IT'S ONE OF MANY GREAT LOVE STORIES THAT CAME OUT FROM GARFIELD; IT'S PROBABLY THE MOST WORLD FAMOUS LOVE STORY THAT CAME OUT OF CENTRAL SEATTLE.

It really was. I just feel so fortunate and then to have children who are part Chinese; it's just such a blessing.

I GUESS THAT'S TRUE, IF YOU HAD BEEN BORN AT A DIFFERENT TIME YOU COULD HAVE BEEN BUSSED TO INGRAHAM AND YOU WOULD NEVER, EVER HAVE MET BRUCE LEE.

Looking back, I had an open attitude from my experiences at Meany and Garfield with different races and just different people, different lifestyles. There were people who came from very poor and very wealthy areas to Garfield, so there were so many experiences. Having that contact with all these different types of people and their families just makes one more open to experiences. I feel very fortunate that way.

WOULD YOU SAY THAT IS ONE OF THOSE THINGS THAT FORMED YOU EVEN TODAY?

Oh, yes, I still have that same attitude. Absolutely.

THAT'S SOMETHING YOU TOOK FROM JUNIOR HIGH ALL WAY ON THROUGH. SOME PEOPLE I TALK TO SAY THAT TIME PERSISTS IN WHO THEY ARE WHILE OTHERS SAY, IT WAS A FEW YEARS OUT OF MY LIFE.

Oh, no. I have very warm feelings about my youth, when I went to school and all the people I met. That's because so many of us have always stayed in touch all these years, more than fifty years. I feel it had a definite impact on me growing in Seattle and being exposed to all those different things. Also, my mother was widowed very young so she had to go to work and take care of my sister and I. We were latch key-kids; we came home from school by ourselves. She did remarry when I was eight, but to a man (pauses) who was not a good man, really. He also did not participate in being a parent to us, not as a dad and not financially at all either.

57

Part of my upbringing was living in a divided household. They had arguments constantly. That kind of shaped me as a person as well. I wouldn't bring up anything controversial because it would just start a big argument. Therefore I'm kind of a person who does not speak up about things and doesn't answer unless asked, just because I don't want to stir up trouble. When I was a kid at the dinner table if somebody said pass the salt, my mother would be, 'What's wrong, there's not enough salt on it? Well, then. You cook it!' There was just constant bickering in my family, so that shaped how I was too.

IT SOUNDS LIKE IT GAVE YOU A REAL NEED AND DESIRE TO LEAVE.

Well, I guess it did. It seems like it when I look in hindsight.

I had met Bruce; we dated pretty much for a year; we did everything together. That was my first year at the University of Washington. He was in his third year and we were spending all our time together. I was taking Gung Fu lessons from him, so we were doing things together.

Bruce had decided that he was leaving Seattle after that year because he was going to join up with a partner in Oakland and open another Gung Fu school. It was a decision-making time—either I was coming with him and we were going to get married or I was not. You know, so part of the decision for me might have been that I wanted to get out of the house but I was already in love with this man, too.

HE MUST HAVE BEEN INCREDIBLY MAGNETIC.

Yes, of course. He was…in personality, he was much like the person you see on the screen in his movies, very energetic, very virile.

DID YOU END UP FINISHING YOUR STUDIES IN OAKLAND?

I did not. We started a family. Brandon was born. We were pretty poor. We really did not have a lot of resources. Bruce was teaching but at that time it didn't bring in much.

Other things were happening at that time too. Bruce was asked to come in to do a screen test in Los Angeles because somebody else had seen him do a Gung Fu demonstration and recommended him to a producer; long story short, we were on the move. It wasn't long before we moved to LA and I had my daughter, and so I had two babies. We were in LA for several years and he did one

TV series. After that he had a great deal of trouble finding more movie roles and continuing to go up in his career. By that time he decided that what he wanted to do was to be an actor…I'm going to end up giving you the whole history of Bruce Lee but you can read about that in a book…

BUT WAS THAT WHAT YOU WANTED? DID YOU WANT TO HAVE A FAMILY OR DID YOU WANT TO FINISH YOUR EDUCATION?

Oh, no. We both wanted to have a family.

SO, YOU HAD WHAT YOU WANTED?

Oh, yeah! We both did. Then circumstances changed and we moved to Hong Kong. He made his films over there and he became very famous and everything.

HOW WAS IT FOR YOU BEING IN HONG KONG?

I loved it. I absolutely loved it. I wouldn't want to live there forever and raise children there, it's very difficult. It's so crowded.

HOW WAS IT TO SHOP FOR FOOD? SO MANY VEGETABLES ARE DIFFERENT.

Oh, gosh. By that time I was schooled in Chinese food. I loved it. Yeah, you bet. Still, it was very hard to be there with small children and be married to a famous person.

OH, BECAUSE HE WAS FAMOUS OVER THERE AT THAT TIME?

At that time over there he was famous but not so much worldwide. There are so many people in Hong Kong in such a small place. You can't walk down the street without being asked for autographs and pictures and everything so it turned into a more private life there—we would stay at home and eat.

DID YOU FEEL SEQUESTERED BECAUSE YOU COULDN'T GO OUT WITHOUT BEING PESTERED?

Well, that was true but more true for him. We wouldn't have stayed there forever. Actually, his last movie was an American co-production. We would have moved back to Los Angeles. That's why I wouldn't wanted to have lived there forever.

THEN AFTER YOU CAME BACK TO LA, DID YOUR CAREER BECOME MANAGING HIS LEGACY?

Well, first of all, Bruce passed away in Hong Kong, and I came back with the children to Seattle.

I thought we would live in Seattle. Bruce is buried in Seattle at Lakeview Cemetery, which is right up the street from my house, so I was already very familiar with it. I thought I would live in Seattle.

I had been gone for ten years and I found out it rains there (laughs). What I mean by that is when you're a kid you just don't notice it. I'd been living in southern climates and also, you just don't go back to high school again. No. Ten years have passed. Your friends have families and they're all doing different things. I had business in LA by that time too settling his estate and all that. In the end, it just made more sense to be in Los Angeles. But I never lost my ties with Seattle. I came back often, still do and just love it; it's a beautiful city. I'm very glad I decided to bury Bruce in Seattle, to this day, because he loved Seattle. I think at some time we may have decided to have a second home in Seattle or something because his very best friends were in Seattle. He loved to come back too. It's not so far for me to go back and forth to Seattle too. I don't really believe I have to go visit his grave to have him part of my life still, he's always with me.

Anyway, I moved back to Los Angeles. By that time, my kids were nine and five and in school and that's when I went back to school. First, I went to UCLA but it was too far, traffic-wise. I switched to the University of California in Long Beach and got my degree in political science, and then I went and got a teaching degree.

Then, the funny thing is, I meet this man. I came to Boise in 1989 to visit my aunt, uncle and cousins who live here. One of my cousins used to be Bruce Cadwell's secretary. She introduced us. So, he lives in Boise and I live in LA. You know, this is geographically undesirable (laughs). Still, we had so many things in common. He's from Seattle and his brothers' friends were the older brothers of

60

kids I went to school with. We just had so many things in common including our experience of growing up in Central Seattle, so it was a good blend and it has been. He's a good guy.

HE MUST BE TOUGH TOO. TO MARRY SOMEONE WHO'S HAD AN INTERNATIONALLY FAMOUS GREAT LOVE MUST TAKE A BIG HEART.

Well, it certainly does. And that's well put. Bruce Cadwell is a very secure man in his own right and accomplished in his profession. He was a stockbroker and so he did not feel that attack on his ego.

Now, it's been forty-two years since Bruce Lee passed away in 1973. There are occasions where I have to make an appearance, or do this or that. It's much less so now because my daughter, Shannon, has taken over handling all things to do with Bruce Lee. Still there are occasions where I have to go to a ceremony but it's very nice because people are so devoted to Bruce Lee and what they have learned from him.

And Bruce (Cadwell) is just great with that. Sometimes he comes with me. We had a fabulous time in Japan when they invited me over there to a screening of *Enter the Dragon* or something like that. Bruce Cadwell is great with that type of thing. He said, 'I've sure had a lot of experiences I wouldn't have had if I didn't meet you.' It's vice versa as well; he takes me to a lot of places. I have played golf all around the world because of Bruce Cadwell, so it's a good partnership.

IT SOUNDS LIKE A GREAT DEAL OF THE INITIAL ATTRACTION WAS DUE TO COMMON SEATTLE ROOTS.

In fact, shortly after meeting we discovered we had both attended Meany Junior High and Garfield. Bruce (Cadwell) is five years older than I am, so we didn't know each other in school. It was definitely an icebreaker on first meeting because we had mutual experiences. Over the years, it has continued to be a connection for us since we know some of the same friends and we visit Seattle together. We both have a natural attraction to the water and like to spend some time there often.

DO YOU KNOW WHAT IT WAS THAT DREW HIM TO GUNG FU?

Bruce says he started Gung Fu because his buddies wanted to try it. His friends had heard of Bruce Lee and wanted to check him out. Bruce (Cadwell) is also a very active man and so martial arts would be right up his alley. I have heard Bruce referred to as the best all-around athlete ever encountered.

AND A MAN THAT HAS A BIG HEART. THERE ARE A LOT OF MEN WHO ARE WONDERFUL PEOPLE BUT THEIR EGO IS EASILY NICKED, SO I'M GLAD YOU FOUND TWO GREAT MEN.

Right! Two great men named Bruce; Bruces are good for me! (laughs) That is very true.

When my son died, that was so…tragic. That was…He had so much promise and so much to look forward to. Bruce (Cadwell) was so supportive. That's the kind of thing that can tear marriages apart and does. He was so…just such a help-mate with everything that went on at that time, which was terrible, terrible.

I AM SO SORRY.

I know. That's a hard one for me to get past. So unnecessary and he had so much to look forward to. Including that he was going to get married seventeen days later. If you ever were to talk to Shannon, I mean, it affected her life as well. She and her older brother they got along so great. You know when something like this happens to you, you lose your husband, or you lose a child (pause) you think you're alone in the world in your suffering. Then you find out that this has happened to other people and you never knew that about them.

Of course, all you have to do is read the newspaper or watch TV—all the people who've lost family members. It's a club you don't want to belong to. There are a lot of people out there who have suffered and been able to go on. It either shatters your heart into a million pieces and destroys you or it opens your heart and keeps them right there in your heart. And it opens you to all the suffering of people all over the world.

WHEN SOME PEOPLE PASS IT DOES FEEL LIKE THEY'RE STILL THERE, SOMEHOW. THAT SOUNDS RIDICULOUS, I PROBABLY SHOULDN'T PUT IT IN HERE BUT I DO THINK IT'S TRUE.

It's true.

DEE GOTO, 23RD AVE

Dee Goto is an author who also kept working (with many others) over many years to make the Japanese Cultural and Community Center in the Central Area a reality. She's grounded in values of family, community history and culture, and is thoughtful, open and kind. Her deep generosity in many ways and in particular to this project has been greatly appreciated.

"I think now that's my purpose in life—to document the history of the Japanese experience in Seattle and the Pacific Northwest."

WHEN DID YOU LIVE IN THE CENTRAL AREA?

In 1960, I had been accepted in the University of Washington nursing program in public health. I worked nine months full-time at King County Hospital before I started school and then worked part time at Swedish Hospital. I came to school here from Oregon because my grandfather wanted me to go to school in Seattle. His roots in America were here.

When I got here and started looking for an apartment, my housemates and I were turned away from three different buildings before we could find one that would rent to Japanese.

IN 1960? IT'S INTERESTING TO LEARN THAT EVEN IN THE CENTRAL AREA WITH REDLINING THERE WERE FURTHER RESTRICTIONS ON RENTING TO JAPANESE AMERICANS.

We ended up living at the Monticello Apartments.

At that time I was studying at the Japanese Language School. My future husband's younger sister was a classmate. I didn't have a car and she offered to drive me home so that's how I developed a relationship with my husband. We married on Christmas Eve in 1961.

ONCE YOU GOT MARRIED WHERE DID YOU AND YOUR HUSBAND LIVE?

On 23rd Avenue, near Holy Names. That house is still there right as you turn downhill towards the university. If you didn't turn, you'd run right into the house.

DID YOU HAVE YOUR DAUGHTERS IN THAT HOUSE?

We did.

WHAT WAS THAT NEIGHBORHOOD LIKE IN 1968?

When we first moved in, a neighbor came over very excited that we were Japanese Americans and were moving in. In 1968, I was unaware of the incarceration problems that had taken place in the Central Area in the Forties.

YOU GREW UP ON THE OTHER SIDE OF THE CASCADES?

Not only that—we went to the incarceration camp to visit and I thought they (the Japanese internees) were having a great time. Back then, we lived on a farm in Idaho. We had relocated before the war and didn't have to go to the camp because we lived outside the restricted zone, which was four hundred miles from the coast.

We visited Minidoka because many of our friends were there. Living on a farm, we didn't have neighbors very close by, so when I visited it seemed like the kids in camp were all having a lot of fun. My mother particularly envied all the craft classes the ladies were taking. Also, she noticed the women didn't have to cook. My twenty-one year old uncle worked hard during the week so he could drive to Minidoka for the Saturday night dances. Despite what seemed like the good times they were having while incarcerated, our family wouldn't consider trading places. We knew freedom was most important.

YOU STARTED TALKING EARLIER ABOUT THE COMPOSITION OF YOUR NEIGHBORHOOD ON 23RD?

There was two Black families across the street and one Japanese family a few doors down, the Hayashis, another Black family three doors down. There were the Vogels, Germans, across the street.

64

We knew everybody for about two to three blocks; we were pretty close. I organized block parties. Our kids played outside with all the other kids, they all were playing in our yard. I had doors open so there were kids running through our house. One day a kid knocked our television off its stand. There were trikes and bikes all over in our yard. I found a photo last night of the kids making a train of these toy vehicles. Because the kids were always playing in the street, I organized a kitchen conference and got all these signatures to get curbing put in on 23rd Avenue so the cars couldn't rush in. That was one of the first neighborhood traffic diversions. Since then, the Department of Transportation made lots of diversionary traffic controls in the streets of Seattle but that was one of the first ones.

IN THE EVENING DID PEOPLE SIT ON THEIR STOOPS TO SOCIALIZE?

No, people didn't sit on their porches at night by then.

WHY WAS THAT?

It was getting a little scary. There was a huge march from the university to downtown. A Civil Rights protest that came by our house. The Black Panthers sort of instigated some things along the route. There was a fear that a Molotov cocktail could be thrown in our windows because we were right on the March route. Anybody who lived on the route was afraid.

THIS WAS IN THE 1970s? YOU WERE IN THE CENTRAL AREA A LITTLE BIT LONGER THAN MANY OTHER FOLKS. IT SEEMS BY THEN THE JEWISH COMMUNITY HAD ALL PULLED UP STAKES. THERE WAS JEWISH FLIGHT, THERE WAS ASIAN FLIGHT, THERE WAS BLACK MIDDLE CLASS FLIGHT AS WELL AS WHITE FLIGHT ALL ABOUT THE SAME TIME.

One night my husband woke up to see someone shooting out the windows of a house across 23rd Street. Because of the unrest in the neighborhood, insurance companies raised rates, then one company was going to cancel our home insurance because we were living in the Central Area, so we had to get insurance elsewhere. And busing was instituted at that time.

HOW WAS BUSING PERCEIVED HERE?

My recollection is that many people didn't like it. I didn't want my kids to be riding all over town. However, my view was different because I had grown up in a rural White area in the middle of a neighborhood that was really anti-Japanese. We had gotten to know our new neighbors and developed new relationships. Over time we got them to respect us. That was really valuable; it gave me a new perspective on Americanism because Japanese Americans were just as guilty

65

of being isolationist. For example, when I came to Seattle I encountered a lot of cliques in the Japanese community. When people come from outside, like myself, we felt isolated and rejected. I had enough self-confidence that I was not intimidated. Still, it's really hard to break into those cliques. They still exist today. I've been here long enough that I could almost be part of cliques, although that's dependent on what social class you belong to. I also have had the experience of different cliques because I had skipped a grade, I was with my class and then also my age group, which were two different groups.

YOU PUT TOGETHER, FOR THE UNIVERSITY OF WASHINGTON SPECIAL COLLECTIONS, A HISTORY OF THE JAPANESE IN THIS AREA, THE ISSEI AND THE NISEI. CAN YOU EXPLAIN HOW YOU STARTED THE HISTORY OF THE JAPANESE AMERICAN COMMUNITY?

I found the community leaders and the stories of where they came from, where they were born, where they lived and so on…The first-generation Japanese were still alive. Of course, there's an immigrant story of why they came to America. I started putting that together. I also had an innate interest in psychology so I wanted to know why people made certain decisions. I went with my instincts and what I found out about that Japanese American experience hasn't changed since; it's stood the test of time.

I think now that's my purpose in life—to document the history of the Japanese experience in Seattle and the Pacific Northwest. That made it important for me to help put together a Japanese Cultural Center. Over many, many years, through the efforts, ideas and energies of myself, Chuck Kato, Ken Sato, Toru Sakahara and Tomio Moriguchi and many, many others, we made a Japanese Cultural Center out of the buildings that had been the Language School and Community Center on Weller. It took initiative and political maneuvering but finally we got it done. In 2003 we got the center and the language school merged and incorporated. It's been moving forward for ten years now and received a million-dollar remodel.

SO, THE JAPANESE LANGUAGE SCHOOL BUILDING BECAME THE JAPANESE CULTURAL CENTER. IT IS A GREAT BUILDING.

It's a hundred years old this year. The first section was built in 1913. It's on the National Registry of Historic Places.

It has a great history, at one point it housed returning internees released from incarceration at the camps.

They just got a Park Service grant to document the families in residence after the incarceration camps. There were twenty-five families who lived there from about 1946 to 1955. Then, it was turned back into a Japanese Language School and Community Center. After the war it was the Japanese Community Service. Genji Mihara was the executive and the president of it then.

Before the war it was sort of a Chamber of Businesspeople and they built the Japanese Language School. They were the organizers of what was called a 'Kenjinkai.' A 'ken' means the various prefectures in Japan and each prefecture has their community organization. If you're from Hiroshima, you belong to that ken, each has a representative that forms a representative body to make community decisions.

The community developed through these organizations. Before the war, mostly these businesses were hotels. During 1890 to 1910, there might have been about ten Japanese-run hotels. The Japanese who worked on the railroads would come back to Seattle on their days off. Probably the hotel functioned as their homes, where they got medical care and so forth. If the hotel was run by someone from a particular ken, all the workers from that region in Japan would use that hotel. My ancestors are from Hiroshima. My great grandfather came here and worked on the railroads in 1897.

I learned from some of my research done during this project about Minidoka that some people make the contention that the reason the Japanese were forced out of the land on the west side of the Cascades was because they were such successful farmers. It allowed white farmers to take those flourishing businesses.

That was mostly in California. That is true, though.

It makes sense because why were people forced into camps on one half of a state and not the other?

67

You see in California the farms were big, but they were small up here. That was true about the big-time farmers so there was some of that, especially because Issei could not own property and in 1921 they also could not rent property, so many farmers lost everything when they went to camp.

ANOTHER THING I LEARNED WAS THAT AFTER MINIDOKA, A HIGH PERCENTAGE OF PEOPLE DIDN'T COME BACK TO THE CENTRAL AREA. I WONDER WHY?

I think (because of) their feelings about the discrimination they'd faced. Some were willing to fight for what they had while others were not entrepreneurial and business savvy so they didn't come back and went to work for someone else. There was a time, even if one had a college degree they wouldn't be hired. The war erased that and Japanese were known to be honest and hard workers. They later proved themselves because by 1980 in Washington, the Japanese were statistically the highest percentage of white-collar workers and per capita income. They were the most educated, they had fewer numbers of children, and they out-married more. The Native Americans and the Japanese out-married more compared to the other ethnic groups.

OUT-MARRIAGE IS WHEN YOU MARRY SOMEONE OF A DIFFERENT ETHNIC BACKGROUND. WHY DO YOU THINK PEOPLE MADE THAT CHOICE?

Because of prejudice, people just wanted to be as American as they could be. Kids of that generation went overboard to be American. Something like nearly ninety percent of Sansei (third generation) out-married where I grew up. On the other hand, as one of the older Sansei, it was still made clear that I socialize with and marry only Japanese. Therefore, my grandfather was known as a match-maker. It was known that if I didn't find someone quickly on my own, there would be negotiations started on my behalf.

I was born over there in 1939. I lived there during the Japanese American concentration camp years. Then, I went to college in Portland. When I left for college I had to take a train because my folks couldn't afford to drive in those days. At the train station a lady came running up to me to ask, 'Are you Japanese?' She said, 'Stand right there. My girls have never met anyone Japanese.' That was my first experience of being a specimen, a curiosity.

AND FOR READERS WHO MIGHT NEVER HAVE EXPERIENCED THAT, WHAT DOES IT FEEL LIKE TO BE MADE A REPRESENTATIVE OF AN ENTIRE COMMUNITY BECAUSE YOU HAPPEN TO BE STANDING THERE?

It was reverse discrimination by that time but we were singled out and made to feel a little uncomfortable. I went to Lewis and Clark College. One time, my roommate wanted to set me up on a date but he said he couldn't go out with me because his parents might not like it if he dated a Japanese girl.

In that sense that's where I was fortunate. My grandpa is one of my heroes. He built churches and he was a community leader. When I was called 'Jap,' and all that, I had a heritage to support me. I felt proud to be called Japanese. My family instilled that into us. Each culture has special cultural traits that help us overcome hardship. That's one of the key things I try to do in developing the Cultural Center here.

William G Lowe, 14th & Pine

To meet William is to be impressed with his sense of purpose, his ability to speak his mind and share his ideas while leaving room for others' thoughts. He has a gravitas, a seriousness of mind and a ready smile. His family was the first Black family to buy a home in Capitol Hill.

"I am still not those epithets, I am walking history. I'm a dinosaur. I've lived it; I walk it; I talk it; I teach it."

You grew up in the neighborhood in the late 1940s?

I was born in Seattle at the old Columbus Hospital in 1946 during the baby boomer time. I'm a dinosaur and a Seattle native. I was the youngest in my class, graduating from Garfield High in 1964. I was sixteen and a half years old; everyone else was eighteen going on nineteen.

How would you describe your neighborhood when you were growing up?

We grew up on Capitol Hill, a block from Holy Names Academy and three blocks from St. Joseph's. We were in an Irish-Catholic, Jewish, Caucasian neighborhood. We were always described as the first Black family on the Hill. There were other neighborhoods at the time that were allowing Negroes, people of color, to move out of the Holly Park and Rainier Vista housing projects.

The Army built one (housing project) the Navy built one and the government built another. This was so when your father came out of the Armed Forces, they had a place to begin raising their families. There was an effort to get into the areas of Madrona, Leschi and even Capitol Hill, which really is the northern extension of the Central District across Madison Street.

When you cross Madison, the demographics were entirely different. There were (real estate) covenants that didn't allow people to sell (their houses) to Japanese. They didn't sell necessarily to Italians, and they certainly didn't sell to people of color. We bought our house from the Schwartz family who owned the marine supply company. There's still a building downtown on 1st and Jackson that the Schwartz family built.

Our next-door neighbors were the Reeds. Barry Reed Sr. owned the hardware store at 23rd and Jackson. The McDougalls lived next door, and the McDonalds lived across the street from us. When you go back and look at the history of Seattle these were families that were in the labor movement. They owned the department stores. We were in a very good neighborhood.

We just didn't know it or appreciate it (because we were kids). All my parents wanted to do was raise their family. They had every intention to keep their yard up, send their kids to school, educate them well and be a good neighbor. That is just how we did it. Over the years other families (of color) began to move in as this restricted/unrestricted attitude was lessened.

I can remember, as a kid, riding from corner to corner on our block because our mother always wanted to be able to see where her kids were. My younger sister and I could ride up and down the street, first with our tricycles and later with our bicycles. My mom could look out any front window and she could see her children. It wasn't so much that you were afraid of your neighbors but at the same time you were cautious because you were colored at the time. It was a brand new cultural challenge not only for them but also for us.

My father's out of Louisiana. My mother's out of Florida. My father came here because of the Army. My mother because of Rosie the Riveter and the Boeing Company. It was that attitude that got you to a better place in life. After my father got out of the Army, he went home, packed a bag and came right back. He always said he'd never seen water so blue or trees and grass so green as when he came to Seattle. No one went to Seattle. Everyone went to Detroit because of the auto industry. You went to Chicago because of the opportunities. If you were going to go west, you went to California; nobody went west to go to Seattle.

BEYOND THE PHYSICAL ENVIRONMENT, DID HE TALK ABOUT HOW IT FELT COMPARED TO THE SOUTH?

Well, there was an interesting dynamic. The West and the Pacific Northwest were not as open, as inviting, as one might believe. There is something called subtle racism. And it is alive and well even in this day. There were people who wouldn't say they didn't like you but they would treat you with a certain amount of disdain or ignore you. There were other people who might be tolerant on an individual-to-individual basis, in a humanistic way, but in a collective way they were not going to be seen as an integrationist, one who was going to align themselves with Negroes. There were other disparaging examples in language that they would use to each other about you.

71

We were higher on the social rank, the African American community, than the Japanese, which was unfortunate but we had just fought a war with the Japanese. Native Americans were seen and stereotyped as being drunks, so they were not going to be in your neighborhood. People of Hispanic descent were seen as illegal even if they had been born in this country. So racism and discrimination were alive and well even in the Pacific Northwest.

I HAD A FRIEND WHO MOVED TO BOSTON AND SHE SAID IT WAS A RELIEF BECAUSE THE RACISM WAS DIRECT. SUBTLE RACISM IS HARDER BECAUSE IT'S INSIDIOUS. YOU DON'T KNOW WHEN IT'S GOING TO COME UP BECAUSE EVERYONE'S NICE TO YOU.

And the reason you're surprised is (that) you let your guard down. We were always on guard. Growing up in our household we were encouraged to achieve. It was also reinforced not to hate but to be aware that you have to work twice as hard because that's just the way of our society. You have to be on guard because when you're not on guard then complacency sets in and then you're vulnerable. Vulnerability will kill you or get you killed.

THE ONLY WAY I CAN RELATE TO THAT IS AS A SMALL WOMAN BUT IT'S DIFFERENT. I ONLY HAVE TO BE AWARE WHEN I'M GOING TO MY CAR AT NIGHT. I DON'T HAVE TO BE AWARE ALL DAY LONG EVERYWHERE I GO. PSYCHOLOGICALLY THAT MUST BE TIRING.

I don't know because I've always been who I am. What it is—it is strengthening. You know that it's unfair; it is what it is. I can do one of two things. I can succumb to it or I can be aware of it and do what I need to do. If I do what I need to do, then this God in Heaven that I serve will make a way. So, I don't worry. I pray. That's what Christians do. The saying goes, if you're going to pray don't worry; and if you're going to worry, don't pray. It is what it is.

So I did not live my life as a second-class citizen. I lived my life understanding I am who I am. My father always used to say, your job is to go to school, not to play sports. Your job is to go to school. I pay taxes so you have a right to go to school and to play in the park. You have a right to walk down the street. I will protect your right to do those things. But you need to do the things I need you to do, to represent us, to strengthen the family name. Your name means something. It means integrity. It means that you're honest, that you don't steal other people's things; that's a family trait. That's integrity. That's motivation.

As you excel and you achieve, that levels the playing field even for those individuals who don't like you or those who hate you. If they cannot out-do you then they have to go to some other means. We trust that it will be legal and if it is illegal we still have rights in this country. So we didn't grow up thinking, 'Oh my gosh, we're poor.' We may have been but we didn't know it. We may have been middle class but we didn't know that either. We knew that our yard, our house, was very well kept. There was a sense of pride and accomplishment in our household. Our name meant something. So when you instill your children with that, there's a sense of pride.

AND ROOTEDNESS.

Absolutely. We knew who we were. Now, you may have an opinion of us and that's fine. I don't live for your opinion. If you like what I do, that's fine. If you don't, that's your problem. I'm going to do it honestly. I'm going to compete. I'm going to be the best I can be. My father always used to say about sports, sports are all played from the top of your shoulder to the top of your head. If I can take the first step and beat you, you'll never catch me. If I can out-think you, even if you outweigh me, I can use your weight against you. If I make a move quicker than you, then you spend the rest of this race trying to catch up. I can't think of a better motivation than that.

IT SOUNDS LIKE YOUR FATHER WAS A VERY STRONG, VERY CLEAR PRESENCE IN YOUR LIFE.

He was a good, hard-working man. He did not mind work, didn't mind going to work, didn't see any overtime that he didn't want. He had a mission. His mission was his family. He wanted a better life for us than he had. He did not come from abject poverty; he came off a farm where there were nine kids. My mother came from a family of twenty-one, she was the twenty-first child. My grandmother was married twice, outlived both husbands, had twenty-one kids. In 1955, we went to the South, got my grandmother and brought her back to Seattle. It was twofold. We had a built-in babysitter but also my mother was able to bring her mother to a better life. That was strengthening.

We were latch key kids, but we had our grandmother there. In the late 1950s everyone in Seattle Public Schools had a dog tag with your name, address, religion and blood type. You could hang your door key on it too. Seattle schools had that to identify kids. There was controversy over that because people thought that was too much information, Big Brother looking at you. We weren't fearful but there was always the idea that government wants to know too much about us. We want to keep a bit of privacy. We didn't want to put Protestant on the dog tag; we were not Protestants.

We were actually Baptists but there was no category for Baptists, so again we had America dictating who you were.

People never called themselves colored. If you go back to the Crayola crayon box, there's no color called colored, so what color is colored? If you called someone who was a person of color 'Black,' those were fighting words cause we weren't black. Skin isn't black. Black is a color. And you aren't White because white is a color. So, what are you? You're Caucasian or you're Irish or you're Irish Catholic or what have you. So what is color? What is colored? It's a category.

Now, every time you had to fill out something, it asked what is your nationality? American. (And they'd say) 'No, no, you're colored.' But colored is not a nationality. And so in our household you did what you had to do when the government forms came your way. But in our upbringing, our sense of identity, my father was from Birmingham, Louisiana. My mother was from a little place called Green Cove Springs, Florida. They both grew up on farms. We had a legacy of family history. Nowhere in our family history did it say we're colored, but if that's the category, then check the box. We were Negroes and that was a category of ethnicity.

When James Brown came out in the late 1960s and said, 'I'm Black and I'm proud,' it was like, 'Oh, no.' Yet, when you listen to the lyrics, it was a great message. In this soulful song he gave identity to a race of people who had been labeled by society, by America, but had never labeled themselves. All the sudden, you take away the stigma of 'Black.' The Black Panther Party gave us Black Power. That was something that America did not know how to deal with.

You can't have it both ways; it's disingenuous. You can't say, 'You're colored, stay in your place.' Then people took what used to be a negative and turned it into a positive. This created a sense of identity and it has power. America was not ready for Black Power.

I WOULD IMAGINE THAT WOULD HAVE BEEN A POINT OF CONTENTION WITHIN THE CHURCHES BETWEEN THOSE WHO WERE OLDER AND FOLLOWED MARTIN LUTHER KING AND THOSE FOLLOWING THE YOUNG RADICALS. IT MUST HAVE SEEMED VERY THREATENING.

Especially because you couldn't identify with it. If you look at what the Reverend Dr. Martin Luther King Jr. did, he built on what Mahatma Gandhi had done (with) non-violent protest. It's hard to have someone insult you and to not defend yourself. It's even harder for someone to hit you and for you to not defend yourself. It's absolutely unfathomable that you would let someone spit upon you and you turn the other cheek. It is just not the human condition. There's a thought process that says, 'When I am hit, I hit back'. It's a defense mechanism; it's self-preservation. It's the first law of nature, all throughout the animal kingdom you have that self-preservation. If you insult me, I insult you back. You hit me, I hit you back. If you hit me again, I hit you twice as hard.

So, all the sudden you take this very dynamic and you say, 'No.' I will not subject myself to that; I will not lower myself to that level. You insult me. I explain why the insult does not pertain to me. You hit me. I walk away. I will not subject myself to lowering myself to your standard, to this physically confrontational animalistic behavior. I won't do that; I'm stronger than you are. Psychologically, it is the strongest thing you can do. Still, it is challenging because how much can the human psyche take when this (violence and insults) comes their way?

We found that there was a movement (around Dr. Martin Luther King Jr.) that sprung up and permeated and was invested in this country. Now, it was not widely endorsed early on. I can remember as a young teenager saying, 'Oh, no. I'm not going to be with Martin Luther King. If somebody slaps me, I'm slapping him back.' But if you think about the psyche, here was something absolutely brand new. Something that we had never experienced before and something that we had to learn to accept because there were so many beneficial aspects of it.

Then you take the Black Panther Party who spoke to the Black manhood of the Black community. If someone hits us we hit them back. We are like a Third-World country in America. You attack us and we will attack back. America has guns; we will go get guns. Oh, an entirely different type of empowerment that spoke to many because some people saw non-violence as too slow a process for change. We live in America where the general consensus is, 'Add water, turn on the microwave and have a meal in minutes.' America has not gotten away from instant gratification, instant change, but real change comes from patience and persistence.

So, IT SEEMS LIKE THERE WAS A HUGE PHILOSOPHICAL DIVISION IN THE COMMUNITY?

There was a division. There was absolutely. Dr. Martin Luther King comes out of the church. The Black Panther Party comes out of the street. There's a line of demarcation that's wide as the Mississippi River. Dr. Martin Luther King is a minister, he's of age, he has a family and he's older. The Black Panther Party is young and vibrant. So you have the old bull talking about the philosophy

75

of change and you have the young bull saying, 'I'll knock something down if something runs up on me. We'll battle.' Oh, my goodness. What a dichotomy.

AARON (DIXON) MENTIONED THAT THERE WERE KIDS THAT WEREN'T ALLOWED TO TALK TO HIM ONCE HE JOINED. AND THESE WERE KIDS HE'D PLAYED WITH HIS WHOLE LIFE. THAT MUST HAVE BEEN TRUE IN ALL THE NEIGHBORHOODS?

Some of it was fear. There's a parent thinking, 'If you arm yourself against America that has an Army and a Navy and an Air Force, you will die.' But you had these young people like Aaron and Elmer, who I know, who talked to Huey P. Newton and others and looked at this revolutionary philosophy.

Then between father and son there are generational philosophical clashes. The father has lived it, worked hard and been rewarded by his hard work. Yet, had there not been this unfair line of demarcation, how much further could he have gotten? Then, there is a young educated son; his father has made sure he has an education, made sure he could walk to school, made sure he had more than one pair of jeans, made sure that he was able to compete. The son thinks, 'I saw what you done to my father and it was unfair. I will not allow that to continue to happen to my father. I will certainly not allow it to happen to me and to the generations who follow me.' So, you have an angry young man. You can call him a Black Panther or revolutionary, you can call him 'young buck' who does not want to see the transgressions that his father may or may not have tolerated, who may have spoken against (these transgressions) and may have been penalized for speaking up. Yet, if a man is truly a man, the head of his household, the carrier of the seed, the protector of his family, how do you reduce that man to something less than human without consequence?

IT SOUNDS LIKE IT WAS A TOUGH TIME TO NAVIGATE BECAUSE THERE WERE TWO VERY DIFFERENT VIEWS.

You were also living in two different worlds. One world by day where you work for the Man and then you come home at night. You look at the positive—here is a family that's growing. (Your children are) asking you, 'Why is our playground not as good as the playground in other areas? Why do we not have the new school books? Why are our science labs secondary, why are our desks old?' So something comes along called Model Cities.

WAS THAT UNDER (PRESIDENT) JOHNSON?

It was. It was meant to try and level the playing field. Then, you look at your history because you're constantly being educated and you see the cheating, the duplicity, the skullduggery and the manipulation that's going on in this America. You ask yourself, 'Why does that happen? Something's wrong here.' We look through the annals of history and we say, 'It didn't have to be that way, if they had just played fair.' We were playing fair.

I WAS READING THAT BOOK ON JAZZ IN SEATTLE, IT MENTIONS THAT LEON VAUGHN WAS TOP OF HIS LAW CLASS. HE WAS INVITED TO A JOB INTERVIEW. WHEN HE WALKED IN, THEY SAID, 'WE'RE NOT LOOKING FOR JANITORS.' SO ALL OF HIS TALENT, ALL OF THAT KNOWLEDGE, AND ALL THOSE OTHER PEOPLE WHO HAD TRAINING AND WERE NOT ALLOWED TO CONTRIBUTE. WHEN YOU THINK OF THAT LOSS OVER GENERATIONS…

What happens to the educated man or woman from the South who comes across the Mason Dixon line and comes to this opportunity in the West and finds that the cultural differences are so subtle? I'm trained to be an educator but when I walk in the room, you only see me as a Negro. You don't even look at my credentials. You just say, 'We're not looking for maids or domestics at this time.' Well, you looked at the package but you haven't taken the time to look at the person, or the content in that package, so you stereotyped a race of people. Why are our young people angry? Because they've watched the treatment of their fathers and their mothers, their grandfathers and their grandmothers, and it continues even in this twenty-first century.

THIS PROJECT HAS BEEN A REAL EDUCATION FOR ME. I THINK THE CIVIL RIGHTS MOVEMENT WAS TO A DEGREE SUCCESSFUL, THE BLACK POWER MOVEMENT WAS TO A DEGREE SUCCESSFUL, AND THE IDEA OF BEING PROUD OF WHO YOU ARE WAS TO SOME DEGREE SUCCESSFUL. STILL THINGS HAVEN'T CHANGED ECONOMICALLY; IN SOME WAYS THEY'RE WORSE.

If not for the Schwartz family, my family would never have been allowed to purchase their house. We get to cross Madison Street, we're uphill from Montlake and Lake Washington. We're living in a neighborhood where they have never seen us before. Yet, we still go to church in the heart of the Central Area. My mother was a fifty-six-year member of the New Hope Baptist Church off of Yesler Street. Our barbershop was still on Jackson Street. We may have shopped at the Safeway on 15th and John Street but we also went to Rev's Rib Place on 18th and Yesler. We bought from Stern's Market, who cured their own meats and made the hot links. We went for those things that were of the South, of our cuisine. We went into the heart of the neighborhood for those things.

ONE OF THE BLESSINGS OF DOING THIS PROJECT IS MEETING PEOPLE WHO WERE THE FIRST TO MOVE INTO A NEIGHBORHOOD, WHO MADE THEIR MARK ON THE HISTORY OF THIS PLACE.

It's marvelous that you're doing this because we did not set out to be trailblazers or to be the first. We didn't set out to make history. What we set out to do was to survive.

The church was one place where people of color, Black folks, could gather. They didn't only gather for worship, we baptized or we christened our young people there, we married in the church (and) we buried in the church. And when there was a crisis, (when) we could gather no place else, we would come to the church.

I can remember in 1961, the great march in Seattle. They had a young minister at Mount Zion, the Reverend Dr. Barry McKinney. You also had a relatively young minister by the name of Rev. John Adams who was the pastor of First AME. The city didn't think these ministers were talking to each other but they were. So you had this young upstart by the name of Rev. Dr. Martin Luther King Jr. come to Seattle. He was a classmate at Morehouse College of Rev. McKinney, so that's how he got here.

Rev. Dr. Martin Luther King Jr. came out to preach for his colleague and he said, 'What's happening out there?' He listened and said we should get together. We should make a statement about the way we're being treated in Seattle. We will make a statement to the department stores about us, (about) adults being followed around the store as if we're going to steal, (about) our kids being stereotyped and categorized. They can't take clothes into the dressing room and try them on. The store said, 'If someone finds out colored people were in those clothes, they won't buy them. If you try them on, you have to buy them.' Well, White folks don't have to do that. Also, we are qualified to do many jobs in the department store but we seem to never get offered anything past the cafeteria or the janitorial jobs. Those are good jobs but (we) were not getting past them. And so it goes, on and on, the redlining and the attitudes.

So there was a march planned on a Saturday. Let me just give you this explanation. Mount Zion is located on 19th and Madison; First AME is located on 14th and Pine. If you come up Madison and down Pine and the congregation from AME and the congregation from Mt Zion would gather at 14th and Pine. Now, if you come from Tabernacle, from Jackson walking west on Jackson, to 23rd to be joined by people from the Institutional Baptist Church, and if you were to continue down Yesler until 14th, they could turn north and be joined by Goodwill Baptist Church. As they came up 14th and Spring they would be joined by Progressive Church, and if they continued across Madison they reach the First AME on Pine. What I'm explaining is that the Central Area and all its churches were joining and walking north. When you get to 14th and Pine and then go down the hill to downtown Seattle, people downtown would see, coming over the hill, thousands of people.

It was my sophomore year of high school, 1961, and there was a great picture in *The Seattle Times* and *The Post Intelligencer* of us coming down the hill on Pine. Thousands of colored folks, Negroes, who purposely walked to Pine Street and Bellevue Avenue and again turned north. There's a significance of always going north, and it's biblical. If you look at the sky and find the Northern Star, you can find your way anywhere. And so, we came across the brand new Denny overpass and filled it with us! And we came down to Stewart Street and turned south into downtown Seattle. The reason being was that at that corner of Denny and Stewart was the Greyhound Service Station. What we were doing was strategically making a statement about this city.

The idea was to come down Pine and 14th here, bringing unity from the Central Area, bringing all the congregations north. Then downtown, as we came across the overpass, is Greyhound, a major employer who wouldn't hire us, and then past that is the Seattle Times building. They can look out all their windows and see us. And then you take Stewart Street and you head back downtown. It was strategically designed so when we went downtown we turned and went up a block back to Pine and there you had I. Magnin, Fredrick and Nelsons, the Bon Marché, JJ Jacobs and Nordstrom department stores. You also had the Federal Courthouse on 5th and 6th.

They had maybe five or six police motorcycle escorts for thousands of people. They thought surely Black folks would tear up something, would riot. But we had been instructed from our congregations. It's a peaceful demonstration. They're going to holler racial epithets at you, they're going to give you the finger, and they're going to spit at you. They were coming out of taverns on that Saturday morning and they're hollering at you, Nigger! Coon! You keep walking 'cause that's not your name. You're on a mission. And even now—I get filled thinking about 1961 (takes a deep breath, eyes shining), because of the success of nonviolence. Because these epithets are not who you are; you know what your name is.

I say this thousands of times because I'm master of ceremonies, or I'm leading a discussion, 'Is there anyone in the sound of my voice who does not know his or her name?' People laugh and say, 'Of course I know my name.' When you know your name you can introduce yourself to someone else. When I know your name I have lessened a part of your fear because now I know you. If I know your name, I can at least call you by your name. I can have a conversation with you and in that conversation we will probably find that we have more in common than we have in a distance. Because these (bodies) are nothing but packages. One day we're going to trade these packages in. What we have in common is that all of us have one heart that pumps red blood. I don't care about the package; that's just a visual. You have one heart that pumps red blood. We have that in common. If I know your name and you know my name, then we can have a dialogue. And that dialogue will lessen those fears that seem to separate us.

The church was our springboard. Many have gone from the church because they think it's anti-quated; it's not progressive. They think it is not connected to what is happening in this world, but we must remember that the only place we had to baptize, to marry, to bury, when we had no other place to gather we had the church: church basement, church parking lot, church sanctuary, church grounds. It was a point where we came together. That march in 1961 proved that if we all met at our respective safe houses we could gather strategically. We had a mighty force, a mighty army and a mighty statement to make.

Mona Lake Jones is a former poet laureate for Seattle and King County. She gave unstintingly to children's education both in the school district and at the Mt. Zion Church. She writes poetry from the heart—if words could be written in sunlight, love and honey, well, that'd be how it feels to hear her read her work.

"So the Central Area to me has always been restrictive because we were almost confined there. Yet, it was a joyful place to be. We had restaurants, we had the churches and it was comfortable. That's because there was a culture that was embracing."

MONA ON THE CENTRAL AREA:

I can remember when the Central Area was the only place we could live. We were trying to look for an apartment. My friend and I had just graduated from college and we just wanted an apartment, we didn't care where it was. We just wanted a spiffy, new apartment. That was not possible. Every place we went they said it had just been rented; it's not longer available. So, we went to the city Human Rights Office because we had gotten real used to having to stand on either side of the door because if they saw us then they simply wouldn't open the door.

WHAT YEAR WAS THIS?

I graduated from school in 1961. So it was about 1962.

OPEN HOUSING STARTED IN 1969?

Yes. My friend and I were a part of making that happen because they used us as a test case. They sent two White women out with the same supposed background that we had and in every instance the apartment was available and they could move in whenever they chose to do so. We were the folks who were out there being used to help make the Open Housing happen because all of that was documented. Ironically, at the same time, my husband had just gotten back from playing in the Rose Bowl and was the big football star. He also was trying to find an apartment and couldn't, although we weren't yet knowing each other at that point. So, at the same time they were testing (landlords) using us two women to make open housing happen, they were also using Joe. He got a lot more press because of his football reputation at that time.

After we realized that people really didn't want us (to live near them) it was kind of frightening to think that if we demanded to be in a complex that didn't want us to be there; we would be two single women (living there).

I THINK THAT'S ANOTHER UNACKNOWLEDGED THING. IS TO BE FIRST IS TO BE VERY LONELY. TO BE THE ONLY IS VERY LONELY. IT GOES AGAINST EVERY HUMAN INSTINCT TO GO INTO A SITUATION WHEN YOU'RE NOT WANTED.

Absolutely. I've been there. I can't tell you how many times I've been there. I cannot tell you how many times I have been the only, the first. Coming from Spokane going to school there at Washington State University, WSU, then coming to Seattle. I mean I have been the first (pause) and the lonely (laughs) lots and lots and lots of times. I can remember when I first realized that people were not going to like me just because of the color of my skin. That was in first grade. I was able to play outside; it was different then. We didn't lock our doors. A little girl came to my house every day and every day she'd say, 'Come to my home with me!' She was just down the alley maybe four or five or six houses away, and Mother would never let me go.

She came so much and for so long that finally Mother relented. She said, 'Well, go ahead. You can go to Karen's house.' I went down the alley with Karen to her house. She says, 'Mommy, I brought Mona home.' Her mom said, 'Is this Mona? Is this whose house you've been playing at every day?' And she jerked her through the door and slammed the door.

I went back down the alley and into the backyard and I saw my mother in the kitchen and then I saw tears start to come down her face. She knew she'd let me down. She hadn't gotten me ready; she'd made the assumption that because that little girl was playing at our house every day that the parents were obviously aware and okay with it. Turns out that they weren't. She sat me down right then and said Mona, 'There are going to be some people who don't like you just because of the color of your skin.' That was just this powerful...I can still...I've told this story I don't know how many times. Every time I tell it, I can still feel the pain that my mother was feeling and the dismay and the hurt that I was feeling because I thought, I've always been nice; I thought you just had to be a nice, little girl and people (would like you) but—no, not some people. So that lesson I learned very early and had this sense of being the only. There was always this little bit of trust and mistrust.

They (my parents) taught us really early before James Brown said, 'Black and beautiful.' They were telling us that there was a beauty in who we were. They would do all kinds of things to find Black dolls that would reflect us. I can remember that being just a monumental thing in the early 1940s when we were playing with dolls. Now that seems so insignificant because you can get any color or kind of doll that you want but not back then. They were trying to help us see ourselves in a positive way. They went through catalogs looking for them.

I'M ASSUMING THAT YOUR PARENTS CAME TO SPOKANE WITH THE GREAT MIGRATION AND THAT YOUR FATHER CAME TO WORK ON THE DAM. WAS THE REST OF THEIR FAMILY STILL IN TENNESSEE?

Yes. They were the only ones who came this way. When my father came out here that summer to help build the Grand Coulee Dam he was making money and decided not to go back (laughs). When he went back for my mother, they were really out here on their own. He was the first Lake (in Spokane). My name is Mona Lake Jones and I was the first Lake that came this way (to Seattle).

SO YOU ALL HAD THAT CORE COURAGE.

Absolutely. No question about it. In, particular, my father. Mother was kind of going along with the program but Dad was adventuresome. He was feeling this was going to be an opportunity for him to make a living, to raise a family in an environment that was not as fearful and prejudiced as where he was coming from in Tennessee and Mississippi.

WHEN YOU MOVED TO SEATTLE DID THEY STAY IN SPOKANE?

Oh, yes. They lived and died in Spokane. When I was growing up, I would come to Seattle all through my grade school and high school because Washington State was small enough then that the Blacks in Spokane knew Blacks in the Central Area in Seattle. That was at the time when almost all Blacks lived in the Central Area. During all of my visits, I'd stay at the Allen's house on

33rd Avenue. My whole reference for Seattle was the Central Area. That was where we came to go to church, and it's where we came to go to the parties; it's where we came to do everything. We'd come from Spokane to Seattle in the summertime and vacation times.

WHEN YOU THINK ABOUT THE CENTRAL AREA WHEN YOU WERE A TEENAGER, HOW WOULD YOU DESCRIBE IT? WHAT DO YOU REMEMBER FROM THAT TIME?

I always looked forward to coming because there were more Blacks living in Seattle in the Central Area than there were in Spokane. So it was like, Oh we get to go meet new kids! Also, the church was bigger. There were more people, there was more to do, there were more parties, more opportunities to have boyfriends and more opportunities to get together socially with folks who are our same age. So, Spokane to Seattle Central Area was a fun (trip), it was something to look forward to.

THAT WOULD HAVE BEEN IN THE LATE FIFTIES WHEN YOU WERE A TEENAGER. AT THAT TIME WAS THE AREA STILL SOMEWHAT MIXED? OR WAS IT MOSTLY BLACK AT THAT POINT?

It was mostly Black. Once you passed the ridge (34th Avenue and east) there would be some differences. For the most part the Blacks were all congregated in that Central Area. Now that's not to say that some didn't live other places (in Seattle) and how they got to I'm not sure. To buy a piece of real estate or to buy a home outside the Central Area was very problematic.

Even after Joe and I were married, we tried to find a house to purchase. It was really difficult to find anything outside the parameters of the Central Area. When I would talk to people on the phone you got pretty savvy about how to maneuver the system. You don't go in person because if you did then you surely weren't going to get an opportunity to (see the house). We would do a lot of business on the telephone. I remember one day a woman Realtor saying to me, 'Oh honey, you don't want to live out there because there are a lot of colored people.' She obviously didn't realize she was speaking to one (laughs). Uh huh. That was…wow! It was probably in the late Sixties when we were trying to find a place to buy. It was still difficult.

So the Central Area has to me always been restrictive because we were almost confined there. Yet, it was a joyful place to be. We had restaurants, we had the churches and it was comfortable. That's because there was a culture that was embracing.

MANY OF THE PEOPLE I'VE TALKED TO HAVE LEFT (THE CENTRAL AREA). THEY'VE MOVED ELSEWHERE. ONE THING I HAVEN'T ASKED MUCH ABOUT IS HOW DO YOU FEEL ABOUT THE FACT THAT WITH THE DISPERSAL, THE COMMUNITY HAS TO HAVE CHANGED?

It has changed. Absolutely.

DO YOU FEEL THAT THE CHURCHES ARE DIFFERENT?

The Central Area now has a whole different feel. You cannot say it's the place where Blacks live and congregate (either out of necessity or out of being forced to do so) or just wanting to be there. It's not that kind of place anymore. It doesn't have the same familiar neighborhood feeling that it offered to African Americans then. We have migrated in all sorts of directions and there is a sadness about it because there is not the sense of neighborhood. There's not the sense of familiarity and support and togetherness and safeness and being in a place where there are a whole lot of folks like yourself. That in itself sometimes is comforting. There's no place like that now for African Americans like the Central Area (was).

That then means that many of the old places are gone. The churches are still there but not relevant as they were because, for instance, the church I go to now is way south in Renton. So the offerings for African Americans in the Central Area are no longer present. The bank has closed, the restaurants have closed and changed. The oldest church, the African American Methodist Church (the First AME) is being squashed by condos and apartment buildings and there's hardly space to park anymore. Mt. Zion Baptist Church is still standing and being attended. Folks are thriving there but many have left. There is an integration that was not present and now a greater diversity exists.

AT MT. ZION?

Mt. Zion still has a Blackness about its congregation but there are lots of others in attendance and the richness of the church service is still the same.

There is nothing anymore in the Central Area that you can say, 'Oh, that's a Black restaurant.' Or 'That's a Black this or that.' It just kind of doesn't exist anymore. Everything, just about everything, is integrated. And there's not a badness about that. There really is not a badness about that because that's what the world is supposed to be like. People should be able to move freely in and out and have relationships with all sorts of people and embrace all kinds of culture with the multi-ethnicity that we strived so hard for. Still, in striving for that multi-ethnic, 'diversity in everything,' there is a loss of…being…enhanced and able to reflect on who you are with people like yourself.

SO IF I CAN RESTATE THAT SLIGHTLY, CORRECT ME IF I'M WRONG, THAT SAFE PLACE, WHERE YOU CAN DROP ALL YOUR MASKS, THAT'S THE PRICE OF INTEGRATION. IT MAY BE INTEGRATED BUT YOU MIGHT NOT ALWAYS BE EMOTIONALLY SAFE.

That's exactly right. Exactly right. I can't think of the Central Area in the same way that I thought about it even twenty years ago. It's happened quickly. It's happened very fast. It's the whole notion of gentrification, taking the old and making it new. That's kind of what the Central Area is now. Every house that goes up is a modern box, tall and skinny. The flavor of the neighborhood is changing, not just in color but in housing. So tradition and culture…I'm always just a little surprised and a little nostalgic when I go through the Central Area. I think, 'Awww, that's where we used to… Awww, that's where this store was…That's where Helen's used to be…That's where we used to go to have greens and catfish. Oh, that's where we used to…' You know, all of those things that used to reflect the Black culture. They're diminishing.

I wish I had taken a photo to say, 'Look!' This is what it is all about. This is what can happen when you grow up around Garfield and Franklin, the Central Area, in and out and around about, so they (my kids) had every possible kind of friend. That's what it should be. Still, I made sure that they knew they were Black, that they liked their Blackness, and they embraced their culture as well. I think you can do it all.

I'm hoping that the Central Area as it changes can offer that kind of opportunity for that old term, 'the melting pot.' I don't want everybody to melt; I want you to be tossed around and still enjoy your culture but be able to enjoy other cultures as well. I always thought when I was growing up…I wrote about it in one of my books; I thought everybody's grandmother baked sweet potato pies and played the blues.

Then I found out through my folks across the street that they go to Scandinavian Night at the Norwegian Center and they dress up in those clothes and they have the best time. So, hopefully in the Central Area those differences will continue to be a good thing. That it won't go from a place where Black people lived to a place where just White people live. I mean, I hope that's not what's going to happen, because that would really, really be hurtful to me to see the dynamic change that drastically.

I SPENT A LOT OF TIME IN NEW YORK. WHAT I LOVED ABOUT IT WAS THAT IT WAS MIXED. IN THE CENTRAL AREA EVERY HOUSE THAT SELLS IT'S LIKE …I KNOW THAT I DON'T WANT TO LIVE IN A HOMOGENEOUS NEIGHBORHOOD EITHER. IT'S NOT GOOD FOR PEOPLE TO BE…

It's not.

…ISOLATED IN ONE SOCIOECONOMIC GROUP WITH PEOPLE. THAT'S NOT REAL LIFE.

Absolutely, It's not. It really isn't. I know when we bought the house here, I was like, 'Oh no.' We had been living in an apartment in the Central Area and we bought a house in Mt. Baker and it was…Wow! The neighbor across the street was White, as was the one on the other, and the right and the left and I thought, 'Ohhhhhh.' And we were trying to raise these two Black kids. I'll never forget the first time a little Black kid climbed over our back fence into the backyard and it was like, 'YESSSS' because I thought I had put them in a pocket of nobody like themselves and I thought, 'I'm going to have to work really hard now.'

DO YOU THINK THAT THESE PLACES WHERE PEOPLE CAN JUST BE HAVE MOVED SOUTH OR HAVE THEY JUST DISAPPEARED ENTIRELY?

I think that they still exist even in the Central Area. People who are now coming to the churches in the Central Area for that kind of community are driving into Seattle (from outside) rather than walking to the church like they used to. There aren't very many (living that close by) because so many have left the area. The church has always been, for Black folks, a place where you can not only exercise your religion, find an understanding of faith and how important it may be in your life, but it has also been a place to try your wings, to get affirmed, to be applauded. While in the broader community you might not get that.

87

So many of us grew up in the church because it was a place of safeness and support. I think it still does that for our kids because it might be the only place they get that. Hopefully, there are other avenues and outlets for that (affirmation) but we use churches to do that for our children. Because if you are not recognized at any point in your life for your talent or your skills or who you are, it's probable that you're not going to flourish. To put kids in a setting, in a church, where we know the intent of church is to be loving and to teach how to be kind. (That's where) our kids get what they need to be strong, to like who they are and to know that they have some talent.

FROM WHAT I'VE READ IT SOUNDS LIKE YOU HAD A PROGRAM AT MT. ZION IN ORDER TO PROVIDE THAT VERY THING TO CHILDREN OUTSIDE YOUR OWN FAMILY.

Absolutely. Yes. I know that there were kids who were kind of out there. We had a lot of kids come to the Ethnic School (an educational program founded and run by Mona at Mt Zion church for many years) who didn't live in the Central Area. They came from Bellevue or from wherever they were coming because they were mixed up for some reason or another. They hadn't received affirmation and they needed to get some information on their history and to see that there were people who have been successful (who look) like themselves. In starting the Ethnic School that was my intent, to put kids in an environment where every week I would have professionals of all kinds come in and talk about who they were, what they did, how they did it and how they got there. All kids were wide-eyed like, 'Really? You're a pilot? Whaat? Oh!' Also, we read literature written by Black authors and invited authors come to talk to us. We got a little money and some computers and film equipment and we even let the kids take the laptops home with them for the week so they could get the feel of technology.

We taught classes in assertiveness, how to look people in the eye and to ask questions and how to speak up and (taught them things) they probably weren't going to get in their classrooms. I knew, having been a teacher and been in a setting very much like what they found themselves in, that they needed those kinds of skills. We did it every Saturday and it was an opportunity for me, personally, to feel some success and some little bit of input in some others' lives.

I THINK THAT MAKES YOU A LITTLE BIT UNUSUAL. ONE CRITICISM I'VE HEARD FROM SOME PEOPLE IN THE BLACK COMMUNITY, OFF THE RECORD, IS THAT THEY SAY SOME PEOPLE GOT THEIRS AND OFF THEY WENT.

I know.

PEOPLE DO WHAT THEY FEEL IS BEST FOR THEM BUT IT'S NICE TO SPEND TIME WITH SOMEONE WHO FELT DRIVEN AND REWARDED BY GIVING BACK.

I think I got that from my parents too. It was always, 'Don't forget where you came from' and 'Don't forget to do what you can for your people.' That's what my mother always used to say. Don't forget your people. So it was ingrained that in some way somehow, you were going to give back. Don't forget the people who nurtured you and who may still need you. We could do with those skills that you've got now.

My hope for the Central Area is that it will not lose its ability to be welcoming to a diverse community. (Diversity) allows folks to understand, to get along and to experience different cultures and for there to be a sense of neighborhood. All that allows families to look out for each other, to care about one another. All of that used to go on in the Central Area.

I THINK THIS YEAR HAS OPENED SOME PEOPLE'S EYES. I HOPE SO.

I think so too. Oh boy, I hope so.

IT SEEMS LIKE THAT IT'S FINALLY BEING REALIZED NOT JUST THE PEOPLE THAT ARE AFFECTED WHO'VE KNOWN THIS FOR CENTURIES BUT FOR THE BROADER COMMUNITY. THEY'RE REALIZING, WAIT A MINUTE THIS KID (TRAVON MARTIN) CARRIED CANDY...

And you're dead?

OR THIS KID (TAMIR RICE) WAS JUST IN A PLAYGROUND...

And you're dead?

OR THEY (RENISHA MCBRIDE) ASKED FOR HELP BECAUSE THEY WERE IN A CAR ACCIDENT.

And you're dead?

I'M HOPING THE CORNER HAS BEEN TURNED.

That would be wonderful.

So, on the subject of the Central Area again, I think that that sense of culture and neighborhood and family and all of that was a beautiful thing in nurturing that positiveness about life.

TRUE, WHAT WE HAVE LEFT UNSPOKEN IN THE CENTRAL AREA IS HOW MUCH JOY THERE WAS. I USED TO WALK MY DOG PAST A CERTAIN HOUSE BECAUSE I KNEW THAT SUNDAY ABOUT SIX O'CLOCK I WOULD HEAR THEM SINGING AS A FAMILY. ONE WEEK I CAME BY, THE PIANO WAS GONE AND THERE WERE BOXES AND BOXES AND THEN THEY WERE GONE AND SO WAS THAT JOY, THE JOY EMANATED FROM THAT HOUSE. I HAVEN'T BEEN TO A CHURCH DURING SERVICES BUT I HEAR THE CHOIR AT ST. THERESE AND THERE'S A LOT OF JOY.

Yeah, there's a whole bunch of joy up in there.

WHAT PEOPLE OFTEN SAY, AS SHORTHAND FOR HOW DIFFERENT IT IS NOW, PEOPLE SAY IT'S SO QUIET NOW.

Yes.

IT'S SO QUIET. I DON'T THINK THEY'RE TALKING ABOUT THE ABSENCE OF SOUND. I THINK THEY'RE TALKING MORE ABOUT THE ABSENCE OF VOICES IN PLAY AND IN SONG AND IN COMMUNITY.

90

Yes. Exactly. Exactly. I remember a little girl would come to our house in the morning because her mom had an early job. She was a little, little White girl. She'd come to our house, this is when our kids were here going to school. In our house when we'd get up in the morning, it was joyful. We'd get up playing music and singing, you might do a dance or two while the stuff was cooking in the kitchen waiting for breakfast to get on the table, you'd practice some dance steps. It was just being Black. That the little girl when she first came she'd just sit at the bottom of the steps after her mother dropped her off. She'd look at people running up and down the steps, she'd listen to the music, she'd listen to my kids saying all kinds of funny stuff and she just was kind of in awe. Just like, 'Oh. What! These people!' I know she was thinking, 'these people!' One day I looked at her, she was down at the bottom of the steps and she was just dancing (laughs). And, oh, she's got it now! She just got acclimated and it just became a part of her morning just like ours. I thought that is beautiful.

She wasn't frightened about it; she just got with it. She got with the way we were moving, and the way we were talking, and the way we were dancing and that music that we played in the morning. We were just the typical kind of Black household, I think. I don't think there was anything different about us but she came from a very quiet, reserved family. I don't know what they did in the morning or how they operated but it wasn't like us. So I watched this transformation in her. I know that she took that away with her as a young woman. As she grew she had to focus on that and know that life can be a little different from yours, but it can sure be fun and it's okay to embrace another little piece of culture, you know, a little difference.

I THINK THAT'S TRUE; JOY IS A STRONG PART OF THE CULTURE.

That's what I'm saying. That's what I've been writing about, celebrating Blackness. There's this one piece and it says:

Ah, it was Saturday morning around about ten and I was passing the barbershop. I just happened to look in and my heart skipped a beat when I saw through the door. I moved in closer so I could hear a little more. And this shop had culture just bursting at the seam and when I tell you what I saw, you'll know what I mean. There were brothers of all ages sitting, waiting in line and each one of them I would describe as fine. And I don't mean fine cause they were short, tall or thin; these were just genuinely handsome Black men. They had love and strength that showed in their eyes and you knew for some just years of living had made them wise. They were grandpas and daddies and uncles and young men just laughing and talking and having great fun. Now, an example of the love that they shared was when they showed the one small son how they cared. For the first time this little fella was sitting in the chair and the barber was fixing to cut his hair. And even with his father standing close by when the clippers were turned on he started to cry.

And then it goes on about these brothers helping this little guy through his first haircut and so forth and so on. It ends as this wonderful story by saying there simply are no others who can take the place of our fine Black brothers.

So I've done that piece (at different events) and the brothers, I mean the Black men, have just hugged me and cheered and cried. I thought about that because I get that same kind of response every time I've done it. And they said, 'Nobody ever says positive things about us. We're in the newspaper when we catch a football, we're in the newspaper when we got to prison but nobody just applauds us as Black men for the kinds of things that we do and give.' And I thought, 'Wow.' I hadn't thought about that really.

TO BE SEEN AS ANOTHER HUMAN BEING AND NOT AS A THREAT.

Yes, yes and yes.

I mean they are (seen to be) such a threat in so many ways. I had trouble trying to understand why they were so happy about (that poem) when they heard it. The first time it was like shocking, it was like, 'Hey!'

MAYBE IT WAS THE JOY IN BEING SEEN. THEY WERE SEEN IN THEIR NATURAL ENVIRONMENT, CARING FOR THIS BOY WHEN PEOPLE DON'T SEE THAT PART OF THEM. SO THEY DON'T GET THAT REFLECTED BACK TO THEM—THAT'S WHY IT MEANT SO MUCH TO THEM.

Yeah, and it was just a natural thing for them. Nobody was pretentious or putting on, they were just going to take care of this little guy. He's getting his first haircut.

I do stuff about women all the time and they appreciate it but there's something about the Black male that when I do work about them, it just gets a whole other thank you response; thank you for validating us and talking about us.

So you're older than the (Black) Panthers were?

Yes. I lived through the Panthers when they were in the Central Area and they were doing the Breakfast Program and all that.

I think the Panthers here were really different than the Panthers elsewhere.

They were very different.

It's interesting because it really depends on who you talk to, some people that didn't know them personally were very afraid of the whole thing. People who knew them personally weren't afraid of them, whether they were White or Japanese or whatever.

Exactly.

From conversations I've had during this project, many understood their anger but felt what they were doing was counterproductive. And so I sense there were schisms and divisions in the neighborhood.

Exactly. We were in that (moment), 'Wait a minute you guys, is all that…necessary?' Because we've been telling everybody to turn the other cheek and be peaceful and all. But also, you had this great respect for their braveness and their putting themselves out there. Besides we were feeling it wasn't working with this peaceful thing. So, we were willing to give these guys this opportunity to be a little on the violent side and shake everybody up. We were okay with that. We weren't going to join in with you cause we're too old already. We're still with the Martin Luther King thing but we're appreciating you. So, go ahead. If you need us to help in some ways, we'll do it in the background or we'll write you a check. But, no, no. We ain't coming down with you to be in that (laughter). That's not where we are.

One of the earlier interviews I did was with Aaron (Dixon) in 2012.

Good. So, where is he in life?

THIS MINUTE NOW (MAY 2015), HE'S AT OXFORD UNIVERSITY IN ENGLAND.

You're kidding.

HE HAS A NUMBER OF SPEAKING ENGAGEMENTS THAT WERE ALSO ARRANGED THERE.

He is still out there. I know he's about five years or six behind us (in age). He was one of those young radicals that were…It was different from where we were but we were respectful of them. Especially when they were doing the Breakfast Programs, how could you not be respectful? And our Black Panthers weren't really…they weren't carrying any guns and shooting up and all that kind of stuff. So, we weren't afraid of our Black Panthers in Seattle.

SOME PEOPLE WERE.

Were they?

SOME ASIAN PEOPLE SAID THEY WERE AS DID SOME WHITE PEOPLE. BUT NO MATTER WHAT THEIR ETHNICITY, IF THEY KNEW THEM PERSONALLY, THEY WEREN'T.

My Joe knew a lot of the guys who were in the Black Panthers so we never were frightened by them at all.

I WONDER IF IT'S BECAUSE IN A WAY THIS BLACK COMMUNITY WAS SO SMALL THAT THE FOUNDING BLACK FAMILIES HAD AN OUTSIZED IMPACT ON THE FAMILIES THAT CAME LATER. THERE WAS THIS COMMUNITY WITH PRETTY GOOD VALUES ACROSS THE BOARD AND THAT PERMEATED. WHEREAS IN PLACES LIKE CHICAGO AND LOS ANGELES WHEN THE PANTHERS OPENED THEIR ARMS TO ANYBODY, YOU GOT SOME PEOPLE IN THERE WHO DIDN'T DO THE ORGANIZATION ANY FAVORS.

Exactly.

HERE THE POOL OF PEOPLE THAT WERE AVAILABLE LARGELY HAD THOSE COMMUNITY VALUES.

Yes. Exactly.

MLK Way
to Lake Washington
Boulevard
between
Madison & East Cherry

Elmer Dixon was an influential member of the Black Panther Party whose childhood interest in medicine drove him to help found health clinics in Seattle that still serve our community. He continues to provide leadership nationally with the Executive Diversity Services. In his warm intensity, you can feel how love and service are the plumb line of his life.

> *"We were very creative in figuring out ways to serve our community based on the needs that were there. And, I think the most effective thing that occurred with us and the community was that we were there, that we were not armchair revolutionaries. We didn't just talk, we did."*

ELMER ON THE CENTRAL AREA:

We moved here in 1957 from Chicago and we started out living on Hiawatha Place, which was a collection of run-down homes on a very small street down off of Rainier Avenue, which was on the edge of the Black community. But the thing that I remember is that, even then, while there were visibly Black people that were neighbors, friends, that there were a lot of Asians in my classes and Whites. And so, it was then a very diverse community. Even though it was predominately Black, and I didn't know that, I just knew that I had friends of all colors.

We moved rather quickly. We stayed there a year and moved up to 24th and Charles, which was almost directly straight up from Hiawatha but was now only a five or six block direct-shot down 24th to Coleman Elementary. So, we were still in that same neighborhood. It was predominately Black but again right across the street from us was Mr. Santos, who was the father of a famous Chicago Cub baseball player, Ron Santos. So, because we were from Chicago and we're across the street from a Chicago Cub player, I mean, that was surreal.

It was really kind of a typical—I would say, working class—neighborhood that had some diversity in it. We then moved after a year, maybe two years, to Madrona. And there we were in the heart of the CD. But we were also, unbeknownst to us, two blocks from the Red Line, which divided the neighborhood where Whites only could live and buy these fancy homes and beautiful homes, and we were two blocks from there on 33rd.

I only had a block to walk to school. We lived across the street from a park. There was a tennis court there. I had friends from all colors of the rainbow, but my two best friends were White and they happened to live across the Red Line. I have a lot of fond memories of those days. I had a multitude of friends though. I had a Filipino friend who was a very close friend of mine, and then I had other friends who were White, and Black and Asian, you know. There was a group that I hung out with—this kind of collective of guys and it was one of the White friends, David, and then another White friend, Kevin, and the Japanese guy by the name of Hugo Kurosi, and myself, and we all took boxing from this guy, Kevin—his dad. Hugo's dad taught us a little bit of Jiu-Jitsu. So, we were kind of doing this young teenage thing where we were getting ourselves, you know, we could be these tough guys, right?

We used to play army in the neighborhood. That was with the other White friend, Mark, and his younger brother. They were really kind of the instigators of this, and then David would come across the Red Line and these army games that we played were quite organized and intense and structured. There was a wooded-area behind these houses. I remember we had a prisoner-of-war camp down there and when we captured someone's team, we would lock them up in the prisoner-of-war camp and then the other team would have to break them out. I mean, it was a really well thought out, complicated process. On one occasion, we spent the night in the arboretum and we were walking through the neighborhood on the way down there with our sleeping bags, camp gear, bazookas and machine guns. We were eleven, twelve, thirteen years old. We were young kids. It was kind of an adventurous time.

When Stokely Carmichael came in 1967, Aaron (Dixon) is the one that told me to come along. He was becoming more politicized and revolutionary and, of course, I always looked up to my older brother. He got me thinking about identity and who I was, which was what Stokely Carmichael inspired; creating identity and the fact that I am Black and to be proud of the fact that I am. I started growing an afro. We became members of SNCC (Student Nonviolent Coordinating Committee) and my White friends and even the Filipino guy, they kind of fell to the side.

They didn't fall to the side in any deliberate way, because we never had a philosophy of anti-White, but we were proud of the fact that we could identify with our skin color and stand up and be Black and not be ashamed of it. It was the beginning, for us, of the 'I'm Black and I'm proud' era. Black is beautiful. Getting engulfed in that, it caused a separation between my friends and I. But I really wasn't aware of it. In retrospect, I think they interpreted it as rejection. I'm always reflecting on tradition and things that happened because they're part of my present and part of who I am. I don't dwell in the past but I think it's important to reflect and so I'm always reflecting. I reflect about Mark and David, often.

I was always looked at as a serious kid. I guess it became natural that when this (the Black Panther Party) came along that I would be in it. And I would be in it seriously, as was my brother. And even my younger brother, Michael. I was in the Black Panther Party from 1968, as a seventeen year old, through 1976, when we detached from central headquarter, and up until 1982, when we continued to operate the Sydney Miller Community Service Center, which was all of the Panther programs up until 1982. So, from a seventeen year old up until I was thirty-two years old, my life was based on revolutionary principle and practices and struggle and fighting back and denouncing fascism and racism. It laid the foundation for me to become a diversity consultant. I didn't know it, but that's what it did; it laid that foundation.

CAN YOU TALK ABOUT THE PROGRAMS THAT THE PANTHERS STARTED AND THAT STILL EXIST TODAY?

Well, we had a range of what we called 'survival programs.' We referred to them as, 'survival-pending revolution,' to address the needs, immediately, that were in the Black community and that were affecting Black people, in particular, but poor people in general. And then, also, to stimulate revolution. To help them understand that they could control the means of production within their communities and that they needed to fight back and resist and take control.

The very first program we started was the Police Alert Patrol, which does not exist today, but that's where we patrolled police to make sure that they weren't attacking or brutalizing innocent Black people. And that was part of our ten-point program. I think that was point number six—(we) want an immediate end to police brutality and murder of Black people by the police. We also launched, later, an effort here in Seattle for community control of police, which included a Citizens' Review Board. There is a Citizens' Review Board today. Now whether or not they will admit that that's part of our initial request, that's what we were putting forth at that time and it got traction.

That was followed by the Children's Free Breakfast Program, because the core of our programs were protecting the very young and the elderly. That program really embarrassed the federal government into providing school breakfasts and lunches. The federal government, of course, will never admit that but that in fact is what happened. We embarrassed them. We were feeding two thousand kids a week here in Seattle alone. And we had these breakfast programs across the country.

We started a free foodbank. We had some of the first free food programs, free food giveaways. We had a free Legal Aid Program, a free Senior Transportation Program, a Busing to Prisons Program where we bussed loved ones to prison that couldn't otherwise get up there to all five prisons in the state. We started a Tutoring Program for inmates at Monroe Penitentiary, which is ongoing today in most prisons. We were the first to do that. And we were helping inmates get their GEDs, so they could get a job when they got out of prison. Prisons weren't providing rehabilitation. They were just housing inmates, and so we launched that effort.

Of course, our free Medical Clinic that we started is still running today. The Caroline Downs Family Medical Center. We launched sickle cell anemia screening. We brought awareness to an issue that was critical to the health of Black people and also high blood pressure screening. We brought awareness to that. This was back in the Seventies and Eighties when we were doing this, but even at a year ago it was announced that there's a cure to certain forms of sickle cell anemia that was finally found. We believe that would've never happened if we hadn't had launched our efforts back in those years.

We had a free Pest-Control Program where we rid peoples' homes of dangerous pests. In fact, Ron Johnson, who was a lieutenant of mine, single-handedly sprayed the whole Yesler Terrace Housing Project because we found when he went into one housing unit and sprayed it, they just moved next door. He got permission from the Housing Department and we sprayed the whole place. All of Yesler Terrace.

There was a lot of significant programs that we started and implemented in the community. We had an environmental cleanup program where we went to vacant lots that were overgrown with sticker bushes and garbage and cleaned them up and eradicated all the rats, so it would no longer be a hazard in the neighborhood. That led to people starting P-patches, because now there was a blank piece of land that was cleaned up and people started planting stuff in them.

100

We had the screening for sickle cell anemia and blood pressure and then we added the third program which was our Summer Liberation School. And we had those run every year. We had students from the University of Washington that would come and be the teachers. The kids from high schools would be their assistants. And we had three hundred kids every summer going to this Summer Liberation School. That was the precursor to the Oakland Community Learning Center, the school that the Black Panther Party started in Oakland, which was a fully accredited school.

So, the ten-point program guided our efforts, guided our philosophy, and we had some thirty to sixty different programs that we had started across the country. One chapter in North Carolina, I believe it was, started a free ambulance program. It had gotten hold of an ambulance and started the free ambulance program.

We were very creative in figuring out ways to serve our community based on the needs that were (already) there. And I think the most effective thing that occurred with us and the community was that we were there; that we were not armchair revolutionaries. We didn't just talk, we did. There were a lot of people talking, a lot of people saying you should do this or do that or listen to my philosophy or listen to this, but people knew that we were about action. We didn't stand around and talk. We went forth and did it, because we stood on principle. And I think that that probably is the most significant thing about the Black Panther Party.

SO, I WANTED TO TALK TO YOU A LITTLE BIT ABOUT THE ATLANTIC STREET CENTER. WERE YOU THERE ONLY AS A CHILD?

Yeah. My return to the Atlantic Street Center was when we were looking to expand the Children's Free Breakfast Program. The very first program, which was a short run, was at the Madrona Presbyterian Church. And that was almost a demonstration of, 'Yep, we can do this.' And so, I—Aaron had a lot of roles for me back then—was to be the breakfast program coordinator, which I was able to hand off to another comrade, Venetta Molson, later. But I was initially the breakfast program coordinator. So, we were expanding the program. We figured five locations, and those five locations were strategically placed in the housing projects: Yesler Terrace, Rainier Vista, High Point and Holly Park. That's where low-income people and a lot of Blacks lived. But we needed one that was still in the CD and so we had approached Mount Zion Baptist Church. We were told, 'No, we have our own breakfast program,' which was really for their daycare center. They didn't want Black Panthers in their church.

We may have approached one or two other locations, more centrally located, and we said, 'No, let's go talk to Ike (the former Director of the Atlantic Street Center).' Ike questioned us and put us through the ringer about, 'What's your intention? What is your purpose?' and we told him, and he said, 'OK, we're going to do it.'

Ike was a very progressive guy, and he took flak from the FBI. They had visited him and tried to dissuade him. But he knew who we were. He knew who we were from when we were kids, and he was always active whenever we took a request to him because he knew us and he knew what we stood for and he knew that we were not just some renegades. He believed in us and supported us wholeheartedly. And there—when we were growing up—there were a lot of Asian kids in that community because it kind of was at the foot of Beacon Hill. And Beacon Hill, of course, has a strong Asian community. But, Ike, when he saw kids walking by the front of his facility, his building, his program, there were Black kids walking by too. We were among them. He wasn't going to turn kids away because of the color of their skin.

And it was the same thing with our breakfast programs. Kids came into our breakfast programs of all colors. They were White, they were Black, they were Asian, they were Latino. We weren't going to turn kids away because they weren't Black kids. And Ike was the same way. So he took flak—I know he took flak from his community. But he said, 'To hell with it.' He had principles and a strong foundation and I think that people with strong principles that stand on the side of righteousness and fairness know each other and recognize each other. We could recognize that in him, and he could recognize that in us.

So, HAVING GROWN UP HERE AND SEEING HOW THE CITY HAS CHANGED AND THIS NEIGHBORHOOD IN PARTICULAR, HOW DOES THAT FEEL TO YOU? HOW DO YOU SEE THAT?

It's like a mourning. It's like a loss; like someone's died. When we were kids growing up here in Madrona, we could go out on a Saturday morning and the park was full of all kinds of kids. There was a Black barber shop. There was the Doll House, which was run by a White woman by the name of Mardie, who hired me. I had my first job outside of my paper route. Across the street from her, was a little record store owned by a Black woman where we could buy our records and tapes. If you went up to 34th and Cherry, there was a soda-jerk joint where you could get sodas mixed and jars of candy from the Black guy that ran that business. There was Brenner Brothers

Bakery down on Cherry and Empire Way, as it was known back then, a Jewish bakery where we went and got Jewish goods. And then back up on 34th there was the laundromat, which is still there, but next door to the laundromat was this little bakery called The Swedish Bakery. And Joe's little supermarket; Joe and May were Chinese immigrants.

It was a collection of all kinds of people within the heart of this Black community. It was seventy percent Black, but it had all these other folks that were still living there—Chinese, Japanese, Jewish, gay, straight. It was a collection of all of these different populations living together in harmony in the Black community. The community was not overrun with drugs, which was a deliberate attempt to drive people out. Our community has been decimated. The influx of wealthier Whites who have gentrified and are changing the dynamic and the makeup of our neighborhood because Blacks have been forced out—it's like a wake every time I come into the CD and look around to see who's left.

It's like a loss of identity. It's a loss of pride. So, that's how it feels. But my roots will always be here and I will continue to work here. I have a business that's based here. I'm moving my residence, because my wife has an illness and she needs a warmer climate, but I will stay connected to the city and connected to my community because I have that pride in Seattle and this—you know, not only Black folks here but progressive Whites, Asians, Latinos—and I'll always have that connection.

Mrs. Frances Dixon worked in the medical field and was married to the greatly beloved Elmer Dixon Sr. of Seattle's Model Cities Project. She was also the intrepid, unflappable mother to sons Aaron and Elmer, who made up Seattle's Black Panther Party leadership. To be in her presence is to admire her quiet, amused incisiveness; she's a gentle, cultured lady with a steel core.

> *"I grew up pretty tough, in pretty tough circumstances. Well, my great-grand-mother helped raise me. That was because my mother worked all the time. But my son, Michael, he says, 'Mommy, you know, you're a survivor.' I said, 'I guess so.'"*

YOU AND YOUR HUSBAND MOVED HERE FROM CHICAGO?

We moved here in 1957 with four children from Champaign, Illinois.

WHAT WAS YOUR FIRST IMPRESSION COMING HERE FROM ILLINOIS?

I just knew it had lots of hills. It was completely different from being in Chicago, or Champaign. Completely. Here it was very countrylike. We used to leave our doors unlocked back then. There was nothing very strange in the news. It was just plain old daily news; you never heard about any robberies or anything like that. I couldn't believe it. Nothing seemed to happen here. Well, until later, of course.

WHAT WAS YOUR NEIGHBORHOOD LIKE WHEN YOU LIVED IN ILLINOIS?

The entire neighborhood, well, we were all Negroes back then. In Illinois, no Whites lived in our neighborhood. Soon as we'd move in, they'd move out.

WHAT WAS IT LIKE, THEN, MOVING TO A MIXED NEIGHBORHOOD HERE?

Not too much (different) because my mother passed for White the whole time I was growing up. My mother's over there (points to a photo on the wall) in that picture. That's me as a baby with my dad. Color didn't bother me at all because my family's all pretty well mixed up, all kinds of color. So moving here with everyone didn't bother me. Still I was shocked. Now, when I went to school in St. Paul Minnesota, I had a little cultural shock moving there from Chicago. When I walked in a classroom, all the kids were predominantly White. I'd never seen that before 'cause all our schools in Chicago were all one color.

WHEN YOU MOVED HERE, DID YOU FIND IT TO BE WELCOMING?

Well, depends on where I went, you know.

YES, A GOOD POINT (LAUGHS).

I never had any problems with anybody, really. I knew that stores were segregated. All the stores were segregated then: the grocery stores; the Woolworth's…The people that worked behind the counter were usually Asian or Filipino. Before we came here we were told it was more of a blue-collar, not a professional-type environment, we were going to enter. My husband graduated from the Art Institute in Chicago. He came from Chanute Air Force Base where he was hired to work as an illustrator, and then Boeing picked him up from there. They were looking for people to come out this way and they liked his work and so they moved us out here. We didn't have to pay our way at all.

HOW WAS IT IN 1957 WORKING AS A BLACK MAN AT BOEING?

Well, they hired him. I don't know. He wasn't looking for them. They looked for him, I guess.

HE MUST HAVE BEEN VERY TALENTED.

Yes. Still, we couldn't live anywhere (redlining). For about two weeks, they used to send us newspapers so we could maybe pick out a house that we might want to rent, or an apartment, but none of those were available to us. We didn't realize it until we came out here.

So when we came out, traveling by car, from back in the Midwest all the way out here, we didn't know how we'd be treated when we stopped at motels. We just stopped whenever we wanted to and never had any problems, ever. Still, then, we didn't know how we'd be treated in Seattle.

YOUR HUSBAND MUST HAVE BEEN A SINGULAR PERSON, VERY UNUSUAL AT THAT TIME TO HAVE CHOSEN TO BE AN ARTIST, TO HAVE GOTTEN INTO THE ART INSTITUTE.

He started in school; in schools they had programs. If they see someone that liked to draw, then they put them in the program and they'd go on Saturday afternoons or Saturday mornings to the Art Institute. That's just what he liked to do.

HE MUST HAVE BEEN VERY GOOD AT IT BECAUSE HE GOT INTO THE ART INSTITUTE, TOO.

Yes, yes. But he was that type anyway; he liked music. He liked classical music and he liked opera and he introduced me to my first ballet. Even though I majored in music I didn't know as much about things like that that he did. He had an uncle that worked at the Chicago Opera House.

I'M SORRY I NEVER MET YOUR HUSBAND.

Oh, he was exceptional. He really was. He had a great personality, great sense of humor. He would say, 'Oh, I love to hear Elmer (their son) laugh.' Have you ever seen a picture of my husband? He was a good listener. Every picture I have of him you could see that he's listening to what you're saying. You can tell.

SO HE WAS AN ARTIST, A LISTENER BUT HE WAS ALSO A FIGHTER. AARON TOLD ME A STORY OF WHEN HIS FATHER WAS IN THE MILITARY. IT WAS REALLY HOT AND THEY ASKED A FARMER IF THEY COULD CUT THROUGH HIS FIELD. DO YOU KNOW THIS STORY?

Oh, well, you know, kids stretch imagination. It was in Mississippi. To understand my husband back then, he had just graduated from high school; he was eighteen. Now, this is just stories because I didn't know him then. I didn't know him until after the war. He had very close friends, well, he had a lot of buddies that he went through grade school and high school. A group of girls and boys who were just one big clique in Chicago. He grew up in Chicago.

106   Chicago has neighborhoods and he lived in what they called Woodlawn. So he and his big group of friends, they all went to grade school together. They were all Negro children, colored children, we were (called) colored back then. The girls would stop by his house. His mother was a perfect homemaker. You know, she never worked until her grandchildren came along,

babysitting, that's all she ever really did. She was always home and the kids would knock on the door, 'Mrs. Dixon, is Elmer (Frances' husband is named Elmer as is her son) ready?' They'd all head off and walk to school together. Sounded like a great time they had. He said for his high school prom, he didn't go to the prom; he went to White Castle. You know that? It's from Chicago. He bought a bag of White Castle hamburgers, ate and listened to music on the radio. That's what he did. That's the type of person he was.

YES, HE DEFINITELY WENT HIS OWN WAY. YOU CAN SEE THAT YOUR CHILDREN GOT THAT, TOO.

Well, we kind of grew up that way. We always had classical music playing or opera. My husband loved opera, the symphony, things like that, so that was their surroundings. And jazz, we were jazz buffs, too. All of his friends, his best buddies were like that, too.

NOW DID HE PLAY MUSIC?

He's not a musician. He didn't play anything. He just liked to listen.

YOU HAVE AN ORGAN OVER THERE.

This is my piano. I'd taken piano lessons when I was five. My mother gave me that when I was sixteen back in Minnesota, so that's my piano.

YOU WERE A MUSIC MAJOR. DID YOU PLAY HERE OR WERE YOU JUST TOO BUSY WITH THE KIDS?

No, I didn't have time to play. I was working.

WHERE DID YOU WORK?

My first job was at Virginia Mason Hospital, the old hospital. I don't think anybody would recognize it now because it was only five stories back then. It was just a brown building on the corner of 8th Avenue. I worked there for five years as a ward secretary. Then I left and worked at a little nursing home around the corner for about a year, part-time.

How it worked back then, (was) you went to a personnel office to see if you could fill out an application and if they could find a job for you. I went to Group Health and they happened to have an opening. Back in those days, all the doctors had RNs working for them and they were trying to fit in assistants, clinic assistants. That's what they were looking for at Group Health. They were trying to start a program. Anyway, they looked at my record of what I did at Virginia Mason Hospital. They thought, well, maybe I might work out. They picked me out of about fifteen applicants or so. They chose me. Mrs. Ross, who was the director of nursing at the time told me, 'Well, I think you can work, but there is someone here that really is not liking this proposition that we're trying to start here.' A doctor, Dr. Fogliano, head of the Ear Nose and Throat Department, wanted an RN with him at all times. He didn't want any outsider that hadn't worked with a doctor before. She said, 'We think we're going to put you there with him, since he doesn't want you (laughs).'

I sat in their office for two weeks until she finally convinced him to try me out, and so he did. The way he did things was so different. When he worked with a patient he just dictated, like I'm talking to you. He was telling what he was doing, what he was going to do. You had to write it down, to take notes. Some of these words I'd never heard before like cerumen (earwax) and epistaxis (nosebleed) and all those kind of things. One day he just said, 'Come in and sit down. I want you to take some notes.' So I did that. I did that. He also did surgeries on that floor, which is unusual. He had set this up his own special way.

There was a surgery suite and there were rooms for patients to wake up. He did adult patients, tonsillectomies…Oh God, I forgot what else he did, but he did a lot of surgeries. So, he had me come in there and I looked at all that blood and gore. I thought, 'Oh my god, I don't know if I can stand this.' I finally got used to it. He had me pick up the hammer and help with the surgeries on the nose and tap all those bones and cartilage out and pull this and pull that. After a while you get used to it; it's amazing. He got so that he was beginning to like me a little bit, you know. Still, he had me in tears quite a few times. I would go behind a door somewhere and you know boo-hoo a little bit, but I wouldn't never let anybody see me. He finally started calling me Fran. And so, he was really nice to me after a while (laughs). Took a while.

AFTER YOU PROVED YOUR METTLE?

I guess so, yes. There was another doctor, too, Doctor Rowan. I worked between the two at the time. And then Dr. Fogliano retired. He was getting older and so I worked just for Doctor Rowan. I worked there, oh, seven years. I was going to work longer, but Aaron's boy needed some attention because he was just a little guy. He needed to get out of that environment down in Oakland at the party (The Black Panther Party).

YES, AARON SAID THAT THAT'S THE ONLY THING HE REALLY REGRETS IS THAT A LOT OF THE FIRST BORN SONS OF THE PANTHERS HAD A VERY TOUGH TIME.

They did, yeah, they did. I had a picture of him (her grandson), he looked so sad, he looked so cute. But anyway his mother brought him back to Seattle for Christmas. My husband and I noticed that he needed some attention. We said, 'We're not going to let him go back down there.' We just decided that. Aaron was already down there and he really didn't mind at the time, I don't believe. I kept him, we kept him for a long time.

I'M SURE THAT WAS THE RIGHT THING.

Oh, I know it was. I know it was.

IT'S A VERY LOVING THING TO DO BECAUSE IT'S A LOT TO TAKE ON A SMALL CHILD.

Well, it's your grandchild. You're not going to let anything happen to him if you've got any decency about yourself. Uh-uh. We kept him and he thrived beautifully.

IS HE HAPPY?

Oh yes, he's a grown man. He went to Howard University for a little while. He was a perfect little child. Really. I used to braid his hair and take him to the store. Everybody said, 'Oh what a pretty little baby.' So I kept him. Also Aaron's wife's mother lived in Seattle. We had worked out a thing where 109 we could keep him together because I had quit my job at Group Health to take care of him. That summer I was fine, but then later I was used to working. I just didn't like being at home all the time. I was busy baking bread and stuff and I thought, 'Well, that's enough housemaid, housewife stuff.'

I saw this Ad in the paper for medical assistants to work at (Virginia) Mason clinic. The clinic that's there now was not there then. It was just an apartment building on the corner and the clinic only had four floors back then, now it has eight, so this was way back. I asked my neighbor, 'I saw this job in the paper. I wonder if you could keep my little grandson for about an hour or so till I can see if I can fill out an application.' She said, 'Oh, yes.' So she kept him (babysat). She knew him.

WAS THAT MRS. MELINSON?

Oh no, this was people who lived next door. That was the Hardings. Bobby was in the Panther Party too. She kept him for me and then they told me I got the job. I said 'Oh, my gosh. I wasn't planning…I didn't think I'd get hired this quick.' I asked, 'I wonder could you wait till later in the year, like summer?' This was in the spring. They said, 'OK, we'll call you.' They never called, so I called them at the clinic. The nurse supervisor girl hired me that day. She said, 'I hope you're going to be here for a while, at least ten years.' I said to myself, 'Ten years?' I was there eighteen years. Then I retired.

DID YOU HAVE AN AFFINITY FOR THINGS MEDICAL OR DID IT JUST END UP THAT WAY?

I think I did because I worked in a Catholic hospital before I moved out here, just as a nurse's aide. I just have a natural ability for it, I found out. I just have a knack for it.

THEN THAT GOT PASSED ON BECAUSE YOUR SON ELMER, HE STARTED A CLINIC HERE (CAROLYN DOWNS CLINIC). I'VE HEARD WHEN HE WAS YOUNG HE THOUGHT ABOUT BEING A DOCTOR.

Yes, when he was younger, we always had our dinner at the dining table, all six of us. We'd talk about all kind of things. I was reminding him the other day. I said, 'Remember Elmer, you said you wanted to be a neurosurgeon and go to the University of Hawaii.' That's what he said. This was when he was still in high school. That was his thing. But anyway, that didn't happen.

110 **WELL, THE PARTY HAPPENED. THE CLINICS HAPPENED. AND THE CLINIC STILL SURVIVES.**

Oh yes, the clinic on Yesler.

So, RETURNING TO YOUR SON ELMER, HE TOOK THAT MEDICAL AFFINITY AND STARTED THE CLINIC.

Oh well, also, he was busy with his music; he played in the band. Elmer's just always been outgoing. When he got in high school he said he was going to be the quarterback for the football team. He was out in the backyard goofing around with some friends and he broke his collarbone. So my husband had to rush him to the hospital. After that he said, 'Well, I'm going to be a drum major.' He's that type. He's tall. He had the hat and everything. He made the perfect drum major.

So, STRONG-WILLED.

Uh-huh. All my children are about a year-and-a-half apart.

OH REALLY?

Yeah, I've had five babies. The second little girl died.

OH, I'M SORRY.

That's all right. And I had them so close. And I never had morning sickness. Never had labor over four or five hours.

WOW.

Never. I was telling a girl at church that and she said, 'What?!' I said, 'Yeah, I never had any problems at all.'

THAT'S A BLESSING.

Mmmhm. Really a blessing. Now what about my daughter? Joanne came before Aaron.

WHAT'S JOANNE LIKE?

Oh she's…the boys are crazy about her; she was very bossy to them. She helped me a lot when they were growing up. They say, 'Remember Mommy, Joanne used to chase us with the broom?'

She would. She'd make 'em mind. She just kind of, I guess, took on some of my tactics.

Michael's the youngest. They're very close. They talk to each other often.

WHAT DID JOANNE END UP DOING FOR WORK?

She just retired last year from the Police Department in San Francisco. She was a 911 operator, dispatcher for the police and later for the Fire Department. She's gotten all kind of awards.

SHE'S ALSO GOT A COOL HEAD.

Oh yeah, she is. Yes, she's very cool. I think that's what they used to call me in college. Some of the guys used to call me, 'There goes Ms. Cool Breeze.' I guess it's just my manner.

DO YOU THINK THEY MEANT THAT YOU DON'T GET RATTLED OR THAT YOU'RE A PERSON THAT'S A NICE COOL BREEZE TO BE AROUND?

I guess I'm just pretty quiet and don't make too much over anything.

YES. YOU DON'T GET RUFFLED.

If I am, you don't know it. For example, I'd been out over to visit a lady after church, the next morning, when I woke up, my foot was killing me. I thought, 'Now what did I do?' But I never mentioned it to any of my kids. Michael came over Monday evening to talk. Elmer comes over every Sunday. I didn't mention it to him. None of them have known about my foot at all. It's finally fine. I figured out for myself it must be tendinitis. Evidently it was. I called the doctor but couldn't get an appointment till tomorrow, so I kept putzing around and finally I got it figured out. It's fine now.

YOU'RE TOUGH.

112

If I make up my mind, yes. I grew up pretty tough, in pretty tough circumstances. Well, my great-grandmother helped raised me. That was because my mother worked all the time. But my son Michael he says, 'Mommy, you know, you're a survivor.' I said, 'I guess so.'

When I was five I took piano lessons. You'd think your mother would take you to the lessons. She took me the first day and the other days she'd walk me to the corner and then send me across the street. I'd have to go up to this Ms. Hardy. I never forgot her. That was my first music teacher.

And so I got used to going places by myself, that you would not let a child do now. My mother sent me to kindergarten. I remember, she always told me, 'Don't stop and talk to anybody, don't let any man talk to you, don't talk to anybody.' I never did. I always remembered that. I remember walking to school in Chicago. Are you familiar with Chicago?

A LITTLE BIT, YES.

Well, the tall building had a gangway that goes underneath the building all the way out to the back and there's some steps you have to walk down. I remember this man calling me, 'Come here little girl.' And I remember running to school. I was always very careful. Then on Fridays she'd walk me to State Street, we lived on Michigan Street. She'd call her grandmother, my great-grandma, and tell her, 'I'm putting Frances on the street car now.' And so she'd meet me at the other end at 95th Street. So I was used to being independent.

I THINK IT'S GOOD TRAINING. IT'S IMPORTANT.

I'd get there and Grandma would be waiting for me and we'd walk to her house. Then (laughs) I was telling this neighbor that I saw Sunday, she's 102, she's also a Frances, this lady that I'm talking about. She asked me, 'Frances, I think about you. How did you do all that? How did you do so many things by yourself?' I said, 'I was just used to it.' So that's my personality, I guess. So I'm perfectly happy alone. I can make it fine.

My mother and dad split up because my dad drank. He had a really good job in the Post Office during the (Great) Depression. That was the job to have. All the doctors and lawyers wished they had a job in the Post Office back then. My Uncle Milt had a good job in the Post Office and he built the house that they lived in. He built it when my mother was little. He bought like four or five lots and he built his house, his property on that. Sometimes my mother used to go out and wash my Aunt Marie's hair.

113

SO YOU WERE ALWAYS USED TO BIG HOUSES LIKE THIS.

Oh yeah, my grandma and I used to sleep in the attic. I used to love it up there cause you could hear the rain.

ONCE SOMEONE ASKED ME, 'WHAT'S AARON DIXON LIKE?' I SAID, 'YOU KNOW, HE REMINDS ME OF A CAT. HE HAS THAT VERY COLLECTED ENERGY.' HE'S TAKING IN EVERYTHING. I CAN SEE WHERE THAT COMES FROM (IN YOUR FAMILY). CATS, THEY DON'T WASTE ENERGY, THEY'RE VERY AWARE, VERY AFFECTIONATE WHEN THEY KNOW YOU.

When they know the surroundings but they're not going to let you know what they're thinking.

SO THERE'S A KIND OF BEAUTIFUL CATLIKE QUALITY.

I think that's probably what they were talking about me at school, just a few boys who couldn't quite put their finger on me.

OH, I BET BOYS LIKED YOU. AND WERE AFRAID OF YOU (LAUGHS).

No, they weren't afraid of me. They just didn't know how to approach me, I guess.

THAT'S WHAT I MEAN. THEY WEREN'T GOING TO COME AND DISPLAY THEIR STUPIDITY IN FRONT OF YOU.

I don't like that type of situation. There's too much forwardness now. I just hate it when everybody's got to do this ego thing, take their pictures. I'd much rather look at older pictures.

(Shows a picture) These are some of my Mormon friends. I first met her when she first came to Virginia Mason Clinic where I worked. We have been friends ever since. When she heard my husband had died they told me she just tore out of work and came right up to my house. I wasn't home. She came as soon as she heard...

WHAT YEAR WAS THAT?

Nineteen eighty five.

OHHH. HE DIED REALLY YOUNG.

He had just turned sixty. And I hadn't quite been sixty.

OH, I'M SO SORRY.

Yes. He got sick. When I met him he had, I don't know if it had anything to do with it, he had a mole on his back. You know, they say watch those black moles. I used to watch it every once and a while to see if it was getting any bigger.

He liked parties. He loved to celebrate anything. Birthdays, Thanksgiving—we'd always have the biggest turkey; Halloween—we'd have two pumpkins; Christmas—we'd have the biggest tree, all that. Even if he got laid off from Boeing, Boeing periodically laid people off, but he would never let me know. He'd always come home with something special. That's the type of person he was. He gave me my first birthday party, big birthday party when I turned twenty one.

SO HE BROUGHT A LOT OF JOY INTO YOUR LIFE.

Yes. He had a great sense of humor. He asked me once, 'Why did you marry me?' I said, 'Because you're so funny, you make me laugh all the time.' He did. He had a great sense of humor.

My husband was also the head of the Art Department for Model Cities, I don't know if you knew that, but he was. After the kids grew up, we started having New Year's Eve parties. The last one we had, we always invited just about six couples, people we were fond of. He was going to build a fire, so he went out in the back to cut the wood. The next day he had a backache, and we just assumed it came from chopping wood. My friend Elaine said, 'I'm spending the night.' So she spent the night and we got up and had breakfast. Elmer was still in his pajamas, which was not like him, then the backache started getting worse and worse. So he had to go to the doctor. He came home and I asked, 'What did the doctor say?' 'Nothing really,' I think he gave him some pain pills or something. I asked, 'Did you take an X-ray?' 'No, he didn't take an X-ray.' I thought that was unusual.

It wasn't getting any better. Now, back then Group Health was over here on the corner (of 34th and Union Street). At that time, they didn't like you changing doctors. So I said, 'I'm going to call up Dr Stever.' Dr. Stever is the doctor who asked Elmer would it be all right with the Panthers if Group Health started this clinic over here. He asked their permission if it would interfere, or bother them, if Group Health moved here…I thought that was a lot of respect that he had for them (the BPP).

Where Amara Is?

Yeah, that used to be Group Health. Once it was an IGA grocery store where Elmer worked. He used to put all the letters (signage outside) up. It was the grocery store where we used to go all the time and get our turkeys and things. The Panther Clinic was right across the street, on the opposite side of the street, where they had their office and what have you. Anyway Dr. Stever knew them, knew Elmer quite well. I thought, 'Well, I know Dr. Stever because I knew him when he was an intern when I was working at Virginia Mason Hospital. I knew him way back then. He didn't remember me that well, I don't think, but I remembered him. I just called up and said, 'He has a doctor, but I would like for you to check him.' So they made an appointment and I walked over there with him, or I drove him because he couldn't hardly walk by that time, his back was hurting so bad.

I took him over there and we sat in the waiting room. The doctor's office was over here (gestures), the X-ray department was upstairs. Dr. Stever took an X-ray and he came back. As soon as he saw it, his whole expression changed. Then Poppy, we called my husband Poppy, he said, 'I saw the way you looked,' he said, 'I knew it was something wrong.' He said, 'Oh, he's got cancer.' He had a big tumor like on his spine, that's why he was having all that pain.

Right away he called up the oncologist and made an appointment. Took him to the oncologist and I said, 'I'm going to have to take a walk while you talk to him.' He was going to talk to my husband by himself. He didn't talk to me. I didn't want him to. After I came back I said, 'What did the doctor tell you?' He said, 'He gave me about six months.' That's how quick this thing was growing. But it was a type of blood cancer, myeloma. He had to be prepared to have radiation and chemo. He handled it very well.

We had planned to go to Chicago that January for him to see the Vatican museum show, all the paintings and we couldn't make that. We postponed it and then found out it was going to be in San Francisco where Joanne lives. He rallied and took his medicine and took his treatments and all that and we finally made it to San Francisco that fall. But he was in an awful lot of pain, he was just in terrible pain. I told them at the clinic when I was working that I was going to have to take some time off because I had to take my husband to get his radiation treatments. This one nurse at the nursing office says, 'Well, we don't have any time.' I said 'Well, whether you have time or not, I'm taking him.'

Word got back to my Dr. Allen, who I worked for most of the time. He was head of the Medicine Department. Anyway, I got a call that afternoon says, 'Fran, you can take any time, as much time off as you want, anytime you want, just tell us when you're going.' His appointments were usually at four, I'd take off at two, call my husband, tell him I was coming home, and to start getting ready to go because he had to get from the bed, around the corner to the bathroom. It took him a good half an hour. I know, he was in so much pain. Well, when I worked at the clinic they said that once they start messing around with your back, you better leave it alone, it's not good. I have a good friend, Elaine, and her back is bad too.

IT SOUNDS LIKE YOU'VE HAD VERY GOOD FEMALE FRIENDS.

I did. I didn't have very many.

NOW FOR YOU HOW WAS IT? WHEN THE BOYS DECIDED TO JOIN THE BLACK PANTHER PARTY WERE YOU WORRIED FOR THEM?

The first time I heard, yeah. The first time we ever heard anything…Now this was before they were in the Panthers, but they were interested in…oh golly, who was that coming to town that was so popular, that was speaking at Garfield. A young person, anyway—he was speaking at Garfield and so they got interested in his talk. Who was that? Good looking. Oh dear, he was well-known, too. He was younger than Harry Belafonte, but sort of in that realm. Anyway, he was speaking at Garfield and that's when they got interested in politics, more or less. All my children went to Garfield and Elmer played in the band. A group of them had stopped at a hamburger place across from the school and for some reason there was some little squabble. I don't know what it was but the police were called. They arrested Elmer among some other kids and they put them in Juvenile Detention.

Another boy, a little older than they were, he called up during the night, 'Mrs. Dixon, Elmer's been arrested.' So that's when I start getting worried about things like that because they had never been in any trouble before. I couldn't hardly go to sleep and my husband took the phone. Anyway we finally had to go (get him). Did you know Rosen? The lawyer?

No.

Well, he was quite a guy. He became interested in these kids and helping them when they got in trouble because they police were, a little, picking on brown children, our kids, the Black kids. Because Michael used to go visit some of his friends and sometimes they'd be running through the street. I told him, 'Michael don't run home because if they see you running they'll think you stole something.'

We always had dinner at five and then of course Elmer would be playing at the band and he'd have to come home during the night. Once, Aaron was up on Cherry Street, he might have just been standing there, and the police got after him. Did they try to arrest him? I can't remember. Anyway, I always remember him telling me, 'Mommy, I told 'em I need to call my mother' and one of them said, 'You don't have a mother,' that kind of stuff. Things were beginning to get very bad, very touchy. So I think that's how they got interested (in the Black Panther Party). Then there was a group of kids who were going to the university down in California (probably Berkeley) to some kind of meeting. That's when the crap hit the fan, more or less.

I used to go in their bedroom and clean it up and nosy around and what have you. I remember I saw that little-bitty clipping about so big that said, 'Black Panthers.' I didn't know what the Black Panthers were but I thought, 'Well, that's kind of interesting. Wonder what that's all about?' So they were getting interested in things like that back then. I didn't know too much about the Panthers.

At that time, in Seattle, a lot of kids in the schools were getting kind of tense about how some of the police were treating the children. One thing led to another. When they went down to the university in California, I remember going up to Joe's (Madrona Food Market), which was a Chinese grocery store up here where we had a little running tab. I got some bread and some stuff for the girls and boys to take with them. I made them some lunch. Anyway, when they got down there that's when they started listening to talks and then that young kid got killed.

I THINK THAT MUST HAVE BEEN BOBBY HUTTON.

I can't remember. So much was going on then. Anyway, my husband used to pick me up from work when I worked at Group Health and he picked me up that day. We were coming home, opened the door and the house was full of young folks, upstairs, downstairs, everywhere you looked there were kids. We looked at each other and thought, 'What in the heck?' but we just went on upstairs. Anyway, they were meeting and forming the Black Panther Party at that time. That's when they picked Aaron. I don't know what year that was.

THEN AS YOU BEGAN TO REALIZE…

Oh, it didn't bother me. I just wasn't that concerned because I found myself getting a little tough about it myself.

SO YOU UNDERSTOOD?

I grew up with racism myself. As if anybody didn't know it. When I hear a Black person say, 'Oh well, I never,' I thought, 'Where in the heck have you been?' You have, or your mother has, or somebody.'

TELL ME MORE ABOUT YOUR JOB AT THE HOSPITAL.

Well…I only worked there three days a week. I was so underpaid and they needed help so bad. It was a teaching hospital. They would, when I first started there—am I talking too long? See once you get started talking, I'll talk. They told me that I had to work, seven or eight days straight and my hours were usually seven to three, three to eleven. Then when Thanksgiving came, we had always gone to Chicago. My husband said, 'Oh no, you have to quit that job. We're going to Chicago. You can't work all those hours.' I told them at the hospital, 'I can only work Tuesday, Wednesday and Thursday' because I belonged to a little housewife's bridge club, which met on Fridays. They needed help so badly they just said, 'That's OK. That's fine.' So that's what I did. My husband got home from work at four and I was home in time to fix dinner for him and the children.

119

We needed a babysitter for that half an hour or hour. I asked my girlfriend who lived in the same project if her oldest daughter, Pat, could watch the children. Well, Joanne was nine then, that's when I decided she could do pretty well. So I had the babysitter for about a week and Joanne said,

'Mommy, I don't like Pat. I can take care of the house myself (laughs).' So I said, 'You can take everything until your dad gets home?' And she said, 'Yeah.' So it was just half an hour you know.

SHE TOOK ON THE RESPONSIBILITY.

She's pretty strong-willed herself. Very, very, very strong.

JACK DUNN REMEMBERED HER AS THE PRETTIEST GIRL AND A GOOD TENNIS PLAYER. THEY PLAYED TENNIS TOGETHER. HE REALLY LIKED HER. I WONDER BECAUSE YOUR CHILDREN WERE KNOWN AS NICE, SMART PEOPLE THROUGHOUT THE CENTRAL DISTRICT, IF THAT DIDN'T HELP TO PREVENT WHAT HAPPENED IN CHICAGO WHERE THE FBI CAME IN AND KILLED EVERYBODY.

Listen, I'm sure Aaron has told you that they were planning to kill them here too. The mayor stopped it.

THAT WAS MAYOR UHLMAN.

I used to go up to the bunker they had on East Spring and 19th Avenue, around there. There might still be a wall there. I don't know…but anyway they (the Black Panther Party) had a house there. That's where they started the clinic, the Free Clinic. They had sandbags all through there.

THEY WEREN'T FOOLISH.

Well, if they had been, they'd have been dead.

EXACTLY. MAYBE THE REASON THE MAYOR WAS WILLING TO STEP UP IS BECAUSE SO MANY IN THE COMMUNITY, LIKE THE STEINBERGS, KNEW AARON BECAUSE HE WAS THEIR BABYSITTER.

I don't think so.

120   **FROM WHAT I'VE BEEN TOLD DOING THIS PROJECT THOSE WHO KNEW THEM REMEMBER THEM AS NICE, FRIENDLY CHILDREN' PEOPLE LIKED THEM. I'VE HEARD THAT FROM MANY PEOPLE: WHITE, JAPANESE-AMERICAN, JEWISH, FILIPINO…**

Yes, mmhmm. They were good (laughs). My husband and I both were good parents, I believe. They had some good manners and so forth. They had respect for other people.

YES. THAT DID PAY OFF.

Mmhmm.

AARON TOLD ME BECAUSE OF THE SITUATION WITH THE POLICE THAT THEY VERY QUICKLY WERE KEEPING GUNS.

Oh yeah, and how did that affect me? Well, I got pretty used to it. I didn't like them, but I did not see them. I knew they were in here somewhere but it didn't really bother me because I used to get very nasty phone calls—people threatening, 'I'm going to kill your children.' I got a lot of nasty stuff like that. Then the police they had ways of hearing what you were saying even. I could spot them. I got so I could spot them over in the park pretending like they were playing tennis. Yeah, they were watching the house all the time and so I got used to it. I thought it was kind of funny.

AND YOU WEREN'T FRIGHTENED?

No.

STILL THE PHONE CALLS…WELL, YOU ARE A COOL CUSTOMER IF THE PHONE CALLS DIDN'T SCARE YOU.

I said, 'Try it' (laughs). Yeah, it didn't bother me, nuh-uh, because we all got pretty tough, I guess. Though, we didn't let Michael join. We learned from World War II, don't put all your sons on the same ship. Although later we knew all the kids were involved.

I WAS TALKING TO MONA LAKE JONES. DO YOU KNOW HER? SHE'S A POET, SHE WAS INVOLVED IN THE MT ZION CHURCH.

No. My kids probably know her, but I don't know those people.

SHE WAS SAYING THAT THE PEOPLE THAT WERE VERY INVOLVED WITH MT ZION…

There were a lot of people who didn't want anything to do with me, us.

SHE SAID THAT THE PEOPLE IN THE BLACK COMMUNITY WHO WERE MORE PHILOSOPHICALLY ALIGNED WITH MARTIN LUTHER KING THAT AFTER DR. KING WAS KILLED WOULDN'T HAVE SHOWN UP AT THE MARCHES AND WERE NOT OVERTLY SUPPORTIVE…

I think they were afraid to. A lot of them were afraid to.

BUT THEY THOUGHT, THE BLACK PANTHERS NEED TO TRY BECAUSE EVERYTHING ELSE HAS FAILED. THEY RESPECTED THEM.

We became very supportive of the children, whatever they did. I remember when there was a riot around here somewhere. I started parking the car around the corner; we had a little white Plymouth. I don't know where I was going, maybe I was trying to see what was going on, but I remember going out. I was going to the store or something. The police were out there hanging around and I thought, I'm just going to sit here in the car for a minute because there's a lot of noise and shooting. The police came to the car and they looked in and saw me, but they said, 'Oh, it's just a lady.' Then they went on so I don't know who they were looking for. It was pretty bad there for a while and my guys, you know, they did some bombing and stuff.

YOUR BOYS?

Mmhmm. Yep. I felt bad. Some places like Joe's, the Chinese place, they didn't bother them. They did not bother them nor the grocery store (the IGA), it was only certain spots that they would bother and they would not bother people like Joe. Joe was really fond of him (Aaron) because they knew him growing up anyway. When Aaron had his first child, the lady there she gave him a beautiful blanket and what have you for the baby. Joe's (Joe's Madrona Food Center) was run by a Chinese American. And Mr. Richlen, who was Jewish, had a store up on 23rd and Union, nobody touched his place either. No. They had certain places that they'd bother. Anyway, that was part of the Revolution, so I went along with it.

122

DID THE NEIGHBORHOOD CHANGE A LOT AFTER THE RIOT?

Yeah, a lot of Blacks were moving out, they started moving out. They said, 'Well, I'm moving south.' (To the south end of Seattle). And I thought, 'Well, move south.' Now, they moved south and now they wish they hadn't moved. They wish they'd kept their butts here.

YES. THAT'S TRUE. NOW, WAS IT THE BLACK MIDDLE CLASS THAT MOVED OR WAS IT JUST A WHOLE SWATH THROUGH THE COMMUNITY?

Well, I don't know. Most people who lived in this area here (around 33rd Avenue in Madrona), we were pretty well middle class. Then others who were farther, a little farther out around Jackson, they might not have been as middle class. Most of the people in this neighborhood, the Melinsons, the Hardings next door, we all got along very well. The church was nice, the Madrona Church. I might have joined that if I'd known it was there before we bought the house. It didn't matter if I was Methodist or not and they still do a lot of work over there. Lots of work.

YEAH, IT'S A GREAT PART OF THE COMMUNITY.

Mmhmm. Now, I'm trying to think how I met my friends…Oh, Joanne was babysitting and that's how I met Joannie Metcalf. I knew the Castles' and Elaine. Once, my husband said about one friend of mine from church, 'You know, you better watch her.' He was a very discerning person about people's characters; he could tell there was something about them he didn't like. He could tell right away there was something wrong with them. She went to our church and one day said to me, she never would come by my house, because, 'You've got that big old black dog so I'm not coming in your house.' So she never did.

YOU HAD A DOG?

Yes, we had a dog. We've always had a dog. In fact, we moved him from 24th Avenue to here. How we got him was…we had just gotten back from a trip to Chicago. I was looking for the kids to come in and have dinner, we always said dinner at five pm and they weren't sitting at the table. I asked, 'Where are Aaron and Elmer?' Then they came and they had this dog with them and we said, 'What are you doing with that dog?' They said, 'That man said we could have the dog.' So we just looked at each other and went on eating and so that's how we got Pal.

123

So anyways, (that lady who didn't like dogs eventually introduced me to) my friend, Pearl. Pearl was always into acting. She and I got to talking and I guess we got to talking so much that we were friends ever since that. Always. She wasn't too fond of too many Black people; I found that out, too. Her people were racist she said; they were Italians from Aberdeen. She was from here but she was…She and her husband used to be Communists. Her husband was a longshoreman, and she and I would talk. Elmer would fall asleep and Dell would be in the bed and we would be talking till three or four o'clock in the morning. She and I—we were just something else. They lived down on Madison. You know where Harrison School (now Martin Luther King Elementary) was?

ON THAT RIDGE.

They lived way up on the top. There were three houses on one side.

I THINK THAT'S PART OF DENNY BLAINE, ISN'T IT?

Around the corner is Denny Blaine; it's part of Denny Blaine, yeah. Well, that's where Elaine lived, down in there. They all lived up in there. They had nice homes. Their houses weren't real big, but they were very interesting. Anyway, Pearl and I became very close friends.

NOW, DID ANY OF THOSE FRIENDSHIPS GET INTERRUPTED DURING THE PANTHER TIME?

Oh no, they were very involved. Are you kidding? That's how I became friends with them. That's why we became friends because I was a Panther member, my kids were in the Panther Party.

DID YOU WORRY? AARON TOLD ME THAT ONE DAY HE WAS TESTING A GUN AND IT BLEW UP—

Oh, that's another story.

HE TOLD ME THAT AFTER A WHILE HE WAS WORRIED ABOUT WHO WAS IN THE PANTHERS (INFORMERS).

Yes. It's just like in the government, it's just like it is now. I don't know who you are. You could be asking me a lot of questions and I don't know anything about you. You could. Or your husband. So that's how things work and things are still that way.

DID THAT MAKE PEOPLE TREAT EACH OTHER DIFFERENTLY AFTER THINGS LIKE THAT STARTED HAPPENING?

I don't think so.

DO YOU DEVELOP AN INSTINCT FOR WHO YOU CAN—

Trust? Yeah, you do. Mmmhmm…with people period.

I INTERVIEWED MIKE TAGAWA—DID YOU KNOW HIM? HE DID THE EDUCATION PROGRAM FOR THE PANTHERS AT THE PRESBYTERIAN CHURCH OVER HERE.

Oh really?

HE WAS TELLING ME THAT THEY COULD KIND OF FIGURE OUT WHO THE INFORMERS WERE BECAUSE ALL OF A SUDDEN THEY'D DISAPPEAR.

Oh you learned that. Oh, is that right?

YEAH, BECAUSE IT WAS CLEAR SOMEBODY WAS INFORMING AND THEN ALL OF A SUDDEN SOMEBODY WOULD DISAPPEAR AND THEY'D KIND OF THINK, 'OK, HAD TO BE HIM, HAD TO BE HER, HAD TO BE WHOEVER.'

Mmmhmm, mmhmm. Well, my friend Pearl, like I said, they latched onto us right away because of our being involved in things like that (the Panthers). They were really up and all of them, even the Gremels. They were always over here. They bought most of their clothes at the second-hand store. He gave Elmer a beautiful raincoat that he'd bought. They were just very nice people. They'd take us out in the evening for coffee in the University District. Or they'd invite us over to their house in the North End; they had us over for dinner several times. We got along very well.

One day we had been out of town, just got back from Chicago and got a phone call. I think it was Elmer, said, 'Mommy, Mr. Gremel's been trying to get a hold of you, his wife, Marjorie, died.' The last time they were over here she was kind of pickled and she said, 'You know, I've got really bad heart problems.' I wasn't paying her any attention and she died when we were away, just like that.

And so her husband said, 'You know, Marjorie has some things I know she would want you to have.' He gave me her typewriter and this old, I still have it up there, Persian wool coat. It was one of hers she'd picked up somewhere, and her little sewing kit that she had all these little things in and all of her books. She had belonged to the Black History Club. Yeah, she was a sweet lady. Just so different. Yeah, those pants she had on, she had this red suit and with those cuffs turned way up here. She didn't care whether you liked it or not. She knew I wouldn't care, or none of my friends.

Pearl was that way, too. She just picked me out (to be her friend). She was crazy about Elmer. Pearl, like I said, was from this family that they was very prejudiced against Black people, but she just didn't pay any attention to them. She was a member of the Repertory Theater. Whenever she was going to be in a play she would invite my family, Elmer and I and the kids, to one of the rehearsals, so we were that close. We were quite close.

She had parties; we were always gathering in her kitchen. She had kind of a smaller kitchen but a big living room area with a fireplace and everything. One time, there was this Black guy there, you really didn't see too many Black people there. He was kind of friendly and he said, 'That's my friend that I came with.' He indicated a White guy. Finally, he whispered to me casually as we were by the stove, 'You know we're here watching you.' They worked for the FBI.

DID THE PEOPLE WHO INVITED YOU...?

No, they didn't know anything about it, uh-uh. Pearl didn't know that. So you never knew who was in your house.

Of course, my kids used to have meetings up at what they used to call the Barn. It was a place there on Madison. There used to be a big warehouse up there. Inside they had a lot of nice-looking old dressers. They'd have meetings up in there. They told me about this so-and-so that used to come up there and they said, 'You know, he's an informant.' They knew he was an

informant. Mmhmm. And another time, they told me about somebody else that was an informant.

But at the party that guy told me. One day, my husband always went to the market on Saturday mornings, the public market. I had bought Elmer, my husband, this red wool cap, a Pendleton cap. So I always knew where he was, because he was a wanderer. He'd wander off and I'd be doing something and then just look for that cap so I could find him. That day, he'd wandered off while we were down there and here comes that same Black guy. We kinda looked at each other. I guess he had to act like he was really following us. He was just warning me. He was just one of those who could tell me they were watching us; he was like letting me know.

WHY DO YOU THINK HE WANTED YOU TO KNOW?

Probably because he's Black, I don't know.

MAYBE HE WAS SYMPATHETIC.

Who knows. Yeah. But he didn't have to do that. I'm sure he was with his friend or some other guys who worked for the FBI. He acted like he didn't know me. But he had told me that at Pearl's house we were being watched. And I'm sure we were.

I'M SURE YOU WERE, TOO.

I'd get phone calls, and they were always watching our house. I could spot 'em. You could always spot 'em. And they were always watching the Panther office there on 34th Avenue. That's when they accused Aaron of stealing a typewriter.

WHAT WAS YOUR HUSBAND'S ATTITUDE TO THE WHOLE THING?

Pretty much like mine; we were on the same page. They would come by his job at Boeing. He lost a lot of chances to getting promotions because of the kids.

YOU SAID THAT AFTER THE RIOTS THE NEIGHBORHOOD CHANGED, A LOT OF BLACK FOLKS MOVED. I KNOW FROM TALKING TO SOME OF THE CHINESE PEOPLE WHO LIVED HERE THEY LEFT ABOUT THE SAME TIME, THE JEWISH PEOPLE ABOUT THE SAME TIME...

The Jewish people left way before that, they moved when we moved in here.

OK, SO IN THE LATE FIFTIES THE JEWISH PEOPLE WERE MOVING?

Well, we moved here in…when did I say?…'57. There weren't too many White people out here. They were all down that way east. We didn't have any White neighbors. The old lady next door lived there; she never spoke to me. Ever. She spoke to my husband, she loved the dog, and she'd speak to the boys, but she did not speak to Joanne and me.

I didn't care. But she'd get on that piano of hers, it was a player piano, and sang. My husband said, 'You hear her singing?' She's sing 'Old Black Joe' with the door wide open. She was something else. She used to raise begonias. She died after she married a guy—a Mr. Seudner. He was a very nice man and after she died, he was gonna sell us that house for nine thousand dollars. But we didn't want it at that time. We didn't want another house. No, but that's the way it was then.

AND THEN AFTER THE RIOTS WHO MOVED IN? DID THE HOUSES WITH ALL THOSE PEOPLE MOVING OUT, DID THE HOUSES SIT EMPTY?

A lot of them did, yeah. That happened even when Boeing closed, you know they said, 'Last one, out turn off the lights.' Do you remember that?

I READ ABOUT IT.

The house right back here was empty for a long time.

128 **DID THE NEIGHBORHOOD THEN FEEL SORT OF EMPTY?**

No, there was people living (here), everybody didn't leave. And I think Blacks started moving out when the riots were coming along, as I recall. I don't know. And I think the housing opened up (Open Housing) more because when we came out here you couldn't buy a house where you wanted, you know.

YOUR HOUSE IS A BEAUTIFUL HOUSE.

This house, my husband was told that it used to belong to that undertaker down there on Pine (now Chapel Bar), I can't even think of the name of it. It was built in '04 so there wasn't a lot of property around here.

WHAT WAS THE NEIGHBORHOOD LIKE, AFTER THE RIOTS?

Then the properties start going up and I guess Blacks started to move. I'm trying to think…when the White's started coming in.

WAS THAT THE SEVENTIES OR THE EIGHTIES?

No, it had to be before, it must have been, well my husband died in '85 so they were coming in before that, before he died, so it must have been the Seventies. I do know when they start moving out, they wanted to move back in and they couldn't because the property was too high. We never attempted to use our house as a way of getting income. We never loaned or borrowed on it.

IS THAT HOW A LOT OF PEOPLE LOST THEIR HOUSES BY PREDATORY LENDERS?

Sure. Mm-hm.

HOW DOES IT FEEL TO LIVE IN THIS NEIGHBORHOOD NOW, WHEN IT'S CHANGED SO MUCH?

Oh fine, it doesn't bother me. It doesn't bother me at all.

WELL, THAT'S GOOD BECAUSE SOME PEOPLE ARE PRETTY UPSET.

Well, they didn't like the White folks moving back in. Yeah, that's true. It is getting a bit White.

Jack Dunn, 31st & Madrona

Jack Dunn was a photographer and firefighter in the Central Area. He crackled with energy and loved exploring mountains through hiking, mountain climbing and skiing. Up until his last days, he rode his electric bike and engaged in his passion for photography. He had a great sensitivity and integrity that his views below reveal and reflect. Jack has passed away and is greatly missed.

"Honestly, though, this neighborhood was the only interesting one in all of Seattle…It's gone through so many changes that no other neighborhood can duplicate."

JACK ON MADRONA IN THE 1940S:

Well, it was a whole new world for me after I moved to Madrona. You might say that at that time I was a 'lil old-hillbilly who didn't know anything about the world but I evolved. I'd grown up in a logging camp near Mt. St. Helens, so I'd only ever seen one Black person in my life. During World War II there was a lot of anti-Japanese propaganda, so I was shocked to see people being friendly with Asian people. During the war a lot of people felt similarly suspicious (since) there had been a lot of propaganda.

HOW DID PEOPLE VIEW THE INCARCERATION DECISION AT THAT TIME?

Well, at that time people trusted the government so if they said it had to be done, well then, people thought they were probably right. There were a couple of newspapers who protested against it, one on Bainbridge Island. But protests were a minority view. The Japanese didn't protest; they went mildly. Maybe inside they were seething, but outwardly they didn't show any signs of protest. It was one of the worst crimes the government committed at that time.

Later, our family became friends with the Kuroses. He accepted me because our wives were friends. He was very bitter after the internment camps so he didn't like White people. We shared a similar political philosophy. I was a protester against the Vietnam War too. And I liked him. His wife, Aki, became a well-respected teacher and a peace activist. It's not often you have a school named after a teacher. She protested against the Vietnam War and her sons were war protesters too. They were social protesters back in the days when the cops didn't like protesters.

Jack on Madrona in the Sixties—The Red Line and The Impact of the Black Panthers:

There wasn't much change in the Madrona area after the war. Then Blacks started buying houses further up the hill towards 35th Avenue. There was what was called a 'Color Line' (redlining), that restricted where people could buy houses. A lot of people talked about wanting to 'Hold the Line.' It was a big hullabaloo. Then the real estate man, Hardcastle, decided the heck with the line and there was a house sold on the other side of 34th. Of course, after that other houses sold. It was very racial here in that respect.

The neighborhood went through real changes during the Sixties. In around 1968, that was the time of what they called, 'White flight.' You should have seen it. The Red Line had been crossed and Black people were buying homes up to 34th Avenue. White and Jewish people were selling their houses at a loss and moving to Bellevue. Then, they realized the commute was terrible and they moved back but had to pay through the nose to get back into a house here.

There was a Jewish family who lived over there on one corner near our house, and when they sold they sold to a Black man who worked for them. So, at that point, there were Black and Jewish families on this corner. At that time, there was no conflict that I knew of; everybody got along, kids always played baseball on the corner.

I couldn't understand the White flight. A lot of the firefighters I worked with didn't live in the neighborhood and they'd always ask me, 'Why don't you move?' Honestly, though, this neighborhood was the only interesting one in all of Seattle. I've always liked this neighborhood and our corner; it's always been interesting to be here. It's gone through so many changes that no other neighborhood can duplicate.

The Sixties were also the time of the Black Panthers here. They had a storefront office on 34th Avenue, behind the fire station. I used to play tennis with a couple of the Black Panthers. I got blackballed in the fire station because I stood up in support of them at a community meeting where the police were talking about a program they'd developed to deal with the Panthers. I said, 'Maybe the program sounds great in your office but on the streets your cops are still beating up Black kids.' When I got back to the station I'd been blackballed. I was told I had better watch my back.

131

Now, the Black Panthers in Seattle was different than it was in other places at that time. See, Elmer and Aaron Dixon started it. Aaron was the head guy but he was mostly in Oakland. Aaron was trying to develop self-esteem in these kids, to give them a reason to be alive and to stand up for themselves as men. They were pretending to be militarized, which terrified the cops, but in reality they were more interested in social issues. That was in part because of the way Elmer ran things here in Seattle. He was well-liked. They started a food program for kids and a free health clinic. There probably wouldn't have been a Black Panther organization here without Elmer or it wouldn't have been the regimented, disciplined organization it was. He kept them out of trouble, he didn't believe in violence.

At the beginning they had a storefront almost behind the fire station. They ran out this awful man—a rip-off artist who sold real estate and everybody was happy about that.

YOU WONDER WHAT IT WAS LIKE FOR THE MOTHERS OF THESE YOUNG MEN IN THE PANTHERS?

They knew. We all knew that the police wanted to shoot them on sight. Aki Kurose's sons were in the Black Panthers and they were in the same position.

WERE THERE ABOUT NINETY FIRES SET DURING THAT PERIOD IN THE LATE SIXTIES?

That's true, but it seemed more like a way to get attention. There was only one big fire, on 14th and Union; it was a big apartment building being built. The fire was started on the top of the building with gasoline, so the whole thing went up. All we could do was stop it from spreading. I thought the fires were just a way of protesting.

Still, though, the fire station got shot at twice. Both times I was in it. The first time it was a shotgun, the second time a rifle. I asked Elmer if he knew who did it. He said he did but he wouldn't say who it was.

There was one night all these police turned up and they were going to raid a house. The wrong house. I told them that. Anyway, the Panthers had already moved and that there were two kids in there renovating the house. They didn't care. The police broke-in the door, guns drawn. I was so afraid that those kids were going to pop up in their sleeping bags and get shot dead. It wouldn't have mattered that they were White; the police were so gung-ho. They actually are sometimes so intent on their plans they don't think. They don't seem to understand control.

JACK ON MADRONA SINCE THE 1960s—THE FIRE STATION AND THE LIBRARY:

There is a sore point for me, though, in this neighborhood about the fire station. It has a long history. Originally, it had a horse-drawn fire truck. In 1919, they rebuilt it for a fire engine. Then in 1973, they closed it and it became a library. There had been firefighters who made a lot of sacrifices and some who'd even died doing their jobs. All that service for the community was ignored when they renamed the building for Sally Goldmark. It bothers me a lot, I complained to one neighbor and he was instrumental in getting a plaque (put up) about the fire station.

WERE THERE OTHER CHANGES IN THIS NEIGHBORHOOD THAT YOU REMEMBER?

In the 1970s, there was an influx of Californians who sold their houses at inflated prices down there. They came up here and started bidding up the prices on houses around here. Taxes went up dramatically. People were very unhappy with that. Then in the 1990s, Microsoft's fortunes came up and that drew a lot of new people to the area. They had money to buy old houses and restore them. Then both housing prices and taxes went up again.

It's still a very interesting place to live. I love living here.

Even at nearly one hundred years old, Fordie's life revolved around service to others. It got him up and out to YMCA meetings, church and frequent two-mile walks. Fordie Ross served his community, his church and his family in a vast number of ways during his one hundred years. He has since passed on and that loss is deeply felt; he left his definitive and optimistic stamp on my life.

> *'I am one who believes that you concentrate not on the bad but on the good, that you build on the good rather than the bad. That is what we have chosen always to do."*

Where did you and Thelma live in the Central Area?

On 32nd Avenue, north of the Madrona Presbyterian Church. In the early 1950s, we lived in a house that had a dirt basement. Every week I would go and get concrete. I finished that floor.

Can you tell me the story of how the Grace Church became part of the Madrona Presbyterian Church?

The Presbytery decided they were going to close Grace Church. They were very firm in their decision. And then they were firm in their decision that if we wanted to scatter to a variety of Presbyterian churches, we could do so. They also extended us the invitation to merge with Madrona Church.

Had the congregation at Grace bought the land the church was on?

I'm sure they had. I don't know for certain. I'm sure they were owners of the land on 22nd and Cherry.

So, the congregation put their own money into buying the land for Grace Church, which was sold. Then, they were told to attend Madrona Church?

One day in 1952 we marched, as a group, to where Madrona Church is located. At that time, it was an all White church with a membership of 144. We worshipped with them that particular Sunday. The next Sunday we went to church, having been instructed by the Presbytery to go to that church, and all of the members of Madrona church had left except eight. Only eight people from 144 had come to worship.

EVEN IN SEATTLE, WHICH HAS A REPUTATION FOR BEING LIBERAL, PEOPLE DIDN'T WANT TO WORSHIP TOGETHER?

That is absolutely correct. They did not want to worship together.

I HEARD THAT WHEN GRACE CHURCH WAS SOLD THAT MONEY WAS USED TO START A CHURCH IN MERCER ISLAND.

That money went to build the Mercer Island Presbyterian Church. Yet, I have to stand up in defense of Mercer Island Church because (fifty years later) they did a superb job in making certain that Madrona was recompensed for the money that went to Mercer Island. They did it not in words but in their actions. Everyone I can think of from Mercer Island Church came every day for five months to rebuild the main sanctuary and the fellowship area. How do I know? I know because I am he who, at seven o'clock in the morning, opened the doors for Mercer Island men and women who worked like beavers (on) behalf of the Madrona Church.

They did a superb job inside and out. Above all there were members of the church who worked even on the roof of Madrona Church. So Mercer Island Church decided they were going to put in new carpet and to do that all the pews had to be taken downstairs. We all had to work like beavers. Mercer Island Church was superb. They were grand. They were great. I can't say too much about how much we appreciate Mercer Island Church for all that they did, the money that they spent and the labor that they devoted. They revamped not only the sanctuary but the Fellowship Hall as well.

That is a sermon of life. It should be always remembered. One important thing is when they repaired it, ninety percent of the church was Black. They did all that for Black people.

SO A WHITE CHURCH IN MERCER ISLAND DID THIS FOR A LARGELY BLACK CHURCH IN SEATTLE?

135

That's exactly what I'm saying. That's absolutely right. The congregation was ninety percent Black when they did the repair.

WHAT DID IT FEEL LIKE WHEN MERCER ISLAND PRESBYTERIAN REPAIRED MADRONA CHURCH? DID IT HEAL THE INJUSTICE?

Oh, yes! We never harbored the injustice. We were bigger than the injustice. In fact, if it were not for the Presbytery we would not have fully known the facts of that injustice. I have pictures of the whole sanctuary filled ninety-eight percent with Black men. Right now, it is ninety-eight percent all White. Most Sundays I am one of only three Black men in the church.

HOW DID THAT HAPPEN?

We all wonder about that.

IS IT A PROBLEM GETTING YOUNG PEOPLE TO COME TO CHURCH?

We have young people; that's all we have, but they're all White.

DO YOU FEEL COMFORTABLE IN MADRONA CHURCH?

That's a tough question to answer. I feel comfortable at Madrona because I am a Presbyterian. I feel uncomfortable because I cannot and do not enjoy the comfort that I desire. I mean by that—that there are no Blacks. I am comfortable as a member of the church. Also as a follower of Christ I have the task of trying to increase the 'Black fold.' I know how almost impossible it is because there are so very few Blacks remaining in that area. There are very few Blacks who can even spell the word, 'Presbyterian.'

DURING YOUR LIFETIME HAVE BLACK PEOPLE BEEN LEAVING THE PRESBYTERY?

No, they haven't left because they had not been a part of it. They haven't been a part because there are more Black Baptists than in any denomination in the world. When I was moderator, I went to every Presbyterian Church to preach. I received an invitation to meet with a special, elite group at the First Presbyterian Church. A day or two before going, something said to me, 'You are talking to an elite group, why not talk about the rules and regulations of the Presbyterian Church?' I was introduced as the speaker for the day. I spoke for twenty minutes about what you do and what you don't do as a Presbyterian. Then, all the sudden I stopped and asked a question—'Who is the Moderator of the Presbytery?' Lord, have Mercy. I was talking to the elite, educated group of White Presbyterians in the church and not one of them, who all go to church every Sunday, not one of them knew I was the moderator of the church. I was the head of the Presbyterian Church. And they didn't even know my name. When we talk about solving the problems of the world…I have encountered many.

When I was young and on my way to college, I rode the freight train to Marshall, Texas. I started walking down the sidewalk to get to school. I was arrested and put in jail. As a Black man I should have been walking in the street. Boy, I have been telling you…

I WONDER WHEN YOU'VE EXPERIENCED UNFAIRNESS, HOW DO YOU KEEP YOUR HEART OPEN?

I do it because I know Christ would command that I do forgive. You will learn as we go along of my deep commitment to Christ.

I'll tell you something strange but it is something that I do. My wife has passed on but every night I pray. Every night I pray. I say, 'Honey, let us pray.' And she is right there. That's my life. She is with me every night when I pray and in my prayer I devote time to mentally listen to what she has to say. I have been working on a project for almost three years and I had been hoping it would consummate this year. Three days ago, I got word that it would consummate. She had worked in the sidelines on it. I would say to my wife all the time, don't get weary we're almost at the finishing line and those were comforting words to her. For a moment, I looked at the dark side because physically she will not see it. But something said to me, Rejoice! She does see all this.

You know, fate is giving us the time to talk. And I rejoice.

I guess, my greatest public achievement got its birth at a meeting in the North End. A man walked up to me and put his hand on my shoulder and said, 'Fordie, I want you to take over OEC (Operational Emergency Center).' I thought, 'You've got to be joking.' He told me, 'The job is yours; the decision has already been made.' So, I went to the director and he told me he was waiting for me. We had an agency, the largest of its kind in the state of Washington. I was its director for twelve and a half years in Seattle.

We had the largest United Way Agency dealing with the needs of people; we provided so much food. I have seen as many as 180 people in line for food. I had food for every one of those 180 people. I had one young man who came in every day. One day I said to him, 'I don't want to see you in two weeks. I want you to have a job.' And before the two weeks were up, he stopped me to tell me he had a job.

We also had a Rent-A-Kid program that was a thriller. People would rent kids to do yard work. It got them off the street, taught them about work and made them good and respectful citizens. We had an agency that everybody talked about.

My wife and I were chosen to represent Seattle at the Seattle Seafair parade in 1962. Then, ten years ago the two of us were chosen as delegates for the Parade of Renton. We were honored guests for ten years. They called a few days ago to tell me we would be honored guests again this year. They did not know my wife had passed.

DO YOU WANT TO TELL ME ABOUT YOUR BIRTHDAY PARTY?

Five years ago, a member of the church said we should have a birthday party for me. Two hundred and two people from all over the state of Washington came for over three hours, wherein I told them the history of my life and all of the many things I had done and accomplished.

When the newspaper closed, I had no job. I said to Thelma that I'm going downtown to look for a job. I went downtown to the National Cash Register Company. The owner told me, 'I'm sorry, we have no openings.' So, I went to a few other places and went home without a job. The next morning I told my wife I was going downtown to look for a job. Again, I went to the to National Cash Register Company. The manager again said, 'I'm sorry, we have no openings.' On the third day, I said, 'Honey I'm going to look for a job downtown' and I went to the National Cash Register Company. On the third day, the manager once again said, 'I'm sorry, we have no openings.' I went to other places and I found no work. On the fourth day, I went to the National Cash Register Company. The manager again said they had no openings. I left and when to other places and I found no work. On the fifth day, the sixth day and the seventh day, when I went downtown, where did I go?

To the National Cash Register Company?

And on the eighth day when I went into the National Cash Register Company the phone was ringing. By then, the manager knew my name and he said, 'Fordie, answer the phone.' I answered the phone and a lady wanted to buy two rolls of paper. I convinced that lady to buy a case of paper that cost over five hundred dollars. And when I completed the sale, the lady told me that she wanted to meet me the next time she came in.

When I got off the phone the manager said, 'Come to my office.' He said very pointedly, you've been here many times and I've told you we have no openings. For the last time, I'm going to tell you again, 'We have no openings.' He got up from his desk, put his hand on my shoulder, and said, 'I heard you make that sale. A job is yours.'

Three years later, I was the chosen employee to go to the national meeting in Dayton, Ohio. So, persistence pays off. I have learned if you are determined and you are consistent, things pay off, if you don't give up. I don't give up. I don't give up on life.

I'm skipping one of the main features of my life. I sold real estate in Seattle. One day a lady walked in and threw five hundred dollars on the table and said, 'Mr. Ross, I have a house that I want to buy. I can't buy it because my husband won't sign the papers and the government, the Federal Housing Authority, won't sell the property unless he signs the paper. You get me that house, Fordie.' She left the money. I went home to think about it. Three weeks later, she came back to find out if I could get her that house. I asked her, 'Where do you work?' She said she worked for Mrs. A on Monday. And another lady's name for Tuesday, and so on through the week.

I leaped to my feet and said, 'You're going to get that house.' When she left, I called the people for whom she worked and told them that on a certain day I wanted them to meet with me at the Federal Office. I asked them to each say how much they loved the woman who works for them because I'm going suggest that the rule be suspended to let her buy that house. We all met there and each one of those ladies spoke for her. I made my presentation and they suspended the rule. The lady bought that house. And I became the Salesman of the Year for that sale.

During all this time I am a member of Madrona Presbyterian Church. You know that Dr. Martin Luther King came to Seattle? He was here one time. He was refused a place to speak in Seattle (voice rises in indignation). He had to speak in a boxing ring.

THAT I DID NOT KNOW. I KNEW HE SPOKE DOWNTOWN.

He was refused the privilege to speak at the First Presbyterian Church in downtown Seattle. Oh, that was common knowledge. Dr. King was only once in Seattle and could not preach in a Seattle church (voice breaks). And isn't that a sad thing?

IT'S UNBELIEVABLE FROM THIS VANTAGE POINT.

Well, it shows that in many instances Seattle has been and is, to some degree, the same as Mississippi. My wife and I decided to have a house of our own so we would travel in our car everywhere looking for an empty lot. Finally, one day we made a turn and this lot (near Jefferson Golf Course) was vacant. Why was it vacant? Because where you're sitting right now was a river. The land where you are right now was a river. I said, 'Maybe we can build a house there; let's check it out.' We got in touch with the owner downtown and he said, 'Heck, I'll sell it to you.' I found that the city would work with me to build a house here. The city worked with me to build a tank in my backyard that is half as big as the lot itself but they helped us build this house. Where my driveway is a bulldozer sank into the ground. It was beautiful to see how they got a bulldozer out of the ground.

Shortly after that, we met a man in Kirkland, Washington. He was a builder and he told us he'd like to build some houses for Black people. I said, 'I've got a lot and I'd like you to build my house. If I got you two customers, would you give me a reduced rate?' He said he certainly would. I got a greatly reduced rate on the construction of my house. I got him three customers. Some of them still live on 32nd Avenue in the Central Area down the street from the Madrona Church.

140

Then, after we moved over here (to Beacon Hill), we learned we were in a neighborhood where Blacks did not live.

WHAT YEAR WAS THAT?

Nineteen fifty-eight. A White man said, 'heck with all of this crap' (redlining) and got a Black family in a house that's right on the corner on 23rd. They were not there long. There is no Black family in this whole area. You talk about discrimination. You talk about the barriers that exist! My wife is dead and there is not one person except the man who lives next door who even knows my wife is dead.

I don't know anybody across the street and nobody across the street knows me. The only person who knows that my wife is dead is the mailman. He came as he did every day and handed me my mail. I told him my wife is dead and that man stood there by that railing and cried. My wife loved the yard; she worked every day in the yard and over time, they became pals.

Since my wife died, I have had as many as fourteen people in this room at one time since her death. I mentioned that I was the president of the Y's Men's Service Club. The eight men from that club came here at seven thirty in the morning to take me to breakfast. And since my wife has passed, of all the people that I know in Seattle over all my years, only two White people have been inside to say, 'I'm sorry.'

Boy, I tell you the world has a long way to go before we solve our problems.

Evan Flory-Barnes is a musician, composer and performer with a deep Central Area history. His joy-filled music and infectious creativity seem to strive to create communion and spiritual development through the joy of creative pleasure. He is radiant—to be his friend is to know a particular type of acceptance and comfort.

"Thinking of the Central District, about coming home from my grandma's house and my dad and mom taking the lake route, because my grandma lived on Harrison Street. You go up past Bush and you go up Denny Blaine and you go down the hill and then you're driving past this beautiful lake (Lake Washington) and you see that every day. And it's inspiring and it's beautiful."

Evan on the Central Area:

When I think about the Central Area, I think about those early days at my grandma's house. I think about my cousin being in a hip-hop group in high school, and we were still in elementary school, with this producer, sort of a Seattle hip-hop legend, named Vitamin D. Now his father and his brother and his cousin are all musicians too. His cousin's Specs One, his brother's Jahon Mikhail and I forget his father's name who was an R&B soul musician. So then there's that influence.

There's being aware of people creating hip-hop music and creating original music, and so when I think about the Central District and its impact, I think about my early childhood and MTV being on, the very early days of MTV, watching all these videos. I remember first seeing *Thriller*, all the Michael Jackson videos, and the Talking Heads and The Police and Men at Work and Toto and then being around kids older than me who were just getting started making their music. And so, making me think about, well, was it something I want to do, but how do I go about it?

Was it easy to sort of dive into music?

You know, I think there's always been a part of myself that's looked at how I got into music as a roundabout way because there was beginning band school programs but I never went to class. I never felt like going to class. I don't know why. I remember when I did, I just didn't like it. So, I didn't count that as part of my musical background. But then when I was in seventh grade, I remember watching that Red Hot Chili Peppers' video *Under the Bridge*. I remember hearing certain songs and just going, 'I want to play the bass.' Always noticing the bass. But then the Red Hot Chili Peppers' song *Under the Bridge* made it, 'OK, it's official. I just want to do this.'

And then a year later, getting an electric bass, when I was at school for a semester at Cleveland (High), starting to play the stand-up bass. You know, I was a beginning-level bass player, but I was hanging on by a thread in the Garfield orchestra—but I had this confidence because I knew it was something I loved to do.

WHEN YOU HEARD VITAMIN D AND THOSE OTHER BANDS, YOU WERE YOUNG ENOUGH—YOU PROBABLY WEREN'T ABLE TO SEE THEM ANYWHERE THEY WERE PLAYING LIVE, SO?

What was cool was in high school when I got in this hip-hop band Maroon Colony. I remember being in middle school hearing about Vitamin D and Source of Labor and all these different hip-hop groups. Ghetto Children was the group that my cousin was in, though he got out of it, while Vitamin D was still doing that. So there were all these different groups. What I remember when I got into the hip-hop group doing shows with those guys and that felt official. That felt like, 'Hey, I'm in a band.' We were doing shows with these guys that I remember hearing about when I was in late elementary through middle school and all the way through high school. So, that was cool.

YEAH, THAT MUST'VE BEEN KIND OF MIND BLOWING.

It was. It was because it wasn't just that they were older and doing music, I also remember how that music hit me and feeling this signature of a time and a place, in particular in Seattle, and really being intrigued by the way Derek—Vitamin D—produced. And that being an influence on me right away; this just wanting to write music that felt that way. So, I got in this hip-hop band in high school and we were doing shows with them and I was getting hip to the sounds that he liked. And those things inspired me.

143

I think sometimes influences are an interesting thing because sometimes people think you're taking down the exact notes or imitating and emulating this exactly. But no, you're absorbing a vibe. You feel the thing in the music, and then you play back the thing that it makes you feel. That's its influence.

It's not necessarily a combination of notes or even a rhythm or—it's just this—your feeling is coming out of you and you're responding with music that is from that feeling. So, it's really interesting to think about those early days of being really young and just hearing this music and going, 'What is this?' This sounds cooler. This sounds like the hip-hop I like to listen to. This sounds cooler than the hip-hop that I'm listening to that's mainstream. It sounds like something else entirely—it feels like me.

RIGHT. IT'S INTERESTING HOW YOU DESCRIBE INFLUENCES—REALLY INTEGRATING FEELING—AND THAT'S A LOVELY AND REALLY PRECISE WAY OF ARTICULATING THAT. YOU'RE ALWAYS TALKING ABOUT THAT OVERWHELMING FEELING AND HOW DO YOU GET CLOSER AND CLOSER TO THE PURITY, THE PUREST EXPRESSION OF THAT FEELING. SO, VITAMIN D AND SPECS ONE—

Specs One—I first heard of him right after college. And I remember (long pause) at the Old Tower Records on the Ave (University Avenue) they had these listening stations and he had his album in there. That was during a time when a love affair with hip-hop was being rekindled. There was also at the Lo-Fi, Stop Biting on Tuesdays—which was these really progressive and forward-thinking tracks. It was in the spirit of what the Vitamin D tracks sounded like. Then there was these B-Boys and there was just this sort of really fertile and inspired and inspiring environment that affected how I wrote music and what I was thinking about musically.

I remember getting hip to Specs One. I thought that he was just this cat around my age or something. It turns out that he's been doing his thing for a long time and he's Vitamin D's elder cousin. So he's been this figure that's such a source of inspiration as far as hip-hop—it goes back thirty years. And I didn't know that, but his album *Return of the Artist*, which came out like in 2003-2004, was this particular marker in time that stands out. Also every other thing I've heard of his has this Seattle signature on it.

CAN YOU TALK ABOUT THAT A LITTLE BIT?

144

Gosh. There's definitely this sort of jazz element to it. It's an element that you hear that people would talk about liking 'East Coast hip-hop'. But it's different than that. It has a tranquil quality about it. And I feel like aspects of Seattle that get overlooked are this kind of humor and this—I call it—this sincere sentimentality.

It's this feeling of place and environment, because just our surroundings—the bodies of water, the giant mountain to the south, the epic mountain ranges to each side, all the green—it conveys that. That sound conveys that. It's more organic than the New York sound, yet it has this awareness of city. It has this awareness of concrete. But it feels more watery and more green—on the Evergreen end and maybe more green on the marijuana end too. It's got this sort of mellow thing. It's got the coffee and the overcast. It's got that combo.

AND THAT'S MAYBE TRUE OF SEATTLE ARTISTS IN GENERAL TOO?

Yeah, I want to bring that forward as a thing. Like how Detroit, or Minneapolis, or LA has their thing. I want to bring that forth as a thing; a signature.

I used to say that Seattle is the home of the misfit adept. It's why when anything from Seattle, or anybody who's even spent time in Seattle, like a Reggie Watts figure who has spent a ton of time in Seattle. I remember seeing Reggie and being, 'This dude sounds like Chris Cornell and Al Green.' It's like, 'Who the hell is this guy?' And then he gets outside of here—I remember also seeing his first solo show. I was in a rock band called the Low Dime and we played at the (old) Crocodile—Reggie Watts opened for us doing, basically, what he's famous for now. I've always asked this question, 'Why does it take the getting out of here to become famous?'

I feel like there's this opportunity to create yourself in a very original way, but in a way that is also grounded. I think when you grow up in an environment that has such grandeur, environmental grandeur, that's your day-to-day. When that's your environment—doing things on a grand but grounded scale—because your everyday is, 'Oh yeah, there's this huge giant mountain, there's this beautiful lake and these beautiful mountains and there's this beautiful (Puget) Sound.' This is what I live with. You live with the clean air and you live with the green and the sky.

I think about two of my band mates in The Teaching. How Jeremy grew up in Colorado—lots of mountains, open sky. Josh grew up around the Great Lakes area and there's a lot of lakes in Minnesota. I feel I've had this combination of both; this water and the mountains. I don't think that's an accident as far as the vibe that is here. The vibe that comes out of the music and the open quality that's there. I think that's always spoke to me. Our environment.

Thinking of the drive home from the Central District, from my grandma's house on Harrison Street. My dad and mom would take the lake route. You go up past Denny Blaine and you go down that steep hill to the lake. You're driving past this beautiful lake (Lake Washington) and you see that everyday. It's inspiring. It's beautiful and it's—

AND IT NEVER, NEVER GETS OLD.

Mhmm.

SO, BEYOND THOSE TWO, WAS THERE A CENTRAL AREA MUSICAL SCENE WHEN YOU WERE IN HIGH SCHOOL AND IN COLLEGE?

Well, I think about what Garfield (High School) is. I mean Garfield could be called the school of the performing arts. I think about that Garfield environment of the orchestra, the jazz band and then the bands that were formed outside of the classes. But I think in regards to the Central District, Garfield is a standard and is a hub for hip-hop, jazz, classical music; people learning that music.

WHEN YOU WERE COMING UP, THE CENTRAL AREA REALLY WAS KIND OF A MUSICAL CENTER. NOW THAT CENTER HAS MOVED SOUTH AND THERE'S A LOT OF REALLY INTERESTING THINGS HAPPENING MUSICALLY AND ARTISTICALLY OUT OF RAINIER VALLEY AND SOUTH.

Yes. It's a trip. There's talk about making Columbia City one of the arts districts. And from the Beat Walk, which has been going on for a long time, to the Royal Room, to Columbia City Theatre, now the Black and Tan in Hillman City, Roomba Notes; and the people live there. Ish (Ishmael Butler) lives in Columbia City. Gabriel Teodros lives in Beacon Hill. I think Vitamin doesn't live too far away from there. Ahamefule (J. Oluo) lives around there. I do too, and that's what I mean. There's all this creativity and I don't think it should just be, 'Oh, we just live there' and then keep to our lonesome. If all that creativity is resting there, and I see it—I mean that's one thing I've been really happy with Mark and the Black and Tan is that they've been like, 'Well—'

LET'S MAKE A PLACE FOR US TO BE TOGETHER.

Yup. And it calls the whole area up to a very high place, and it's really exciting, and it's open and it's full of possibility. Again, there are viable venues anywhere.

YEAH, THE CENTER OF GRAVITY FOR MUSICIANS HAS MOVED FROM THE CENTRAL AREA TO COLUMBIA CITY. AS SOMEBODY WHO DABBLES IN HISTORY, TO ME IT'S A LITTLE BIT SAD THAT YOU HAVE THESE MULTIGENERATIONAL FAMILIES WHO'VE CONTRIBUTED SO MUCH TO MUSIC AND THEY DON'T LIVE HERE ANYMORE. BUT THAT IS THE NATURE OF CITIES—THEY GROW AND THEY CHANGE.

What I also see happening is sort of a redefining of venue space. I feel that can take hold in a new way here. I feel every neighborhood should be an arts district in Seattle. I feel there's a way to do it, because there's so much of it that's associated with drinking and noise, and it doesn't have to be that.

What I know is that everybody likes to hang; everybody likes to enjoy themselves. Everybody likes to feel like they belong, or think that they have an insight into the under-culture that's going on. Everybody feels like they want that. And so how do you remind people that they truly want the cultural experience? Because you're not trying to convince them of something. It's not just, 'Hey, come see my band because it's a band I'm in.' There's a confidence I have for the things I do. It's soul enriching.

CREATIVELY ENRICHING.

Yeah, I want that to be obvious for people. I think people will spend—I don't know how much—an arm and a leg to go to something they know and then be up in arms whenever they have to pay five dollars for a so-called local artist. I don't necessarily look at the world's stage as more meaningful or more powerful than someone that is performing on the local stage.

147

IT'S ALWAYS INTERESTING TO TALK TO YOU ABOUT THE POTENTIAL OF SEATTLE AT THIS MOMENT. THERE'S THIS SENSE THAT MAYBE YOU DON'T HAVE TO GO TO NEW YORK BECAUSE WHAT WE HAVE HERE IS SPECIAL IN ITS OWN WAY.

Yeah, I think it becomes you go to New York because of the environment of New York, but not because you have to to be a successful artist. I think about Bill Frisell. The guy lives in Ballard. He plays with everybody. I think about Dave Matthews; dude lives in Wallingford. He does his Dave Matthews thing. You can see him hanging out at the Sea Monster having a whiskey and just hanging. Those are two cats, top of their unique fields, just doing their thing. Neither of them are from here necessarily, but have made such an impact just having a home here.

I think that what needs to be broken down is this hard idea that if you don't do X, Y, and Z…I think Macklemore broke down that idea. *The Heist*. Independent of the music, I mean I love the music on that album, but independent of it, those guys have their finger on the pulse of something. It's taking what they already were doing, for crowds that were in the hundreds, and then knowing that this hypeness, these anthems, these sounds, resonate with a broad amount of people. Selling out Key Arena two or three times and being from here… I've been one of his strongest supporters, because I'm like, 'What is that?' He doesn't have the pop machine behind him. Working with Ryan (Lewis), he's super intune with that pop zeitgeist. He's super in tune with the formulas. And they inform his formula. But it wasn't like there was some dude—

WITH THE A&R GUYS—

Yeah. And they created something that resonated over and over and over—something that was new.

AND UPLIFTING.

Yes. That's to be celebrated. Independent of aesthetic preference, that's someone that shattered the notion that you have to get out of here. You do have to get out of here as far as touring and bringing what you do to the world, but you can be (from) anywhere. In a way, it's exciting. It's exciting that it's breaking down, and if you're going to push the message of City of Creativity or City of Music, then really be it. It shouldn't be one neighborhood.

148

HISTORICALLY, THAT'S A TOUGH THING I THINK FOR THIS CITY. THERE'S STILL THAT LITTLE VILLAGE THINKING INSTEAD OF 'WE'RE A METROPOLITAN REGION.'

Then what makes people come? What is that thing here? What is that thing that makes people come here? What is it? I mean, it's always interesting being from here, born here, and wanting to know what draws people and then also having this narrative that's constantly—that's shared (outside of Seattle) about the place you come from but that doesn't fit who you are. That's a very interesting thing.

A LOT OF THE PEOPLE THAT I HAVE MET, TRANSPLANTS, COME HERE BECAUSE THEY KNOW THEY CAN BE THEMSELVES HERE. AND THAT SEEMS TO BE TRUE—THAT SENSE THAT YOU CAN BECOME WHO YOU WANT HERE WITHOUT AS MUCH CONSTRAINT. I THINK THAT'S A THREAD TOO.

It's an expanding, growing thing that's redefining itself and it's in such flux that what it meant to be in Seattle, even in 2013, is different than what it is now. I think the vantage point I have is that I've grown with the city. The early Nineties were a period in my growing up. They weren't the glory days. There's a lot that I love about that time in my life. There's a lot that's really beautiful and hilarious memories.

BUT LIKE YOU SAID IT'S NOT THE GLORY DAYS FOR YOU. THOSE WERE JUST THOSE DAYS.

There's a thing that I feel I've been getting into more. It's just an attitude. It's like cooking, for in-stance. Yeah, having awesome ingredients is awesome; having technique and know-how is awesome. Because I've had a lot of food that has a lot of fancy things involved in it, but it doesn't—there isn't this feel.

I mean, I get reminded of that eighty-twenty thing my friend Greg Lundgren said. Eighty percent talent, twenty percent confidence here. Whereas a place like LA (is) twenty percent talent, eighty percent confidence. But I think this attitude—let the chill and the sincerity be in the music. I've never liked when being at a certain place in New York or in LA gives a person a little sign-off because of their associations. I've never been into that. But there's a certain thing about when you can play, or when you are at a certain level of your powers, that has nothing to do with where you are or who you've been associated with. We have something going on here. I want for myself, and for the city, to own its attitude.

149

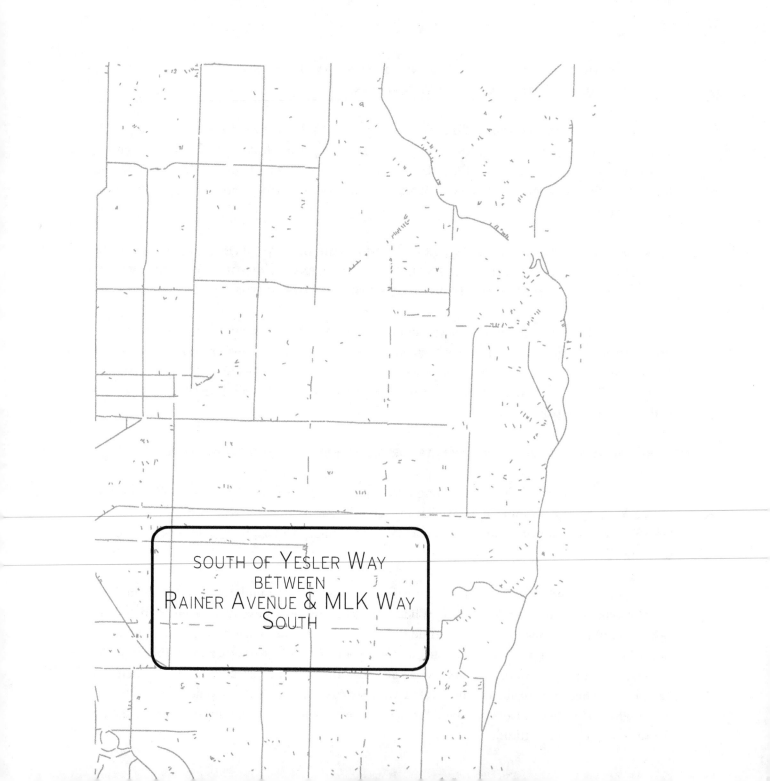

SOUTH OF YESLER WAY
BETWEEN
RAINER AVENUE & MLK WAY
SOUTH

Mike Tagawa is a former Metro driver and Black Panther minister of education. He's a wonderful example of how the unsung often have great stories. He joins and contributes to organizations with his full energy and intelligence from serving in the Armed Forces, to being minister of education in the Black Panthers, to volunteering to fix guitars and instruments for elders in care facilities. He thinks deeply about how his ancestry and history gifted him with both entré and exclusion—depending on the moment and the community.

"One interesting thing about this topic to me is that it's always been known as the Central Area. Yet, those of us who grew up here always called it the CD. People would ask, 'What does the CD mean?' and we would say, 'Well, it means Central Area.' It was always kind of a joke amongst us, so some of us would just answer that question with, 'The CD, that's the Central Area."

How did being from the Central Area affect your life?

To begin with, my maternal grandparents came from Japan. My mom, Masako Nagashima, was born in America. Her husband, my daddy, Takeo Tagawa, was born in Hiroshima. They got married and then had kids. Prior to 1942, we were living in the Central Area on about 18th and Yesler.

With the war they shipped us out to the concentration camps. Our family initially was sent to Puyallup staging area and then to Minidoka in the high southern desert of Idaho. On the West Coast, Japanese Americans from southern Oregon and north were shipped to Minidoka, (those south of Oregon) were shipped south to Tule Lake.

My family was in Minidoka until 1945, so I was born in a concentration camp in February 1944. I was eighteen months old when we left the camp, so I don't remember anything about it. When we moved back to this area, of course, we didn't have any money or any means to afford to live as we had in the Central District. We had to temporarily reside in the Renton Housing Project. A lot of those old housing projects are still there. We were there until I finished third grade.

Then, we moved back to the Central Area in the Rainier Vista Housing Projects. The Rainier Vista projects were a little fancier than in Renton but there was no mistaking that they were projects. I went to Columbia Grade School, in Columbia City, until the fourth grade. We moved a lot from near Colman Elementary, to near Providence Hospital at the old Washington Junior High School. After that I went to Garfield High and graduated but only because I went to summer school.

The Central Area at that time was a real potpourri. There were a lot of Blacks and Asians and a lot of Jewish kids. The Central Area used to be the home for the Jewish population of Seattle. That's why there are so many Jewish temples in the CD. Those buildings, though, aren't Jewish temples anymore. There were Jewish businesses like Brenner Brother's Bakery on Empire Way (which became Martin Luther King) and Cherry Street. A lot of people are surprised to learn all that because they think of the Central Area as being a Black neighborhood. Yet, there were so many Asians and so many Jewish people at that time.

Back in the 1950s into the early Sixties people from my class of 1962 were almost blissing out because everybody got along: Blacks, Whites, Asians, Filipinos and the few Chicanos. Garfield High School at that time was known as being this great, integrated school. Everybody loved each other. Everybody got along. It had quite a reputation for being the school with all different races. Yet, nationally, the late 1950s and early Sixties was when the divisions in the country, well, people started becoming aware that the country was divided. This was putting us on a road to trouble. The segregation in the Deep South was going to have to be eradicated. People were going down south and protesting; there were bus boycotts.

Up here in the Central Area during the late 1950s, we all knew about that but it didn't seem quite real. It just seemed like something very far away. It was something that we really couldn't relate to. Those of us who were politically astute were a little bothered by it and concerned. But here, at that time, it was just normal to have great race relationships. Everybody got along. There was interracial dating.

152 There was no problem because most of us stuck together in the Central Area. We didn't walk around or drive around to other parts of the city. It was a whole lot different when I was a teenager than it is now. Now, there's more mobility. Back in those days, you stayed in your own neighborhood. You didn't have access to a lot of things; certainly you didn't have access to computers and knowledge

of things all over. What you knew about was what you read in the newspaper or heard from friends. Today, even little kids have probably more knowledge available to them than we did as young adults. It amazes me how sophisticated little kids in grade school are compared to us back in high school.

Still, we knew there were problems elsewhere and Dr. Rev. Martin Luther King came to Garfield High School to talk. We knew elsewhere that race relations were bad, that the Deep South was a hotbed of racism and violence towards Black citizens. In comparison, the Central District was like Nirvana. Everything was good. Everything was just perfect.

After I graduated, I joined the Air Force. By June, I was down in San Antonio, Texas, at Lackland Air Force Base marching around in the hot sun in a fatigue uniform. I went from San Antonio, Texas, to Greenville Air Force Base in Mississippi. I went from the most integrated neighborhood and the most integrated school in the country to Greenville which was known as the very epicenter of all the racism. The next place I went to for more tech school training was in Montgomery, Alabama. Finally, I was stationed in Sacramento, so I'd go to San Francisco and see all the hippies and to Berkeley to listen to the protesters.

I get born in a concentration camp, go to the housing projects, go to the Central District, go from the best, most integrated high school in the city and then into the deepest part of the Deep South with the most problems and from there then end up in the hippie capital where a cultural revolution was taking place. The whole thing was just extremely fortunate, and was almost like a dream state, to see that whole spectrum, you know?

CAN YOU TAKE ME THROUGH WHAT THAT WAS LIKE? YOU GO FROM A PLACE WHERE RACE, AT LEAST FROM YOUR PERSPECTIVE, WASN'T AN ISSUE TO THE DEEP SOUTH. THAT MUST HAVE BEEN VERY SHOCKING.

It was. For instance, on our way to Greenville Air Force Base, we had to stop at a restaurant. The sergeant in charge said, 'Alright, this isn't like what you guys might be used to wherever you came from in this country. We're going to go to this restaurant after hours because they don't want us coming in in a mixed group during normal hours. You guys can't all be sitting together; we got some Negroes and some White guys, you know, different races here. They don't like that. They don't want us bringing a mixed bunch of people into the restaurant during business hours. After hours, we get the whole restaurant to ourselves.' Then, there was a 'Colored' and a 'White' bathroom. At first we all thought that was kind of a big laugh, because we were now really in the heart of Dixie.

I should mention here that some of the guys who joined the Air Force with me were from Garfield High. There were a bunch of Black guys that joined and I met other Black Air Force guys from all over the country. I had become good friends with them. I was running around mainly with the Black guys. They were all from the North and from areas that all weren't as segregated, or blatant about it, as the Deep South. We would laugh about that kind of stuff, even though underneath we realized this is deadly serious. I mean, literally deadly serious. There were a lot of violent deaths in the Deep South.

WHAT WOULD HAPPEN IF YOU WERE BY YOURSELF?

This sounds very strange to everybody that I tell this to. I didn't feel any more (pauses) uncomfortable in the Deep South than I did here in the Central District. This was a very strange thing for me, because I had a lot of friends who were White and a lot of friends who were Black. I would go into town with the White guys, no problem. I could go into every single restaurant; we went bowling together. Then when it came to do something that might be good, I would go into town with Black guys.

I would never have any trouble with the Blacks or the Whites when I went into town with either group. The people in Greenville didn't seem to know quite where to put me, so I could go into town with either group. The officers would tell us don't go into town as mixed groups, White and Black guys because you'll be asking for trouble. You won't have the protection and the sympathy of the people on the base. Some of them White boys wanna kill your ass. So, don't be tempting fate just because you know what is morally right. When you're around people who are ignorant and racist, they don't follow any higher level of thinking. They just think, 'Hey, look at that! A bunch of White guys and colored guys together. We should go kick their ass.' Don't do something that's going to agitate them. The Black guys can go into town together, and the White guys can go together. They didn't know quite where to put me, so I went into town with either group. I got treated well by the White merchants and all the people I would meet in Greenville, because I met a lot of civilians.

154

When I went to town with the Black guys, they were befriended by the people in the Black community. A lot of the food-service workers in the mess halls were Black, and they were very friendly towards the airmen. When I went into town with the Black guys, we went to a lot of dances. It was a dry county, but you could buy your own booze and sit there in the bottle club. They would give you a glass for a dollar and you'd pour your own booze into it. All these civilians, they treated me just fine. They were just as wonderful and loving to me as anybody. And the White people were the same way too. It was very interesting for me.

YOU WERE ABLE TO KIND OF PASS NO MATTER WHERE YOU WERE. YOU THINK THAT WAS PARTIALLY THE UNIFORM?

No, because when we went into town we were wearing civilian clothes. We never wore our uniform to town. It was the same way in Montgomery, Alabama. There was only one incident I remember. A bunch of us, all Black except for me, were walking towards the Capitol Building in Montgomery, Alabama. I think it was probably on a Sunday, the city was basically shut down. All the shops were closed. A car came by, slowed down, full of White guys. They said, 'AAAAAY, look at there man! There's a bunch of niggers! Man, look at 'em, a bunch of niggers out there!' Then there was a slight pause, and then one of them in the car yells, 'There's a Jap too!' Of course we're all, 'Fuck you guys.' We were talking shit. They were giving us the finger and yelling about niggers and Jap and all this stuff. Then, they just drove off. That was the only real incident I had in Montgomery. Same thing, I would go into town either with the White guys or with the Black guys.

As a matter of fact, the only time that race was an issue (for me) was when I went to town socially. I went to town with the Black guys to a Black college there. There was a dance there one weekend. We got to the door to pay admission, and when I got to the guy taking admission he asked, 'Are you with these guys?' I said, 'Yeah.' He said, 'Uh, nah man, You can't be comin' in here.' I said, 'What do you mean?' And he says, 'You ain't colored man. This is for colored people. This is for Negroes, and you ain't no Negro, man.' I said, 'Hey man, I'm with my friends. A couple others came up and said, 'You can't come in here.' That was the only time that I had any discrimination practiced against me was when the Blacks wouldn't let me into the dance at the college there. As far as going into a town full of White guys, never had any problem.

DID YOU EVER TRY TO GO TO ANY LOCAL DANCES WHERE IT WOULD HAVE BEEN WHITE?

No. None of the White guys seemed to socialize with the population like the Black guys did. In Greenville and Montgomery, Alabama, the Black guys seemed to flow easily into the community, become a part of the community and go to events in the community. The White guys always were just 'the guys from the base.' They didn't socialize as much with the population. It was just very interesting to me that it was that way.

I always noticed um…Blacks have a tendency to be more friendly and open to people that aren't necessarily part of the community just because they recognize people as human beings, that we're all together, whereas White people tend to be more inhibited. Black people tend to be less inhibited about socializing with other brothers and sisters than White people, and certainly way more than Asians. In comparison, Asians can be so stuffy and a bit uptight. Now, I'm making some stereotypes here. But you know, these are kind of generalizations that I've noticed are pretty true.

WHEN YOU WERE AT GARFIELD YOU SAID EVERYBODY WAS FRIENDS WITH EVERYBODY. YOUR PARENTS DIDN'T GROW UP IN AN ENVIRONMENT LIKE THAT. HOW DID THEY RECEIVE YOUR FRIENDS?

No problem at all. My daddy died when I was nine years old. He died at Firland's Sanitarium… It was a tubercular sanitarium that was located up there between 150th, 160th and 15th in the North End. It was a huge complex where all tubercular patients from around the northwestern states went. My father contracted tuberculosis after we got out of the camps. He was a great outdoorsman. He was known in the community as being a great fisherman, one of the best fisherman ever. He won a lot of awards. He used to work at Tashiro Hardware down on Prefontaine Place and Yesler. That was a big place for the Japanese community, because that was Japantown before the war.

My daddy used to work down there; he used to make split bamboo fly rods. Daddy was always out fishing. He was fine when we got out of the camps, and then he contracted tuberculosis. At Firland's they did some exploratory surgery on him and he died. I tell this to people and they freak out and don't believe that could have happened. He died from the cocaine used as an anesthetic and it killed him. He had an anaphylactic shock and he died.

After he died, we moved into the CD. Now, my mother was raising five kids plus her own father. Her father, *ojii-san* or grandfather, was still living with us. She went from being a housewife to doing nursing assistant work in various places around the Central District. That really was too bad because when Mom graduated from high school she was valedictorian. My mom was just brilliant but she ended up being a housewife and with no real skills. After Daddy died she was left with the task of taking care of six people. It was a tough life for her. We didn't have much money in our family; I'll tell you that. That's why we lived in the Central District and in housing projects.

WAS YOUR FAMILY A PART OF THE JAPANESE COMMUNITY?

All the Japanese families knew each other. All the kids knew each other. We all went to school together at Washington and Bailey Gatzert, Coleman, Cleveland, Franklin. As far as being part of the social fabric of the Japanese community…since Mom was a working mom and not having a daddy, our family wasn't part of the movers and shakers of the Japanese community like some more well-off families. All the Japanese families knew each other; it was very easy that way because we were contained.

DID YOUR FAMILY PARTICIPATE IN ANY OF THE RELIGIOUS COMMUNITIES?

Mom made sure that we went to church. We went to the Faith Bible Church up there near 18th and Yesler, and then we went to the Japanese Presbyterian Church. But, because Mom was by herself we didn't do a whole lot of social things with the churches. Hardly at all. A lot of families didn't either.

JUMPING BACK TO MINIDOKA, DID YOUR MOTHER TALK TO YOU ABOUT HER EXPERIENCE THERE, OR WAS THAT SOMETHING THAT WAS NOT SPOKEN OF?

She didn't speak much about it. When I was growing up, the elders, our parents and those old enough to remember the camps, tended not talk about it. It was like they were ashamed of it. When they would talk about it they would talk about it among themselves but they would not usually talk about it with us kids. I always thought it was kind of strange that they wouldn't tell us about it.

I understood why later, a lot of them were ashamed. It was about honor. They had basically been told, 'You guys are a bunch of sneaky, disloyal Japs and goddamn spies. You're the ones that killed

157

all our people over in Pearl Harbor with that Jap sneak attack.' They heard that and faced that when they got out of the camps and came back to Seattle. They faced a lot of bullshit like when the White population put signs up saying, 'Jap Go Home,' or 'Jap Stay Away.' So there was a lot of reluctance to talk about the camp. It wasn't until roughly the late 1970s or Eighties when they started talking about reparations that the Japanese elders started really becoming more vocal. They talked about how horrible it was. Even in that time some people were saying, 'Oh, we don't want any reparations. We don't need any reparations. Let's just forget about it.'

What was interesting to me was for years their attitude had been embarrassment because we were the enemy; we were damn Japs. It was like they almost believed that we really were the enemy and deserved this because we were Japanese. That really irritated my ass, but once they got over that, then they started taking on this attitude like, 'Hell yes, I was in the camps and we survived. We did good. We made the best of it.' Then, it started becoming a matter of pride for a lot of people. Not because being in the camps was a good thing but they survived it and made a better life for themselves. They came back and fully recovered and showed the goddamn government and all those racist sons-of-bitches who we really are. And they were proud of it.

SO THEY LIVED AND THRIVED?

Absolutely.

NOW, WHERE DID YOUR POLITICAL CONSCIOUSNESS COME FROM? CLEARLY THAT WAS A BIG MOTIVATION IN YOUR LIFE.

I started getting really political when I was at Travis Air Force Base and I used to go down to the Bay Area. I love American traditional music and traditional blues. Lo and behold, I was in one of the hotbeds of traditional American music in the folk clubs of Berkeley, California, and San Francisco. Folk music was a big thing back then—everybody from the Kingston Trio to the Brothers Four and all that. Hearing them made me realize that they're singing an old traditional song from the Deep South. I'd wonder, 'Who wrote that?' So I went out and explored.

It appealed to me because it sounded so real. It sounded to me like it's part of their culture, a part of their growing up, a part of their life, a part of their lifestyle. When I was listening to these great blues singers who were still field hands…The Carter Family was the same way; they were doing stuff for their friends and family. They were sitting around in their home and then that music became commercially viable for them. That kind of music appealed to me, whether it was Black or White, because it sounded right, it sounded sincere.

The Bay Area was just great, but also there was all this stuff on the campus of Berkeley. In 1965, I saw Joan Baez. Once on the campus of Berkeley there were tens of thousands of students there yelling and screaming about all these political things: end segregation, end the war, free speech and all that. I had an inkling of that but then I started realizing that there were huge, major issues going on. That campus might have been unusual because back at the base and in other parts of America, everything was fine. There wasn't any racism. There was no need for integration. People didn't need to get involved in things like free speech. The more I started to think about it the more concerned I got about it. I was left leaning. I supported the idea of integrating the faculty of Berkeley and getting more minority students. By that time, I was coming to a close of my four-year hitch in the Air Force; I was getting pretty political.

When I was in the Air Force I was a psychiatric ward medic on the closed psychiatric ward at Travis Air Force Base. Back in those days, in the Sixties, Travis Air Force Base was the main embarkation/debarkation point for servicemen going to Vietnam. All these medical patients would land in Travis Air Force Base. If they had psychiatric problems that were really bad then they would come up to F3; that was the ward that I worked on. Seeing all these guys from the Navy, the Air Force, the Army, Marine Corps, even some (south) Vietnamese coming from bases in the United States where they had been getting tech training and they cracked up. Well, it struck me as odd that they would take a Vietnamese soldier and bring them all the way over here. I figured, if it's something that can't be treated in Vietnam and he is one of our allies, then you better take care of him; he's wounded or screwed up because of America so you better take care of him.

159

DID YOU HAVE MUCH CHOICE ABOUT THAT?

You mean about becoming a psychiatric tech? No! When me and my friend joined up together, Vince Matsudaira, we both kind of had the idea that we would get on a flight crew being Boom Operators. They're the guys at the back of these fuel tanker airplanes that feed this long boom into airplanes and do mid-air refueling, because that's what Vincent's brother Mitch did when he was in the Air Force. But we didn't even come close to getting any flying status.

I didn't get exactly what I wanted. But looking back at where I went: Texas, the Deep South, and then in the Bay Area, I think, I was one lucky son-of-a bitch, because I got to actually step there into those moments of history.

WAS THERE ANYTHING IN PARTICULAR THAT YOU SAW DOWN SOUTH THAT YOU THINK REALLY BROUGHT HOME TO YOU WHAT IT MEANT TO LIVE DOWN THERE?

We were driving into Montgomery one day, and we're going down the highway and there's a big old billboard. It has a huge graphic of this guy in a Ku Klux Klan outfit on his horse with the ropes flying. It read, 'The Ku Klux Klan welcomes you to Montgomery, Alabama!' I thought, this is what it's like in the Deep South. It was just sort of a wakeup moment. This is not like Seattle.

WHEN YOU WERE IN TRAVIS AIR FORCE BASE, GENERALLY EVERYBODY'S PRETTY CONTENT WITH THE STATUS QUO. YET, YOU'RE DEVELOPING SOME RADICAL IDEAS THAT THE ANTI-WAR MOVEMENT WAS INTERESTING, THAT RACIAL ISSUES IN THIS COUNTRY NEEDED TO BE CONSIDERED, AND MAYBE THE STATUS QUO WASN'T REALLY SUCH A GREAT THING. DID THAT CREATE PROBLEMS FOR YOU?

It created a problem for me in a way because after I started getting political. I became more distant from the guys that I used to hang out with a lot. I was pretty much going down to the Bay Area by myself to go to these rallies. I was taking this anti-war position and being supportive of protests in the Bay Area on my own free time. I think that had something to do with the fact that one day I went to work in the psychiatric ward and they said, 'Mike you're not working here anymore. You've been assigned to the squadron.' What that meant was the squadron commander and a first sergeant, the First Shirt, would just have you do little chores and things that needed to be done around the squadron area.

So you go from having a position of responsibility to being a floater?

To being a floater, but that meant I worked Monday through Friday as that was the officers' and First Shirts' hours. Big guys get the weekends off, and the flunkies like us have to pick up slack for the other seven days, but because those guys were now in charge of me, I worked Monday through Friday, eight to five. I got to trim and mow the grass, do whatever things needed to maintain the barracks. That's the way I finished out the last month or so of my Air Force career. I asked why, and they'd say, 'This is best' and nobody knew why. The First Shirt didn't know, the squadron commander didn't know.

Do you suspect that they really didn't know, or do you suspect that they didn't want to tell you?

They didn't want to tell me! They had to know, this is the military, this is the Air Force! Everything's on paper, everything's done for a reason. But they never told me, and I've never been able to find anything, and I tried again just not too long ago to get something through the Freedom of Information Act from the FBI and nothing.

And you came back after your service?

I got discharged and came right back to Seattle.

And you would have been about how old then?

I would have been twenty two.

So you were a little older than some of the Panthers.

Yes. I got discharged in June of '66. So it was a little over two years, 1968, until I joined the Black Panther Party here.

DO YOU THINK THERE WAS A CONNECTION BETWEEN YOU BEING BORN IN A CONCENTRATION CAMP AND YOU BECOMING A PANTHER?

Yeah. I think that figured into my psyche, that we—because of our race, our ethnicity—were thrown into a concentration camp. In other words, we were treated badly because we were different. That's exactly what's happening to all my Black brothers and sisters who were getting treated badly. They had been lynched and persecuted ever since the 1600s when they first started bringing them over here. It's only because of their race. It was very easy to identify with that.

Having grown up in the CD, I wasn't thinking strictly about it being a Black, White, yellow kind of thing. It was like we were all the same people, you know? These were my friends. When I joined the Black Panther Party, I was married then. My wife and I were driving through the arboretum, and we could see all these people marching around. So we pull into the parking lot and watched, and it was the Seattle Black Panther Party. They were doing drill practice there.

The thing about discrimination—it's always based on so many things other than just who you are. It has to do with things particular to a certain community or perception of how things are from an economic standpoint or a cultural standpoint. I think of America and all the different groups that have suffered. You know there was a time when the Irish were looked upon as being the scum of the earth on the East Coast. Now Asians are starting to get a little more respect, but for a while they were the sneaky Japs and money hungry grubbers. These stereotypes and prejudices go in and out of fashion. To me, from time immemorial, there's always been this stuff. It just kind of shifts back and forth, but it never goes away; it just kind of changes its shape a little bit, and we're gonna have it forever.

There's a production of the Mikado with an all-White cast in Seattle. All the Japanese roles are being played by White people who act stereotypically. Now, if they tried to do this with blackface, they know that wouldn't go over; there would be riots in the street. The perception still is that Asians are passive and they're going to put up with this shit.

WITH SOME OF THE JAPANESE AMERICANS I'VE TALKED TO, THERE'S THIS VERY CLEAR SENSE OF THE AMOUNT OF PRESSURE THAT THEY FEEL FROM THAT COMMUNITY. YOU CLEARLY CHOSE NOT TO LET THAT AFFECT YOU.

I've always felt like, you got to do what you think is the right thing.

DID YOU GET ANY PUSHBACK FROM YOUR FAMILY ABOUT THE PANTHERS? A LOT OF PEOPLE WERE AFRAID THAT THEY MIGHT GET SHOT.

Well, my little sister Kathy (who passed away about a year and a half ago), she was very supportive. She said, 'Right on!' Still, she was kind of worried when she found out about it. And my brother too, he was kind of OK with it too. They might not have been activists themselves, but they supported equality, anti-war protests and supporting the community. My mom was kind of worried. She wanted me to be careful. My mom was just a wonderful, sweet person. When I was younger, I had a lot of conflict with Mom because I was crazy. She was always saying, 'Calm down!' After I got out of the Air Force I came to a resolution with Mom about having been a crazy kid. Still she was concerned about the Black Panther Party. Once, my then wife's mom, when were having dinner she paused and asked, 'Mike, did I see you on TV?' I said, 'Me? I don't think so. Why would I be on TV?' I thought she was joking. Laying it down for me she says, 'I thought I saw you on television the other day. I saw this protest at this place called Bluma's Delicatessen in the Central Area. They showed all these Black Panther Party people with guns lined up on the street. I thought I saw you there.' I'd never told her about being involved. I was just thunderstruck. I said, 'Yeah, that was me.' I wasn't really paying attention to the fact that the news crews were up there so I didn't know I was on TV. She just thought in a little silence. Basically she said, 'Well, I understand being involved in those kinds of things, but just be careful. Just be careful because we love you.' That was all I ever heard of that.

DO YOU THINK THE TV STATIONS PICKED YOU OUT BECAUSE YOU WEREN'T BLACK, OR DO YOU JUST THINK YOU WERE NOTICEABLE TO PEOPLE WATCHING TV BECAUSE YOU WEREN'T BLACK?

I think I was just noticeable to people because I was the only one who wasn't Black.

163

WHY WAS THERE PROTEST AGAINST BLUMA'S? IT WAS A JEWISH BAKERY RIGHT?

It was a Jewish deli near Garfield High on Cherry Street. Now, it's a little barbecue joint. Apparently someone started selling drugs out of the Bluma's there. Well, that was one of the main things we were against. They eventually opened up another place on 1st Avenue after they were basically chased out of the Central District. For years, Bluma's Deli was a staple of Garfield students on their lunch break. It was a great place to go. After my years in high school, I guess it had gradually gone downhill.

I HAVE THE FEELING THAT, FROM LISTENING TO PEOPLE THAT THERE WERE SOME WHO TOOK IT UPON THEMSELVES TO CALL THEMSELVES BLACK PANTHERS AND RUN AROUND SETTING FIRES AND HAD NOTHING TO DO WITH THE PANTHERS. IS THAT YOUR IMPRESSION AS WELL?

Well (long pause) did you ever hear about that Rainier Beach incident? We went down to Rainier Beach High to shut down the school once. At that time, it was a White high school with a few Black students, now everybody thinks of Rainier Beach as a Black high school.

The few Black students were getting picked on and discriminated against by the staff. That's why we went down and invaded the school. I think Aaron (Dixon) talks about that a little bit in his book. We ended up going down there and chasing the principal out, or he ran away from us when we marched into the office with our guns. Then, we had a little discussion out in the middle of Henderson Street with the police. We had Black brothers and sisters down near the park standing by with their guns. Aaron and Bobby (either Bobby Harding or Bobby White) and the three of us were talking to the police sergeant. That helped define the Black Panther Party and brought attention to the party so that got people interested in joining.

At the same time, in the neighborhood some people were interested in taking things to another level of radical politics, becoming more actively involved instead of just signing petitions or going on marches. Some people took it upon themselves to do some pretty radical things in the Central District, and for better or worse, they would say they were representing these various organizations. It's hard to say who did what, but in reference to your question about who was setting the fires and shootings and stuff, a lot of what was ascribed to being Black Panther Party activities…Well, for a while Seattle was known as the fire capital of North America.

There were more fires set in Seattle than any place. There were a lot of shootings and a lot of fires set in the Central District. But who knows who was doing it?

Some people think that a lot of it was Black Panther activity, some people think that it was activity by other groups like the Black Nationalists or the Weathermen or others. The best I can tell you is that (at that time) there was a lot happening.

ONE OF THE PEOPLE THAT I TALKED TO WAS A FORMER FIREMAN, JACK DUNN, WHO USED TO PLAY TENNIS WITH THE DIXON KIDS, PARTICULARLY WITH AARON'S SISTER. HE WAS THE ONLY PERSON IN THAT FIREHOUSE (NOW A LIBRARY ON 33RD) WHO WAS FROM THE NEIGHBORHOOD AND KNEW THE DIXONS. IT WAS HIS IMPRESSION THAT SOME KIDS WERE CALLING THEMSELVES BLACK PANTHERS BUT HAD NOTHING TO DO WITH THE PARTY. IT WAS THEIR CHANCE TO MAKE TROUBLE AS TEENAGERS DO, BUT THE PANTHERS TENDED TO GET BLAMED FOR SOME OF THAT.

Yeah, Bobby White and I went one time to Washington Junior High School just to be a presence walking around the school. I remember seeing these kids in black-leather berets and calling themselves Panthers but they were doing stupid stuff like bullying people and stupid shit. There was a fair amount of that. Then, there were also those guys that Aaron referred to as 'summertime Panthers' who would show up at our rallies and marches so they could be seen marching down Cherry Street with us. But if there weren't going to be a lot of people to see them and take pictures, then they wouldn't show up. They wanted to show off, but when it came to doing classes, political education classes up at the church on 33rd there would be very few people who would show up.

WAS THAT MADRONA PRESBYTERIAN?

We used to have political education classes there. It would be very rare for me to have more than two or three brothers or sisters come into the political education class there. So, that's the interesting thing about it (all the people claiming to have been Panthers).

I'VE HEARD THE READING WAS RIGOROUS IN THE POLITICAL EDUCATION CLASS?

We wanted it to be rigorous and we wanted to talk about topical things. I'll be completely honest, the political education classes I did, I could see it right away. Now, see I was twenty-four years old.

So you were a little bit older.

A lot of these guys were between eighteen and twenty-two. A lot of them hadn't been around much. They didn't know about Franz Fanon or *The Wretched of the Earth*; they didn't know about a lot of stuff. They knew about racism and segregation, about the Black Panther Party and police violence.

I remember early on bringing out a book and wanting to talk about it, but seeing that wasn't going to work. It was not going to hold their interest; it was not going to be something they could relate to. That was really important, being able to relate what we were talking about, tying it in with the community and what they're going to do in the community and for the community.

Some of the political education classes I taught didn't follow that list of Black Panther books. It was instead talking about how the Black Panther Party works in the community. How what we do in the community is the important thing, and tying it together on into the large picture of racism and the history of racism in this country with violence against Black people, about how Black people have to fend off this aggression against them and be their own leaders. That's what I taught in my classes. I'm not exactly sure what Bobby Harding and Bobby White did in theirs, but from talking to them over the years, I'm pretty sure they did about the same thing.

It was almost like an impossible task to talk to all these young people about WEB Dubois, or Franz Fanon, or any theories. It was, instead, let's have a discussion about what we're dealing with and what we can relate to. This is despite the long list of books from the Black Panther Party, at least up here in Seattle. Now, I think all over the country in all the Black Panther chapters I'm pretty sure that a lot of it looked really impressive when you looked at the book list. Still, when it came down to having the political meetings and the political education classes, a lot of it had a lot to do with talking about the shit going on in the neighborhood and how it relates to history. It didn't go into a lot of discussion of all these intellectual books by all these scholars. I can tell you that.

MAYBE YOU AND AARON WERE ALSO DIFFERENT IN THAT YOU WERE READERS.

We might have read a little more than these guys. It's hard to hold somebody's interest and attention when you're talking about stuff that's theoretical. When you talk about what's going on in the neighborhood, when you talk about experiences they had and their mother, father, sister, and brother had, then you can get them interested and involved. We had to keep it relevant, something that they could relate to. If they couldn't relate to it, after a while, I wasn't going to talk about it. There was no point. It was just wasting time. I think the attendants of these Black Panther Party political education classes was a reflection of that. There were more people in the beginning, but once they saw what the classes were about, interest dropped off real quickly. There weren't a lot of people who showed up for the classes.

NOW, I KNOW AARON WAS DETERMINED AND SOMETIMES AFRAID. HE'S TALKED ABOUT IT IN HIS BOOK AND IN HIS INTERVIEW. HOW ABOUT YOU? DID YOU FEEL YOU WERE FOLLOWED AND DID YOU FEEL PHYSICALLY AFRAID DURING THAT TIME?

No, I didn't really feel that at all. I didn't feel like I was being followed. I felt like there was a couple of times where we were being observed and followed by the Seattle Police, when we were out there putting up posters for rallies or selling papers. I never felt threatened or felt there was any danger. I guess I felt like there weren't many other people that can mess with us because we might shoot back at them. What're they going to do in front of witnesses and crowds? They knew we were armed to fight back. Cops that just want to practice their racism or to fuck with you aren't going to with someone that has a gun that may be more powerful, a rifle or a shotgun, that can outgun them. Remember, back in those days, generally we had firepower that was equal or better than the cops'.

Nowadays, cops have these special units. They've got bulletproof vests and helmets, high-powered rifles; they've got everything under the sun. Back in those days beat cops carried a .38 Special. They didn't have all these special SWAT teams and all that. I think that's why a lot of us were able to go around and be seen and visible in the party. Marching down Cherry Street without a permit, carrying guns and rifles, and they never messed with us. They would follow us, check us out, there's a cop car here and there, but they ain't saying, 'Get off the street' or pushing us. They do that to people they can pick on.

167

M
I
K
E

T
A
G
A
W
A

MAYBE THAT'S WHY IT WAS SO APPEALING TO YOUNG PEOPLE. THEY HAD SEEN PRIOR CIVIL RIGHTS MARCHES WITH PEOPLE FROM CHURCHES GETTING YELLED AT AND SPIT ON. HAVING SEEN ALL THAT, THE PANTHERS WERE MORE ATTRACTIVE BECAUSE YOU WERE BEING RESPECTED. YOU WEREN'T BEING SPIT ON.

Yeah, because for one thing all these marches and rallies and such were in the CD, so most of the people that were there were Black people, and there was a palpable sense of pride and anger. You could just tell that even if they didn't want to join the party or carry a gun like us, they could relate to it. They could maybe, vicariously, be a Panther. They knew what it was like to be fucked with by the police or the authorities, so when they saw us it was like, 'Right On!' We got a lot of support that way. People would come out on their porches on Cherry Street and clap; kids would run alongside of us.

IT MUST HAVE BEEN A GREAT FEELING.

It was a great feeling. The politics and the energy levels back in those days were intense. You could just feel the adrenaline running for a lot of the things that we used to do.

ONE THING I ASKED AARON WAS ABOUT HOW MANY JAPANESE FAMILIES AND BUSINESSES GAVE MONEY TO SUPPORT THE BPP BREAKFASTS AND THE FOOD DRIVES. HE SAID HE'D ALWAYS WONDERED WHY. MAYBE IT WAS INTERNMENT. DO YOU THINK THAT MIGHT EXPLAIN THAT?

I think some of the contributions we got from Japanese Americans was because some families could look at The Black Panther Party and think, 'Here's a group of people that are standing up to the United States government.' The government that suppressed you because you were a minority, because you're different. Here is the Black Panther Party saying, 'You ain't gonna fuck with us anymore.'

Stephanie Ellis-Smith is as warm as she is smart, as interesting as she is interested, especially in cultivating an artistic community in her adopted home of Seattle. She has done important work in the arts, civic engagement as well as in the field of science and medicine.

"I still hope with the growth we don't lose that essence of the city. Things change and alter. That support and generosity is very special and unique to this area. I hope that there are many people coming after me with new ideas. I hope that they will be as easily supported."

WHEN DID YOU MOVE TO SEATTLE?

In 1994, that's about twenty years ago last month.

YOU WERE A SCIENTIST AT THAT TIME?

I was working in laboratory research building my publication history. I was applying to grad schools and my husband had just finished applying to grad school; he's a Russian historian. We decided to move up here from Los Angeles and I began working at the University of Washington right away in HIV in Virology.

THAT MUST HAVE BEEN INTERESTING WORK.

It was actually quite fun, quite fun.

THEN YOU STEPPED AWAY FROM THAT?

It was a circuitous process. I was looking for a biochemistry genetics program and then I realized post-docs were few and far between, so there was no work for me. My husband was looking for a teaching job in Russian history, and we were trying to find a university that could take both of us, which was highly unlikely. Also, I was working a lot, maybe ninety hours a week in the labs. We were just married so it was very unromantic. I never saw him. I thought, well, maybe I don't want to do this as this would be my future for the next fifteen years, at least. I was applying to graduate schools and I withdrew all my applications. I decided I wasn't going to go through with it. I was going to do something else but I had no idea what. All of my life I thought I was going to be in science or medicine. It was a very scary time.

THAT'S VERY COURAGEOUS, TO WALK AWAY FROM ALL THAT WITHOUT KNOWING WHAT COMES NEXT. THIS MUST HAVE BEEN ESPECIALLY TRUE AS YOU MUST HAVE BEEN A VERY FOCUSED STUDENT TO HAVE BEEN IN SCIENCE OR PRE-MED?

I was. I was very driven. Yet, because of that I had almost no marketable skills. I didn't know how to use a fax machine. I didn't know how to use a multi-line phone. I had no jobs like that. All of my jobs were highly skilled but in a really niche area. I literally didn't qualify for most jobs, so that was very disconcerting after all the education I had.

Long story short, I ended up being involved in a catalogue raisonné project, which is an art historical endeavor, for the artist Jacob Lawrence. It resulted in a two-volume catalogue of his life's work. All of his paintings, drawings, and art works were located, many had been lost, and those were newly located and photographed.

A catalogue raisonné is the definitive compendium of a lifetime output; they are very prestigious books for artists. I didn't know anything about art history when I started because I was a science person. This was the first catalogue raisonné that was ever done for an African American artist.

It was wonderful; it was an amazing experience. The best thing about it was that my husband and I became quite close to the Lawrences (Jacob and his wife Gwen) and spent a lot of wonderful time with them. They became like surrogate grandparents for us in this town. This was truly amazing not just because of who they were as artists but also who they were as people. They were just lovely, lovely people to get to know and to be around.

It was through that experience that I began thinking about African American art, history and culture. About how all three of those things became intertwined as well as the impact that they had on American culture at large. That realization was because of the time spent with Jacob and Gwen.

LIFTING SOMEONE INTO THE OFFICIAL NARRATIVE BEGINS TO BREAK DOWN THAT IDEA THAT THERE WERE NO IMPORTANT ARTISTS OF COLOR. I WOULD IMAGINE YOU THOUGHT ABOUT THAT DURING THE CATALOGUE RAISONNÉ.

Yes, it was clearly apparent looking at the trajectory of art criticism around his work. It was very fascinating to see. He was considered late Harlem Renaissance or perhaps was at the very tail end. Yet, he did benefit from that level of interest and the exoticism that came from that in its heyday. He rode that wave initially. Then came the 1950s, Abstract Expressionism became the vogue. Lawrence was still doing figurative art, making statements. However in the world of the critic, Clement Greenberg, Lawrence was sort of marginalized even though he was part of the New York scene. Now, to be sure, he had his followings and his followers. He was respected but he was not part of the 'hot, young things' coming up at that time, the Pollocks and all that. Then through the 1960s and the Seventies with the Civil Rights Movement when a lot of work became more political, Lawrence was more of a quiet voice of change. He wasn't quote-unquote 'angry;' he wasn't making big, bold, brash statements. He was making important quiet statements. Like a lot of people with the back-to-Africa sensibility and ideas, he spent some time in West Africa. From that he made some paintings that weren't necessarily Afro-centric, so he was again a little on the outs. With all that, he ended up moving to Seattle.

I always thought, though any art historian could completely argue this point, that given the way Seattle is and was as a Black community I imagine for him it was a very safe move. Earlier, you alluded to the Black Panthers not being the same here as they were in other places. Seattle is just not loaded with all the baggage as intensely as other major American cities with larger Black populations. I think it was possibly that he could get out of that New York City fray, when he moved here. Boy, from New York to Seattle, Seattle then was not the way it is now, it was really totally…

IT WAS COMPARATIVELY NEARLY A TOWN…

It was like a town, it was out of the way, off in the hinterlands. To me, when I was reading and thinking about this, it always seemed to me that he was placing himself in self-exile, self-banishment. In a way, he was able to be to be nurtured and supported and was able to think more on his own and more clearly.

I just found the Black community here to be very…I just found it to be fascinating and interesting and very strange. I'm from Los Angeles; it was very foreign to me at first.

COULD YOU EXPLAIN MORE ABOUT THAT FOR SOMEONE WHO DOESN'T HAVE THAT PERSPECTIVE?

Well, sometimes it's hard to put a finger on. For example, I remember not too long after we arrived here, someone was giving me a tour around and they said, 'This is the Central Area; this is the ghetto.' I was from LA, so I thought, 'Seattle does not have a proper ghetto, there's no respectable 'hood here.' It would have been much better if Los Angeles had been like the Central Area.

It seemed to me to be a middle-to-working-class neighborhood, not really rough here, from my perspective, coming here from all of the drive-by and gang shootings. People said there are a lot of shootings in the Central Area and around Rainier Avenue. I was thinking, 'Well, that's nothing compared to LA.'

IN THE EARLY NINETIES IN NEW YORK CITY, IN ONE DAY YOU COULD HAVE THE SAME NUMBER OF PEOPLE KILLED AS IN SEATTLE NEARLY OVER A WHOLE YEAR…

One day in pre-Giuliani New York.

HICH ISN'T TO SAY THERE AREN'T REAL PROBLEMS HERE, THERE ARE.

There are, but it's a question of proportion, of perspective. I just found it to be so jarring. It was very, very different. My parents wondered, why are you here? To be fair, we didn't think we'd stay here. We thought this would be a pit-stop till we were on our way to the next thing. We're in an interracial relationship and were married in 1993. That was a very, very bad time to be an interracial couple in LA between the OJ (Simpson) trial and the Rodney King (riots). It was actually quite dangerous; we had many threats (made against us) there. It was just a very weird place and time.

172

FROM BOTH SETS OF COMMUNITIES?

From both sides.

THAT'S AWFUL.

We came up to just visit and saw there were a lot of interracial couples and families here. It was quiet.

AND ALL THE SUDDEN IT'S NOT A FACTOR IN THE SAME WAY.

Not at all, it was like no factor at all. And that was weird. We were so jittery. It's almost a cliché but we were on edge. Once someone was gesticulating to us from his car, and coming from LA at that time with the drive-bys my husband said, 'Don't look, someone is by our car.' He sped away but that person sped up, pulled up and yelled, 'You have a flat tire.' We thought they were trying to harass us because it had happened constantly in LA. We said, 'Oh, sorry!' Those people must have been thinking, 'What's wrong with you?' We were just trying to get your attention for the last two miles; your air is low in that back tire. Being in Seattle was a very different, very happy change, but it took some time to get used to.

ANOTHER THING I LEARNED WHILE DOING THIS PROJECT IS THAT THE PERCENTAGE OF BLACK HOME OWNERSHIP WAS HIGHER THAN IN ANY OTHER CITY IN THE COUNTRY AT ONE POINT. WHEN YOU COULD OWN YOUR HOME, THERE WAS A SENSE OF CONTROL OVER YOUR LIFE. YOU COULD PROVIDE AN ENVIRONMENT THAT'S DETERMINED BY YOU FOR YOUR CHILDREN. YOU COULDN'T BE FORCED TO MOVE OUT BY A LANDLORD SO IT GAVE A KIND OF ROOTEDNESS TO THIS COMMUNITY THAT WASN'T THE CASE IN OTHER PLACES.

I think you're absolutely right; it's a very, very good point. It also says a lot about what's happening today with rising property values, which is arguably a good thing on one hand for the people already in, but to try and get in it's obviously getting harder and harder. I hope that doesn't change that sense of ownership and rootedness. I mean, of course it will, and it already has even in the twenty years I've been here. I've seen a huge change with the influx of immigrants especially Black immigrants from Africa. I think the Black community here has been forced to open itself up more than it ever

173

has before because it's been a very enclosed insular group, as is normal in a city with a small number of Black citizens. When new people move in, like myself, try new things, foist new things and expect participation in different aspects of civic engagement—I do think that does change the nature of the community and what people can expect.

Did you feel welcomed when you came here?

I didn't.

I've met lots of Black transplants, newly arrived here, and it seems common not to feel welcomed where that wouldn't be the case, say in the South. It's really hard to come here and meet people.

That's very true. Most of CD Forum's audience was newbies and what we called all the Black Misfits, all the unaffiliated Black people. They are happy living here and don't need a huge Black community to feel complete but nonetheless would like some sort of connection. So not being able to break into the Black community of Seattle—I mean, none of my close Black friends in Seattle, none are from here.

What inspired you to create the CD Forum?

As I mentioned before, the initial inspiration came from the Jacob Lawrence project. Well, let me back up a step. My job at the catalog raisonné was to do some location work but mostly I had a team of fifty photographers both nationally and internationally to re-photograph all the works, the originals that we found. To do so required me to contact the owner or the owners' representatives, the curators at museums. I got to talk to a lot of people with that. I was so impressed when I would get them on the phone and talk about the work to hear their stories about how they got it, and what it means to them, from all across the social economic spectrum, across ethnicities, nationalities. It was amazing to me how this work that was very Black, it was about the Black experience and how all these different people got what they needed from it.

It is profoundly humanist work too.

There's a niche aspect but it's very broad at the same time. I just thought that was so interesting. I had never really thought about the Black experience being so universal in many ways. That made me think, 'Well gosh, other people must feel that way.' There are other artists—I mean, as wonderful as Jacob was, he's not the only one. I started thinking, 'Who else does that?' That was the artistic focus of it.

As far as the Central District and Seattle, during our early years here we had our first anniversary in 1994. My husband gave me Quintard Taylor's book, *The Forging of a Black Community*. I was so blown away by that book because I was trying to get a sense of who are these people? Where am I? It was so amazing to me and so different that people had been here for ages; the loggers and the sense of ownership in the community. Maybe that's because the numbers overall have been relatively small as compared to other cities, there's a lot more freedom here: voting rights, home ownership. Yes, there was redlining but there was redlining everywhere at that time—still here they were voting and owning houses at such a high rate. I found that to be really interesting and really foreign to my own experience regarding how Black communities get started.

The CD Forum was about pairing those two ideas, those two concepts. I thought Seattle and the Central District in particular was such a rich and nurturing place for art in general and about how Black people in the community have been able to take advantage of that, to use it. Despite the bumps in getting the Forum started, and people not being sure what I was doing and why, especially as I had come from LA, it was relatively speaking an easy place to do this because it was just so ripe for it. People ask me would you do this in LA? I don't think it would work in LA. Honestly, one, there's too many competing entertainment options, and two, it's too big.

EVERYTHING IS MORE DIFFICULT THERE.

And things and people are not accessible. When I first left my (science lab) job, I was looking for things. I don't know what possessed me to do this but I was looking for all the famous people who lived here in the phone book, when we still had phone books. There was Jacob Lawrence listed in the phone book. Our then mayor, Norm Rice, his address was in the phone book. I thought, 'Oh, my God.' I called my husband and he said, 'That can't be the real one.' I said, 'No, it is! I read in the newspaper, this is his address.' When I started the Forum, we had a Black mayor. I was just doing random things so I called the Mayor's Office and an assistant answered. I said, 'I sent some material to Mayor Rice. I want to follow up.' Then, he answers the phone. I think I hung up! I didn't think I'd speak to him, I just thought, 'Oh my God—where would that happen?' Could you call Bloomberg's office and have him pick up the phone? I was shocked by that. It totally caught me off-guard; everything was so accessible. I say this to folks who want to start artistic projects, if you really want it here, you can really get it.

That's one thing that I hope CD Forum did, and I hope we can do more of, is create a platform for local people to launch into new things. I always try to encourage people to take Seattle by storm, completely wring it out, take every ounce it has to offer and then move on. There is actually a lot here. There are a lot of important people here.

Yet, going back to the early days of CD Forum while it was a challenge to get going, I have to say after twenty years I've benefited tremendously from the warmth of the community. People from all backgrounds, once they understood what I was trying to do, that I wasn't a nefarious California person with horns coming to destroy their way of life; I've found the community to be so supportive. I felt so welcomed.

THAT'S THE WEIRD FLIP SIDE: PERSONALLY PEOPLE DON'T INVITE YOU INTO THEIR LIVES, BUT THE LARGER COMMUNITY ITSELF IS VERY GENEROUS ABOUT SUPPORTING ARTISTS AND ACTIVITIES. HERE, COMMUNITY THINGS JUST SORT OF COME TOGETHER PRETTY EASILY AND NATURALLY.

I hope with the city's growth, which generally I support, it's only selfish, I'm not thinking of anything larger, I'm just a big city person; I still hope with the growth we don't lose that essence of the city. Things change and alter. That support and generosity is very special and unique to this area. I hope that there are many people coming after me with new ideas. I hope that they will be as easily supported.

I hope that now I'm at a place where I'm not working, at the moment, but still involved in the community, I'd like to be able to continue to help support the new: new ideas, new things people try out. It's so important to keep an area vital and to keep people thinking and not to get too settled in whatever is considered normal. That is funny for me to say being married to a historian who is very rooted in the past, but I'm a very future-oriented person.

176

The Honorable Richard A. Jones grew up a block from Garfield High School and attended Seattle University and the University of Washington. He has served Washington state as a lawyer, prosecutor and King County and US District Court judge. He is a man of intellectual depth with a tangible aura of warmth and generosity. He offered meaningful encouragement when this project seemed endless and thankless.

> *"In many ways, I look at what's happening now across the United States. I look back at how we grew up in the Sixties and Seventies and it's almost as if we're returning back to what we had before...as if that's the only way to try and make change come about."*

Were you born in Seattle?

I was born in Seattle (at) Providence Hospital (now Swedish Hospital, Cherry Hill). I grew up on 22nd and Jefferson, right around the corner from Garfield High School.

Is the house still there?

The house is still there. I encourage you to go see it. It's 410 22nd Avenue, in the middle of the block. It's a very small house. When our family first moved there, it was a one-bedroom house. It had an upstairs, which we all affectionately called the Attic. Our family had moved there from the projects in Bremerton. I was the eighth kid born into the family. So, imagine ten people in the house with essentially one bedroom and an attic. It made for very close, confined quarters. Still, we got along.

What impact did growing up in the Central Area have on who you became?

One of the gifts that the Central District gave was that it put me in an environment where I really learned how to deal with a lot of different cultures, a lot of different folks, a lot of different histories and backgrounds. The community I was raised in really looked like the rainbow coalition of life. Yet, my block was almost one hundred percent African American. There was only one Jewish family around the corner from us.

In the larger neighborhood, there was a little bit of everything in our community. That has helped me over the course of my life, as I learned that there are different cultures, that people respond differently and react differently. It's helped me, not only in the different types of work I've done in the past, but it's been an enormous benefit to me as a judge.

I WOULD VENTURE A GUESS THAT IS NOT A GIFT THAT'S REPLICATED WIDELY IN FEDERAL COURTS ACROSS THE COUNTRY?

I can tell you that (laughs) without question. I attend our judges' conferences and when you look at the sea of faces, the representation of diversity is not that great. The bulk of people from ethnic backgrounds at these conferences are a lot older than I am. They are senior judges, then there's a big gap. A big concern is what's the future (of the higher judiciary) going to look like because the bench really makes a lot of determinations about what happens in this country.

GIVEN ITS SIZE RELATIVE TO THE ENTIRE CITY, A DISPROPORTIONATE NUMBER OF PEOPLE FROM THE CENTRAL AREA HAVE BEEN PHENOMENALLY SUCCESSFUL. THAT'S DESPITE STARTING FROM POVERTY. WHETHER IT'S LIKE DOROTHY AND FRED (CORDOVA) WHO FORMED A NATIONAL ORGANIZATION, OR MARTIN SELIG WHO STARTED VERY HUMBLY AND BECAME AN ENORMOUSLY SUCCESSFUL BUSINESSMAN NOT TO MENTION ALL THE ARTISTS…THERE ARE MANY, MANY EXAMPLES FROM THE CENTRAL AREA AND PARTICULARLY GARFIELD (HIGH).

That might have been because of the expectation that we weren't going to succeed because we grew up in the Central Area. I can't tell you how many times I would get into a conversation and when people would hear you lived in the Central District, it's almost like you were looked down upon. It seemed to be assumed that you came from a lower class or a dangerous part of the city. That was the antithesis of my experience as a young child. My life experiences growing up in the Central District helped form who I am as an individual today. The challenges particularly during the Sixties and Seventies had a profound effect in terms of my growth. Seeing how people were treated, how people had to fight for just the barest existence and expectation of where they were going to go in life.

WERE YOU OLD ENOUGH TO BE ABLE TO SEE DR. KING WHEN HE CAME?

I was old enough but I went away to boarding school when I was thirteen years old. So, I was in and out of Seattle for about four years after the age of thirteen.

WHAT YEAR DID YOU LEAVE FOR BOARDING SCHOOL?

I graduated from eighth grade in '64 and I graduated from high school in '68.

THOSE WERE PRETTY TUMULTUOUS YEARS.

There were huge changes. I'd come home once a month and in those one-month time periods, there was just so much change happening in the community. In just two or three years, the growth was phenomenal. Some of the challenges came when the Vietnam era started. There was Black Power, the Black Rights Movements started popping up, Black Pride started developing in a profound and positive way. People felt so much more enriched and better about themselves because now you did have a voice. You could have a collective voice, and that collective voice was dependent upon you and your neighbors and the community that you grew up in.

LET'S SAY HYPOTHETICALLY YOU HAD STAYED INSTEAD OF GOING TO BOARDING SCHOOL—WHAT DO YOU THINK YOUR RELATIONSHIP WOULD HAVE BEEN TO THE BLACK PANTHERS IF YOU WERE IMMERSED IN THAT?

Don't get me wrong, (despite) the fact that I was gone I was immersed when I came back home.

CAN YOU TELL ME A LITTLE BIT ABOUT YOUR BOARDING SCHOOL, WHAT WAS THE RACIAL DIVERSITY THERE?

When I got to St. Martin's in Olympia, one hundred percent of the African American population just about shared locker space. There was a kid that was right next to me; he was the only other African American. What they were trying to do was trying to diversify the boarding school. They had created scholarships that were combination of diversification and grades. That school…it changed my life. I learned how to get through tough times, how to deal with people who weren't hateful but

179

they were just insensitive to other cultures so they'd say things that were completely racist. I would challenge people; there were always discussions.

I had two sets of clothes I would wear—the school clothes with cuffed pants and for at home the platform shoes and the look that everyone was wearing in the neighborhood. It was just a whole different experience. I would catch the Greyhound bus to Seattle and as soon as I could ran in the house and change my clothes. I would go out and hang with my boys. We'd just go run the streets.

I WONDER ABOUT WHAT IT COSTS YOU PSYCHICALLY AND EMOTIONALLY TO HAVE TO FORGE YOUR WAY THROUGH ALL THESE MISUNDERSTANDINGS AND MIS-READINGS. THE RESULTING AMOUNT OF STRESS, I CAN ONLY IMAGINE THAT IS HARD.

I grew up in such a culturally diverse neighborhood in the Central District. I had the comfort of home. I could go down to my neighbor's house down the street; that family was Filipino. I could go down to another friend's house who was Chinese; another one was Japanese. Everybody on my block was African American. There were all these different cultures with different-looking people. It was a degree of comfort with ethnicity. Then, all the sudden you are extracted from that zone of comfort and are transported into a different world where everyone around you is one hundred percent White.

I got a great education. I can also tell you there were challenges because of the stereotypes people had about African Americans, about the ideas of your career prospects or life opportunities. I had a coach for college counseling. I would sit outside his door waiting and hear what he had to say to the two people in front of me about their college opportunities. When it was my turn he said, 'Well, Richard I think you have a better chance of going into trades than wasting your time on education because for a colored kid with a college degree—what are you going to do with it? If you go into the trades, your dad had a good living—he took care of your family and you'd have a great career. You could be a foreman or a supervisor.' That's where he capped my potential. I had a smart mouth in high school so I called him a couple of names and walked out of his room.

SO NOT ONLY DO YOU HAVE TO DEAL WITH THE SPLIT OF BEING IN THIS SCHOOL, THEN YOU HAVE TO DEAL WITH THE SPLIT OF ALL THESE CONVERSATIONS THAT YOUR NEIGHBORHOOD FRIENDS ARE PROBABLY DEEPLY INVOLVED IN. THOSE WORLDS COULDN'T HAVE BEEN FURTHER APART.

It's funny because I would come back over the summer months. During the summer, I would have changed in terms of what I'd absorbed in my own neighborhood, in my own community. I would come back to school and then have to readjust. Not that you were a sell out, not by a long shot, but you had to readjust. They had to readjust too, to you as well, because your thought process had developed, and you would interact with folks in our community with different topics.

SO YOU BECOME YOUR OWN NORTH STAR.

In many ways you have to be. You have to be. That's the work we do every day here (at the federal court). You're not being cavalier with the approach you take to the law; you have to follow the law. At the same time, many times you have to steer the ship when there is no law, there is no authority so you have to make the determination (of) which direction, which way we're going to go with it.

There were fascinating things that took place at some of my places of employment. Walt Hubbard used to be the director of this program called CARITAS, Community Action Remedial Instruction Touring Assistant Services. In my freshman year of college, I got a job there. Shortly after that, Bob Santos took over. He and I go way back 'cause he taught me boxing when I was in grade school. I've known his whole family since I was in fifth and sixth grade.

Later when I worked there, Bob set the program at St. Peter Claver Center. It was open opportunity for diverse thought and community activity. Bob's always been a community activist. We had our own responsibilities—recruiting tutors and bringing kids in. We had breakfast programs; we did a little bit of everything for this program. We were surrogate parents for some of the kids who didn't have fathers. We put on Halloween parties for the kids who didn't have any place to go. We gave out Christmas gifts. So, it was pretty much non-stop. Even to this day some of the kids who saw us as surrogate parents (they were six to eight years old and we were eighteen to twenty), they still come when they get in trouble. They still call when they need help; they still need assistance.

We also had groups coming through there, like the CCA, Central Contractors Association. That was Mike Ross and Tyree Scott. They would come in and meet. For the first two meetings we would come in and listen to what was being discussed. Their approach was similar to the Dr. King approach of non-violence—just go to construction sites (and carry signs). So, you'd hear these conversations and sometimes we would go and march and then come back. At one point, things started to change. There was (a) huge, big meeting. A big group of folks came up to St. Peter Claver Center and talked about what the activities were going to be. The discussion started to include perceptions of what violence might occur. I saw folks, kids, that morning before they left, perfectly healthy, perfectly fine. I'll never forget one kid came back and half his face was swollen from a gash on the top of his head down his cheek, with part of his mouth and nose damaged. And Tyree brought him in and said, 'This is what happened. This is what violence we face.' Some of those kids had been in jail.

Then everybody in the community was just shocked and outraged. All he (Tyree Scott) was doing was just trying to get the jobs for people. He wasn't doing anything but saying, 'We're a peaceful march. We're a peaceful demonstration.' Then the people in the Central District were so upset and angry about the violence, that changed how they approached demonstrations.

We had other groups there like the War Without Peace Council and other people were calling in bomb threats. I remember one time running through the building, telling people to leave but they voted they were going to stay. I had to get the kids out of the building. I ran through the building and went to the bathroom and there was a shoebox in the stall. So I ran back and shut the building down. The bomb squad came in and someone had just to disrupt things, had taken Silly Putty, ran a wire around it, and tied it into a clock to make it look like it a legitimate bomb. It was just to disrupt the meetings taking place. I grew up with people trying to fight for peaceful causes and then you saw these reactions of hate, trying to stop positive movement, positive growth and positive development. I think it's also the fear people have about the unknown.

As I said earlier, we lived on 22nd right across the street from Garfield High School. And I remember a group called the Students For Democratic Society, SDS, went to all the inner city schools—Garfield, Franklin, Meany and Washington Junior High School. They collected a whole bunch of different folks, and they came over to Garfield High School. It was completely peaceful in the afternoon. People were giving speeches. The SDS gave a statement on what they were trying to achieve. SDS left around six-thirty (pm) or so. Folks had been there for a couple of hours. Then, about dusk, a helicopter flew over while people were playing drums and other people were giving speeches.

Again, it was completely non-violent. When the helicopter flew over, the Seattle Police Department said, 'This is unlawful assembly. You are directed to disperse. You have five minutes to disperse.' The helicopter flashed the lights all over the place to try and intimidate people into leaving. It just reinforced the commitment to *not* leaving. This is our neighborhood; (we) weren't doing anything wrong. We had the right to assemble.

I ran across the street and jumped the back fence to tell my parents what was going on over here. I remember looking over at the end of the block and I saw a cop car on 22nd and Jefferson. I ran to the end of the block and as far as I could see were police cars. They were four deep. It was a riot squad, they were moving in. I ran back to try and find my friends and let them know what's about to go down, to give them an exit strategy in case it starts going crazy. Before we even had that conversation the helicopter came back. It looked like a scene out of Vietnam. They started shooting tear gas out of this helicopter. So much of it landed, it was difficult to see. I remember people getting hit in the face with tear gas. I remember people running, trying to throw away the (canisters). Then, more police came and they were shooting tear gas too. It was just total chaos. The guys that I was with—everyone just split up because it was just pandemonium.

I remember just running up Terrace, all the sudden I heard a gunshot. I hit the ground; lay there for a while and when I didn't hear (it) anymore, I literally crawled back home. When I got home, I saw police officers coming up the street, they were six plus, they had riot sticks, they had their (riot) gear on. The police were picking up every glass bottle out of fear people were going to make Molotov cocktails or throw bottles at people. They told me, 'Go in your house.' On the front lawn of my house I said, 'I live here.' I don't have to go inside my home. I have the right to stand on my front porch.' Then, one of the officers made a move towards me. I had to run in the house. And so, it was that type of action that caused a reaction.

All the sudden, the more aggressive and violent activity started (rioting) and that lasted for several days before things finally started to cool down. So you have to reflect back and ask if the (police) approach had been different, not responding with aggressiveness and violence, would that crowd simply have dissipated on its own? Unfortunately, it didn't work out that way. It, though, helped me in terms of formulating my own ideas about what's right, what's wrong, and the freedoms that people are supposed to have in this country. In many ways, I look at what's happening now across the United States. I look back at how we grew up in the Sixties and Seventies and it's almost as if we're returning back to what we had before…as if that's the only way to try and make change come about. I'm certainly not advocating violence because I have to deal with individuals that are charged, possibly criminally, depending on what they've done. At the same time, when you are up against the wall—you feel that there is no hope; you feel that there is no recourse, then you figure we have to do something. That enormous frustration makes people feel they have to do something. And so, I pray to God that we can do something in a way that is positive, that's energetic, so that it benefits everyone, so that people don't resort to violence to try and bring about change.

THE PANTHERS COME UP IN ALMOST EVERY INTERVIEW. SOME PEOPLE FELT THE VIOLENCE WAS COUNTERPRODUCTIVE WHILE AT THE SAME TIME THE PANTHERS WERE DOING POSITIVE THINGS. THEY WERE MAKING A STRONG STATEMENT BECAUSE BEING NON-VIOLENT DIDN'T PROTECT DR. KING. STILL, IT SEEMS LIKE THERE WAS A SPLIT IN THE NEIGHBORHOOD REGARDING THE PANTHERS. DID YOU HEAR THOSE CONVERSATIONS? DO YOU REMEMBER WHAT YOU THOUGHT?

The difference for me was I grew up with a lot of people who became Panthers. I didn't have that fear that something bad was going to happen to me, or to our neighborhood. Besides, the Black Panthers used to have parties all the time. They were good parties.

YEAH, I'LL BET. I KNOW AARON (DIXON)…

(laughs) Aaron, Elmer, Michael…There were so many different folks and their hearts were trying to do the right thing. They just saw that doing it through non-violence wasn't necessarily going to bring about change. There were discussions; we've tried the Dr. King approach, we've tried the non-violent approach and we want folks to know that we're prepared to do violence and to defend ourselves if we have to. There were sandbags in the windows in the Black Panther Party offices. That terrified people because people looked at the Panthers as some kind of terrorist organization back then.

184

In our neighborhood, in our community, there was a clearly defined split. Some saw the Panthers with fear that taking a violent approach would cause retaliation against the whole African American community. That was realistic because if a few were causing problems the reaction from outside forces might be that everyone might have to pay. There was that component that said we can be much more progressive without the threat or fear of violence. Then there were those who said we've tried that approach. We're not getting anywhere; we're not getting there fast enough. Some of the components that came from the Black Power Movement on the more aggressive side were positive, they instilled pride in us. I mean, we could wear naturals (hair), we could wear our style of dress, (we could own) our comfortableness in terms of who we were as Black folks. We could take comfort in knowing that we were a people making progress.

Look at all our history. Part of the Panther's education program was to teach kids pride—to feel that we do have a history whether or not it was taught in the schools and to understand, you do have a history. The Panther's education program taught them Black history and indoctrinated them about our history. We do have a history and that was certainly not a bad thing. A lot of positives came out of that experience back then.

I TALKED TO MIKE TAGAWA. HE RAN THE (PANTHER'S) EDUCATION PROGRAM WITH ANOTHER MAN. HE IS OBVIOUSLY (OF) JAPANESE (DESCENT); HE WAS BORN IN THE CAMPS (MINIDOKA). SO HE UNDERSTOOD THAT TO UNDERSTAND WHAT WAS HAPPENING IN THE NEIGHBORHOOD, THEY HAD TO MOVE FROM THEORY TO RELEVANT DISCUSSIONS ABOUT HISTORY. THAT WAS WHERE THE EDUCATION PROGRAM ACTUALLY WORKED.

Another example will be Larry Gossett. He and Bob Santos were called the Gang of Four. He's got a book out now. People could look at them and say that group of radicalized individuals, look at the benefits and positives just those two folks brought into our community: Bob Santos and Larry Gossett.

In Mr. Ike Ikeda's interview he said that, 'because we are so few (minorities in Seattle) we had to reach across the aisle.' Whereas in Los Angeles, with big groups of ethnic communities, there is not that reaching across the aisle in the way there was here. Not only were our Black Panthers very different, I think that reaching across the aisle and finding a common cause was very different here. As people get dispersed, it's my fear that working together as an ideal gets lost.

I look at the Central District now…the neighborhood has changed so much. It doesn't look like the same neighborhood. I know you've heard the whole discussion on gentrification in the Central District. It used to… it was all ethnic. It was just a completely diverse population. That's transitioning.

Now it has transitioned to a point where the economy is a driving force. Now, it's chic to live close to downtown, close to buses, close to educational opportunities, close to your job…it's not even a question of…could the Central District boom. (Back in the 1960s) It was a little bit of everything.

Yeah, it's sad to see the things that you really love and think are special moving away. A lot of the people I've interviewed no longer live in the neighborhood. Still, (pause) each person in a way contributed to that history.

For most people, you're taking on assignments and projects, pursuing your own career or what you want to do in life. You are not trying to make history. You are not trying to be a leader. It's just you see something that needs to be done so you go and do it. You see people that need help and you help them. Then you see folks that grew up the same way you did and it's a question of reaching back and lifting up. It's not a question of saying, 'I got mine; you get yours.' That's not what we learned in the Central District. We grew up as a family.

It's interesting listening to you from the moment you got involved with Peter Claver Center and you chose a major, there is this clear through-line of wanting to be involved in making change.

I really believe that the gifts that I've received, the work I've had the opportunity to do, these were gifts and because they're gifts we've got a responsibility not just to say, 'I've got mine, you get yours.' We have a duty and an affirmative obligation to try and reach back and try and help as many kids and many other people as we can to help get to their dream. If you're not, then you've completely failed, you have completely failed at what you can accomplish in life.

THE FIRST GIFTS YOU RECEIVED HAD TO HAVE COME FROM YOUR PARENTS. YOU SHOWED ME THE SAW AND THE TIMEPIECE IN YOUR OFFICE BEFORE THE TAPE WAS ROLLING, SO CAN YOU TELL ME ABOUT THE GIFTS YOU RECEIVED FROM YOUR FATHER?

Sure, sure. When people talked about what we've got in the Central District, I didn't have to go out my front door because it came out of my house. I saw how hard my dad worked. I saw how hard my mom worked. My dad was always passionate about us getting an education. He was also passionate about us—whatever it was that you wanted to become in life. He used to say, 'I don't care if it's a ditch-digger, if it's a truck driver, it's a carpenter, a doctor or a lawyer, I don't care what it is but whatever it is you're going to become—but if you're going to do it, you be the best at whatever it is.' He used to have this saying, 'Once the task has once begun, never leave it until it's done. Be the labor great or small, give the job your very best or not at all.'

That was his mantra. You talk to any of the kids in the family and they all knew that exact statement. That was it was all about. When you felt kicked down or beat down, you had to figure out how to do the very best you can to make this right. Sometimes you feel like giving up, you think about how Daddy had to push. He had to take care of eight kids. Any little stuff you have to worry about is insignificant compared to what he had to do.

Daddy was a mentor in so many ways; he talked about Black history before I even knew what Black history was. When we were kids, he'd talk about Ralph Bunche, he'd talk about Satchel Paige, he'd talk about Frederick Douglass. Even in his own world, education was important; he took correspondence courses at the Chicago Technical Institute. They'd send him test or study materials and he'd have to complete a test after he'd worked all day long. He'd study. When he'd get his grades back, he'd say, 'See this, boy? I worked all day and I still got an A.' It wasn't a question of just talking about how to get an education, it was look at what I have to do to get an education, to continue to advance what I can do.

WHAT KIND OF PARTNERSHIP DID HE AND YOUR MOM HAVE?

They weren't always on the same page…My mom had to work very hard to be sure we got a quality education. I saw the places she would work and the circumstances. She had to work as a maid or as a nurse's aide just to send five bucks down to the boarding school. I knew that meant she had to work a few hours to get that five bucks. So she had her own way and her own style of doing things. She was the disciplinarian also, so everybody had real clear lines of what you could get away with and what you couldn't get away with. You couldn't get away with too much in our household. I wouldn't say they were always on the same page in terms of parenting styles or what they were doing. Still, in terms of wanting the kids to do well, to have a good opportunity in life, that was pretty clear. That was pretty clear.

YES. WHAT WERE THE GIFTS THAT YOUR MOTHER GAVE?

I'd say the gift my mother gave me was her hard work ethic. My mother worked hard 'cause you figure in terms of raising and feeding that many kids. And that house was always immaculate. My mom was so (laughs)…had such a fetish about keeping the house clean. She had plastic runners on the carpets. She had plastic on the furniture (laughs) because she thought whatever you buy was supposed to last a lifetime. We didn't have the resources to go and buy something two and three times.

SINCE YOU WERE SO MUCH YOUNGER, WERE YOUR OTHER SIBLINGS STILL IN THE HOUSE WHEN YOU WERE GROWING UP?

When I was a baby, up to my first three or four years, the older sets were in transition in terms of moving out and doing different things. They were in their mid-to-late teens, around that age. Most of my childhood was coming up with my two sisters, the two sisters above me. But at the very beginning, it was everybody (in that small house). I mean, my crib was the top dresser drawer. Everybody just worked out where they were going to sleep and live in that house. The attic had no heat. We had a coal furnace in our home until I was in high school. Welch's Fuel and Hardware was over on Jackson. They'd dump a half a ton of coal in the front yard. We'd put out a canvas and they'd dump the coal out and then we'd go out and try to put it…

188

IN A COAL CHUTE?

No. Just a window. We'd just throw it in the coal bin; that's how we'd heat the house. Daddy would make a big fire before we went to bed and then the coal would burn out overnight. He'd get up in the morning and try to make another one before he went to work. There was no turning up the thermostat, turning the heat up. You had to make that fire. That's unheard of in modern times in the United States, supposedly. At the time, we just thought that's how everybody lived. So it was no big deal; that was just our existence.

BY THE TIME YOU WERE FOUR, IT WAS JUST YOUR SISTERS AND YOU IN THE HOUSE?

I think so. I think just about everybody else was out or if they were there I wasn't paying attention because I was too young. I look at pictures and I see family in and out of the house at different events. Or somebody would come back into town and everybody would come over.

HOW MUCH OLDER ARE YOUR TWO SISTERS?

Let's see. I'm not really good with numbers. They're about three and six years older than I am.

THEY WERE ENOUGH OLDER THAT THERE WOULD HAVE BEEN FOUR PEOPLE TENDING TO YOU. SO, YOUR EXPERIENCE WOULD HAVE BEEN VASTLY DIFFERENT THAN YOUR OLDER SIBLINGS.

Yes, absolutely. Absolutely. Totally different. We even came in a different time; they were born mid-to-late 1930s, with the economic conditions back then. They were coming up in the tough times. They were coming up before civil rights, before Martin Luther King, before some of the Civil Rights Movements in this country. That was some of the toughest times that Black folks in this modern generation, of those that are still alive now, had to contend with.

Two of my sisters passed away and two brothers have passed away.

I'M SORRY.

189

There are still four of us left, one sister is in Seattle, the other one lives now in Anchorage. I've got a brother who's in California.

HOW OLD, ROUGHLY, WAS YOUR DAD WHEN YOU WERE BORN?

He was…fifty, fifty-five, something like that.

YOUR MOM WOULD HAVE BEEN ABOUT FORTY?

My mom's age is the eighth wonder of the world (laughs). Nobody really knows how old my mom was. She was adamant about not letting anybody know how old she was. I've seen my brothers' and sisters' birth certificates and there was an eraser burn where her age was listed. She just didn't want people to know how old she was. She was amazingly beautiful even deep into her life, smooth skin. She had all the old approaches to keeping smooth skin. I thought olive oil was lotion until I got into high school because she would put it on her skin to make it so soft. At school it was one of those cultural shifts and I asked why people were cooking with olive oil. And they looked at me like I was absolutely insane. There was always a bottle of olive oil in the bathroom because that was lotion (laughs), and so it was greasy but put a little bit on, just rub it in.

(LAUGHS) WAS SHE SECRETIVE IN OTHER WAYS? IT'S ONE THING TO NOT TALK ABOUT YOUR AGE BUT IT'S ANOTHER TO GO TO YOUR CHILDREN'S BIRTH CERTIFICATES…

She was…that was her thing. You see, my mom didn't grow up in this country.

OH, SHE DIDN'T?

She was an immigrant. My father was born in Charleston. My mother was born in Bocas del Toro, Panama. I actually had a chance to go down there in the past eight years. It was amazing. It was the same way as she had described that community. The same lifestyle exists. We stayed at a place down there on the beach. These boats would come in with the long sticks, and the women had clothing (piled) on their heads. These women were doing what is called 'day work.' They would get on these boats; that was the little community ferry system to go over to the port across the river. These long boats would go across the river and there was something serene, slow-paced and relaxing about that environment. The young kids who were all going to private school all had on uniforms. The simplicity of that lifestyle, everything was geared around water commerce. It's not a big city at all. They have enormous poverty there. It was just the way she described how it was when she was a child. When I went back, it was almost the same thing today.

DID SHE HAVE FAMILY HERE?

Her father was a seaman and he got his citizenship. Then she, with her brothers and sisters, got their citizenship. Many of them were still down in that area or in Panama. She had a couple of aunts and an uncle in the United States but we had little interaction with them when we were kids. They'd come into town. We'd see them for a little bit and that was it. She'd write them all the time, but we didn't have anything other than the telephone or a postage stamp to stay in touch with folks back then.

DID YOU SEE YOUR FATHER'S EXTENDED FAMILY AT ALL?

We were pretty much alone in Seattle. We had aunts and uncles in New Jersey. My dad had a couple of other sisters but then people couldn't afford to travel, traveling across the country, certainly not flying or the train.

WAS THERE ANYTHING MORE YOU WANTED TO SAY ABOUT BEING IN LAW SCHOOL?

Law school taught me so much. I'd say the only other experience to mention is that we came in just after Defunis. Defunis was a Supreme Court case that said White students were not admitted because of affirmative action efforts on campuses; when I first came to university.

WHAT YEAR WAS THAT?

It was 1972 to 1975 when we came into school. I remember my first day at law school. Again, I'm not condemning the University of Washington. Anyone who knows me knows I bleed purple. I'm a die-hard UW Dawg Husky all the way. I'm proud of the fact that I have an education from the University of Washington and the contacts, and my commitments to the University of Washington.

Still, I think it was a different experience because when we came in we were affirmative action babies. I think a lot of UW professors didn't know what to expect. Would that mean there was going to be some diminishment of the quality and caliber of work that we could provide? They wondered about our performance, if we could succeed in law school.

DID YOU GET THE FEELING THAT THEY WANTED YOU TO SUCCEED?

Ah, it depended on the professor. I know the first time I walked into class, I won't say which class, I clearly remember it was that old *Paper Chase* style of classroom—the tall chairs, the heavy wood. I walked into the classroom and had a leather coat, an apple hat on and a T-shirt.

AN APPLE HAT? THAT'S THE ONE WITH THE BRIM?

It had a little lid. That's what we called them back then. So I walked all the way to the front. I wasn't going to sit in the back of the classroom. I was going to sit right in front near the professor. I walked all the way down. The professor came all the way down the stairs. I was just getting settled, so I took my hat off. I had my hair in braids. I remember he put his books up and he turned and stared at me like an alien just walked into his classroom. He just stared and our eyes connected. He looked at me and I looked at him. He just put his head down and then it made me feel a little bit uncomfortable. I said if there's any discomfort, that's on him; it's got nothing to do with me. It was because of what was going on at that time, naturals and braids. I had another experience a few weeks or a month into law school. I had two jobs when I was in law school. I went to the dean and said I know I can't work the first year of law school. I need authorization to work so I can pay my rent or I need the law school to write me a check so I can. He said, 'We don't pay your rent in law school.' I told him I had to get authorization to be able to work or I need you to give me a check. He told me that he couldn't give me authorization to work. Then, he started giving me all these lectures about the structure, and the challenges—you can't succeed if you work, you'll fail in law school. We finished the conversation. I didn't have a check. I didn't have permission but I kept on working because at that point I didn't have any options at that point to survive.

During my first year of law school I was working at the CARITAS. Then the second and third year I had a job at the US Attorney's Office, law clerking. Because I was trying to make money on both ends (of the day) I would do accounting work for Mr. Santos, Bob Santos. He let me do the bookkeeping for CARITAS because his brother had retired and he was getting too old to do it. He said you could come do the bookkeeping in the morning and do the tutoring at night. So my law school experience was: I'd go to CARITAS in the morning then I'd rush over to law school and when my classes finished I'd go back to CARITAS and work until we closed at about eight o'clock at night. That was the first year.

The second and third years I'd go to CARITAS in the morning, then go to school and then I'd go work at the US Attorney's Office until about five or six and go back (to) close up CARITAS at eight pm. It was a non-stop cycle when I was in school. My grades suffered but I still did okay.

I remember I had a challenge in one course in civil procedure. I went in to talk to the professor. There was a kid ahead of me who sat in front of me. I'd seen this kid's grades so I knew I had better grades than him. I overheard their conversation, 'Oh, you have a strong tradition of lawyers in your family. This is just a speed bump; don't worry about this, just go study. You'll do well.' Well that took enormous pressure off me, because I knew I did better than he did. I should get the same type of advice so I'll be out of here in five minutes. I walk in and he pulled my test out. He says, with no other conversation, 'Let me explain something to you. There are those people who have a desire to become a surgeon and they don't have a steady hand, and there are those people who desire to become a professional musician but they don't have a musical ear, and there are those people who desire to become lawyers, do you get my drift?' That was the extent of my coaching, so I felt like I got kicked in the stomach. All the effort to get into law school and everything else, nothing counted.

I'll tell you I had the biggest pity party on the planet. I walked over to Red Square. It was pouring down rain and I was ready to just cash it in right then. I thought, if this is what law school is all about, if this is how they think we're supposed to succeed here…I thought, they can have it. I will work at Boeing or at the Post Office. I will do something else. I'm not going to put up with this. I walked around in the rain for about ten or fifteen minutes, getting soaking wet. Then something just clicked on. I thought, I'm not going to let one person define who I am or my destiny. I walked back over to school. I got a withdrawal slip. I walked back to his office and (knocks on table) said, 'Would you sign this?' He said, 'What's this?' I said, 'It's a withdrawal slip,' and he said something. I said 'No, the only communication we need to have is for you to sign this. We don't need to have more communication, period, for the duration of my existence in this law school.' He signed it. I walked away.

Then, because I had taken most of the course material, the following quarter I had to ask another professor. I explained to the professor that I had to withdraw. I didn't go into all the detail but I told him I wanted to challenge the course. He was very helpful in terms of coaching and mentoring and all the things you'd expect from a professor. He was absolutely wonderful, the consummate idea of what a professor is supposed to be. He authorized me to overbook at twenty-one hours that quarter which was unheard of in law school especially if you had two jobs and he let me challenge the course. This meant I had to come in and take the final exam and turn in a couple of other assignments. I passed (hits the table) without any problem. I did well in his class.

It was another one of those occasions where you have to figure out and dig deep when you run into challenges or confrontation to figure out another way to get around this—don't be afraid of it and don't run from it. That's the way you have to plan your life and live your life.

THE FIRST JUDGESHIP WAS AN ELECTED ONE SO YOU HAD TO DO THE WHOLE CAMPAIGNING?

And the way it came about, I wouldn't recommend it for anybody. I was working at the US Attorney's Office at the time. I had practiced law for nineteen years. I wanted to do something different while staying connected to the courtroom, so the only next logical step was to become a judge. I went through all the evaluations you have to do. The week I finished the last evaluation, Judge Sullivan, Department Seven, King County Superior Court passed away. That following week on a Tuesday was his funeral.

Now, there was a community grandmother named Freddie May Goucher, don't know if you've had a chance to meet her. She was like family to us. She called up and said, 'I know you're trying to be a judge. Did you put your application in to become a Superior Court judge?' I said, 'Well, Freddie, today is Judge Sullivan's funeral.' She said, 'What's that got to do with you putting your resume in?' I said, 'Just out of respect for the man; today's his funeral.' Freddie's words were, 'Look, fool, if you don't send in your application a thousand other people are going to send in their application today. Get your resume down to Olympia.' That was Tuesday, so I faxed my resumé on Tuesday. On Wednesday, I got a call from the governor's office. On Thursday, I was interviewed by the Governor's Office. On Friday at eleven o'clock, I was appointed a King County Superior Court judge. Sunday night was my effective last day as an assistant federal prosecutor though I still had two weeks of commitment to wrap cases to try and wind them down. The following Monday, I was sworn in as a King County Superior judge and I had to put a campaign together. That meant at lightning speed; everything was happening during the campaign. I was working, closing down my cases and my files, and walking down the road, and all the sudden—you're a superior court judge now. It was overnight.

HOW'D THAT FEEL, THE FIRST TIME YOU PUT ON THAT ROBE?

The first time I put that robe on, I was walking down the long hall to get to court from my chambers—it happened so fast. I stopped midway down and I thought, 'What the hell are you doing?' This is absolutely insane.

DID YOU FEEL WELCOMED IN THE FRATERNITY OF JUDGES?

Oh, absolutely. Absolutely. Many of those were people I had known before or had appeared before. Many were former colleagues. For example, several of the federal judges here: Pechman, Lasnick and Ricardo Martinez, all current federal judges; we all started off as King County prosecutors. They were already on the bench, they are also all now federal judges so you had a built-in set of colleagues walking in the door and everybody was really collegial in terms of wanting you to succeed.

THEN YOU NEVER FELT AS A JUDGE EXCLUDED OR TREATED DIFFERENTLY?

No, no. You had lawyers test you. I don't think that was race specific; a few times it would be but with lawyers, it doesn't make any difference. Once they saw what your style was and how you performed as a judge then they learned lessons pretty quick about what you would tolerate and what you wouldn't tolerate.

Then, the federal experience is totally different. Someone once described the process of being a federal judge as like a live autopsy because once you start the process and you put your name in the arena, other people are controlling your life. They're poking around in your life; they're exploring

195

every avenue of your life. They had six or seven FBI agents, not just for me, that's for everybody, and they're running around talking to people to complete your background investigation. That's because these jobs are so few and the information we receive is so vast—so enormous and so sensitive so they can't afford to have somebody they don't have utmost confidence in. So when I say it's a live autopsy, they explore everything: everything you've ever done, where you've lived, where you've traveled, every speech you've given, every paper you've written, every opinion you've written, every decision you've made, everything's open to inspection.

People told me about the security issues; there's no privacy when I became a federal judge. If you worry, you can't function. What you can do is focus on what you can control right now, on what's in your hands, the work. You control the work, let that take care of itself. The least amount of my energy would be dedicated over here (gestures to the left). All of my energy would be dedicated towards the work. We work on big cases. When the Ridgeway case happened, for example, I couldn't worry about what was going to be on TV or what was going to be on the newspapers or broadcast across the planet. I told myself, you focus on what's in front of you. You have absolutely no control over the rest of it. Control what's in your hands. You can only control what's in front of you and let that take its own course.

WELL, THAT'S A TREMENDOUS ACHIEVEMENT.

It's a process but once you get on the other side: the opportunities, the types of cases and the caliber of people you get a chance to work with—it's the best job on the planet. The best job on the planet.

I LOVE IT WHEN PEOPLE SAY THAT BECAUSE NOT MANY PEOPLE HAVE THAT LUXURY.

I know. It's a lifetime appointment so you better be happy doing what you're doing.

Cecile Hansen, Duwamish Longhouse East Marginal Way

Cecile Hansen is the fiercely determined and deeply kind chairperson and activist for the Duwamish people at their Longhouse on East Marginal Way. Not only is Seattle named for the Duwamish Chief, but without the gifts of the tribe to the first White settlers, the city would not even exist as it does now. The Central Area was a part of their territory, so all of us in Seattle are greatly indebted to—and living in—the home of the Duwamish Tribe.

> *It makes me imagine how they were surviving, about every day of survival and how it was to live at that time. I can't go anywhere that I don't think about how my people lived here, especially along the rivers.*

Could you explain where the Duwamish homelands were?

Oh, we gave up about 54,000 acres that would comprise Seattle, north of Shoreline, up to Edmonds, and all through South Park over to roughly where that Freeway 167 is (in Renton). That is our territory; that is all the land that we gave up.

Our people traveled by canoe, so back then, it was all along waterways. We're talking Lake Union, Elliott Bay, Lake Washington, the Duwamish River and the Black River from Tukwila over to Redmond. When they made the Locks (in Ballard, the Hiram Chittenden Locks) that dried up the river and our villages at that time.

It also destroyed the means of sustenance and fish habitat.

Well, at the time everybody laughed about it because when the river went down there was all kinds of salmon there for the taking. It must have been quite a thing everybody was laughing and they were taking up the fish. What they did, though, was they killed that (Duwamish) village (on the Black River) in Renton because you couldn't live there. Well, they could live there but their river was gone. The Black River was gone.

CECILE So it took away not only a source of water but also the entire livelihood of a people. It was an enormous ecological and cultural tragedy.

It was but we survived.

HANSEN Do you know where the burial grounds were?

There were burial grounds by that village (Renton) and up the hill. I'm certain it's under houses now. There's another burial ground in Renton. Well, a lot of our people are buried there on the ridge. There's a cemetery up there where a lot of our people are buried.

Is there one on Foster Island in the Arboretum?

I'm sure there is. It sort of drives me crazy, it bothers me a lot that they're building bridges there and tearing up the territory (in the arboretum). That was part of our territory too. I am very sure that there are remains and spirits there too. I believe that even though no one thinks there's anybody there. The spirit of our people is there.

There's a famous quote from Chief Seattle, your Great-Great-Granduncle: 'Even the rocks that seem to lie dumb as they swelter in the sun along the silent seashore in solemn grandeur thrill with memories of past events connected with the fate of my people, and the very dust under your feet responds more lovingly to our footsteps than to yours, because it is the ashes of our ancestors, and our bare feet are conscious of the sympathetic touch, for the soil is rich with the life of our kindred...' How do you relate to that statement? You live in Seattle. How do you feel about the spirits in the land here?

Well, I really do believe. Across the street from where we are sitting in this Longhouse—(it) is a documented National Historical site. There was a Duwamish village there. When our people passed, they were buried up on the hill (above the longhouse) somewhere. I find this story amazing. We tried to find a place to have our own home. We tried in Renton but couldn't find a space. Someone offered us a little tiny piece of acre but you couldn't build anything, well, maybe an outhouse. Then, we tried at Fort Dent. Meanwhile we were going through the process of

198

documenting not only our history but trying to work with the city to build a longhouse, our own home. That fell apart because they said we could build but we'd never have the land.

I told this gentleman that we'd been renting and that I'd always hoped was we would find a place where we could have headquarters and an office. So this gentleman friend of ours asked if he could look for some land for us. I said, 'Sure go ahead.' He said, 'It's time you have some property.' I thought nothing of it. Then, he helped us secure two-thirds of an acre. This gentleman was an elder, a White man who owned a lot of property. He was the landlord of a lot of houses across the street; this was all a development of houses here. There were a lot of houses and a little tiny dirt road here. A man named George and his wife gave ten thousand dollars of his own money to buy the two-thirds of an acre. So through their efforts, the two-thirds of an acre is paid for and the building is paid for. That gives you the dream and the vision. We did it.

DID YOU KNOW THEN THAT THERE WERE THE REMAINS OF A VILLAGE AND THE MIDDENS OVER THERE?

Yes, we knew that. In fact, the Port of Seattle owns that land there and we wanted to build over there and they said no.

THAT'S THE HEARTBREAKING PART OF THIS STORY OF WHAT THE INTERTRIBAL FIGHTS HAVE COST THE DUWAMISH.

I believe as Indian people we're all supposed to work together. Just because you have some casinos doesn't make you brilliant. Still, I always hope. I don't have any problem with tribes having casinos if they in fact do use the money to take care of whatever they need on the reservation. However, I know they use the money to lobby against us. I know it must go on.

I don't go back to DC (anymore). I did that for many, many years lobbying and knocking on doors trying to get support as we were going through the process of our acknowledgment. Finally, we went to the National Congress of American Indians, a national organization, and lobbied there. We went to Affiliated Tribes too. Eventually, I decided I don't want to go to these meetings anymore because they're not supporting tribes anymore. When I got involved in the 1970s, there was thirteen tribes trying to prove their identity. Today I don't know why any Native American has to prove their identity, if in fact they were here first.

CECILE HANSEN

IN THE CASE OF THE DUWAMISH IT'S BEEN DETERMINED THAT YOU'VE BEEN HERE, YOU ARE DIRECT DESCENDANTS AND YOU HAVE PROVED THAT IN COURT.

Yes. Yes.

CAN YOU EXPLAIN HOW THE DUWAMISH SEE ANIMALS DIFFERENTLY THAN OTHER PEOPLE IN SEATTLE?

I believe that the Creator made animals for us to take care of and to honor. This is especially true of the eagle. We have high regard for the eagle. I notice when I am traveling with my sister that the eagle always shows up. We say if the eagle shows up we are being blessed anytime we're traveling. I believe even though we existed on the deer and the fish and everything, you have to respect that gift of sustenance. Today, what really concerns me is that the fish are disappearing from the sea. I guess people don't care. I don't just mean the Indian tribe, I mean everybody. The fish is not plentiful anymore.

WHEN YOU WALK THROUGH PLACES LIKE PIONEER SQUARE WHERE THERE WAS A DUWAMISH VILLAGE THERE FOR TEN THOUSAND YEARS, WHAT DO YOU THINK ABOUT?

It makes me imagine how they were surviving, about every day of survival and how it was to live at that time. I can't go anywhere that I don't think about how my people lived here, especially along the rivers.

Today, our Duwamish River is a Superfund. Still, I imagine the villages where they all traveled by canoe from place to place. They survived but it must have been pretty tough. We're so blessed today—we got a roof, we run to the store and we can cook at home. You know they cooked outside. They smoked their fish and meat. They survived by taking the cedar off the cedar trees and then making garments and hats and then using the wood to make paddles. It was hard work. It wasn't easy, not like today, you walk into a store and buy what you need. They were so intelligent, don't you think? That basket right there it's a clam basket. Woven to drain beautifully with just enough space woven to get the water and sand out.

IS THE TRIBE INVOLVED IN TRYING TO CLEAN UP THE DUWAMISH RIVER?

The tribe is not on the River Coalition. If we were, there would absolutely be no fishing on that river. It really irritates me one hundred percent that the Muckleshoot are allowed to fish in that Superfund river. We would really dig into all those who might have been messing up the river.

I WOULD IMAGINE THAT AS THE TIDE GOES IN AND OUT, THERE ARE STILL ARTIFACTS BEING DISCOVERED. DO YOU GO OVER THERE?

No, I can't. That's the Port of Seattle.

YOU CAN'T GO OVER THERE EXCEPT AS A PRIVATE PERSON?

No. Well, they'd let us have gatherings there. I have no respect for the leadership of the Port of Seattle because, in their stupidity, they gave our artifacts away. There reason was, 'We don't exist' (without federal recognition). We were told we would be able to have our artifacts back. They should never go to any area other than Seattle. I don't have any respect for those kind of people. They gave the artifacts that were from the Duwamish village on the river there to other tribes. They belong here in the Duwamish Longhouse and they gave them away, which is disgusting.

TO RETURN TO ANOTHER THING CHIEF SEATTLE SAID, 'AT NIGHT, WHEN THE STREETS OF YOUR CITIES SHALL BE SILENT AND YOU THINK THEM DESERTED, THEY WILL THRONG WITH THE RETURNING HOSTS THAT ONCE FILLED AND STILL LOVE THIS BEAUTIFUL LAND. THE WHITE MAN WILL NEVER BE ALONE. LET HIM BE JUST AND DEAL KINDLY WITH MY PEOPLE, FOR THE DEAD ARE NOT ALTOGETHER POWERLESS. THERE IS NO DEATH, ONLY A CHANGE OF WORLDS.'

Well, the spirit goes on. I think his spirit is around. I'll tell you a story, I haven't even told this to my kids. Before I got involved with the tribe, I was staying at home taking care of my house, raising my kids, getting involved in their sports, cooking for my husband who worked for the Port of Seattle (laughs). That was a long time ago. I was busy. I had my own garden. My brother would bring me salmon. I had a smoke house in backyard. I would smoke fish. I love smoking fish. So, in about 1974 our people were fishing in the river here—my cousins and other Duwamish people, tribe members. My brother came to my house very upset because he had been written a citation by the State Fishery. They said, 'You can't fish here.' He responded, 'I'm Duwamish.'

201

He told me, 'You got to get involved and go to a few meetings.' I went with him to the state fisheries and got interested in the issues with the tribe. I joined an organization created to help small tribes called, STOW. They helped small tribes with policy and financial (advice) in every which way they could. It was a good organization. We still remember them after all these years. I sat there as a delegate for the tribe. Now, my brother and I are part Suquamish on my mother's side so he decided he was going to join that tribe so he could make a living fishing or at the Sawmill because that's how he took care of his family. That went on for twenty some years. Then my brother died. It was really devastating to (the) Indian Country when he fell off his boat and drowned in Tulalip Bay.

OH, NO. I'M SORRY.

It was really, really sad for everybody but we kind of laughed at his funeral because it was like he belonged to all these tribes—so many people claimed him.

Now, to get back to spirit. The year before he died we went to a powwow in Everett. He got me this chain, I think it has the Lord and the Blessed Mother on it. I have that pendant in my car. I think when he's there in spirit it flips over. Why does it do that? It's him saying, 'I'm here.' The other day I got in my car and it was flipped over. So, I said, 'OK. I know you're here. All right (laughs).'

My point is the spirit of our people—they're around us. I really truly believe that. When people go into the large room here at the Longhouse, people say it's so peaceful. Before we ever opened it up, I had this place blessed inside-and-out. We don't want any harm to come to anyone who comes here. We're here to be peaceful. We have peace here even though we're dealing with a lot of injustice. So this place was blessed inside-and-out and it was said to us after that was done that our people are so happy that we built this place. Isn't that marvelous? They are thanking us that we're here. So, they are here.

Jackie Lawson has used her intelligence, abilities and sensitivity in her ceaseless work as an archivist and with the Black Heritage Society. In the late 1960s she and her husband, a genial Seattle police officer, lived just blocks away from the Black Panther Party.

'We didn't realize that at the time but we found out. The guy said, 'I won't sell to color,' which hurt me deeply. Then we came back to the Central Area and started looking and found a darling little house that is still there; it is still a darling little house."

When did you live in the Central Area?

If the Central Area includes Madison Valley, I've lived there since I was born. We first lived on 26th Avenue, then we moved to the 400 block of 29th Avenue North. That house is still there.

What was the neighborhood like when you were a child?

It was probably pretty much the same because I know some of the people that still live there. But there were several nationalities, I guess you could say, living there. The boys across the street and next door were Swedish and Norwegian. My best girlfriend was English, her mother actually was from England, although my friend was born here. My other best girlfriend was Italian. It was quite a variety of cultures. The people next door were Nicholsons; they were from Norway.

Did the children play together?

Oh, yes! We didn't go into each other's homes. That was one thing that none of the parents, my parents or their parents, would allow. We weren't allowed to go into the houses. We played outside in the streets. We did a lot of kick-the-can and all of those childish games.

WHY DO YOU THINK PEOPLE DIDN'T GO INTO EACH OTHER'S HOUSES?

I have no idea. I didn't know at the time. In my case, as the years went by, first I would have to know the parents and the parents would have to know me. Now, I was allowed into the little English girl's house next door because she was right across (from us); we shared a driveway. We knew her well enough. My parents knew her parents well enough. I think that was the only home I was in. Maybe once I was in Joanne's house; she was Italian. Joanne's parents I knew very well. He was a shoemaker right on 29th off what is now Martin Luther King Avenue. He had a shoe-making place there so he was very well known in the neighborhood. Maybe I went in Marianna Sandi's once, but I was scared to go in there. I didn't really know her parents.

WHY WERE YOU AFRAID TO GO INTO THAT HOUSE? WAS IT A DARK HOUSE, OR...

No, her uncle or her father, I forgot which, had this really deep voice and it used to frighten me. He was a very good friend of my uncle's. Oh, he was a big man. He just kind of scared me. You know how little kids are.

WERE YOU AWARE, AS A CHILD, OF THE GREAT DEPRESSION AT ALL?

I was affected by it, although I didn't realize it was the Depression. We always shopped at the Goodwill. Daddy taught me how to put soles on shoes. We had an old foot form that my grandfather had used when he was a shoemaker or a shoe repairer. My clothes were always homemade—my dresses and everything. I never thought about our lives as being deprived. We all wore second-hand clothes and hand-me-downs. It was just the way it was with everybody.

DO YOU REMEMBER YOUR MOM MAKING YOUR CLOTHES? WOULD YOU GET EXCITED?

Only the one dress, I have a picture of it. She and I are standing in front of the big ol' car. She has on her Sunday clothes and her little hat and I'm standing there with my hands on my hips. I was so proud of that little dress with the ruffles. Usually, they were made out of a stock pattern; we had the same pattern. Yet, I never had dresses made out of flour sacks. I think I may have had underclothes made out of them. The dresses were always very inexpensive little flowery prints. Different dresses in the same pattern. I still never thought about us as being poor.

204

Where did you go to church?

The First AME. My grandfather was one of the trustees, one of the founders of the church. The original stone on the church, I don't know what they've done with it, his name was on it. As was his brother-in-law, who is also his wife's brother-in-law.

The current city boundaries for the Central Area don't include the First AME.

Well, the First AME was out of the way.

Yeah, the city considers that Capitol Hill. But you can't really account for the history of that community without the First AME.

In fact in my book, *Let's Take a Walk*, I put it in as an extra note because the walk described ended at the top of the hill on 19th Avenue or 20th, so I had to add, 'Farther down is First AME.'

You went to high school at Garfield High. What year did you graduate?

Nineteen forty-six.

So then you were you in school when your Japanese classmates would have all disappeared?

I was in grade school at that time. I remember I was at Longfellow and the principal had called us to an assembly. He announced that our Japanese neighbors were going to be sent away. We didn't know why or understand it. I remember all of us started crying and that's all I remember about it. I think that was 1942.

Did you have any friends that were in your neighborhood that were Japanese?

205

Oh yeah, we had a lot. My friends were younger but some of the older kids were Japanese. One of the boys from the neighborhood, it was rumored that he went back and joined the Japanese Navy. The Kosakas were Japanese, Yuji and Aibo, those were their nicknames; they had longer names.

They were very close friends with my brothers—Yuji was my brother's best friend. Interestingly enough, in the late 1970s my mother started going to Senior Services or something having to do with her rent. Her agent was Yuji who had come back from internment. Here was Yuji. It was exciting for all of us to know that some of the kids did get ahead.

WHAT HAPPENED TO THE JAPANESE HOUSES AND BUSINESSES DURING INCARCERATION?

I couldn't help you at all. I was young. I know that one group of Japanese friends had the big grocery store right where the new MLK Avenue cuts across Madison Street. They either lived right there at Arthur Place and East Madison or across Madison, which would have been 27th Avenue. There were several Japanese families that lived there. I don't know about their businesses; I don't know about their homes. I just don't. That store that I'm talking about wasn't taken over by anybody, it was just demolished by the city.

MLK WAY WAS BUILT THAT EARLY? I ALWAYS FIGURED IT CAME MUCH LATER.

Oh, it probably did. I don't remember that well. I hadn't paid that much attention to it until I start doing research on my own.

WHAT DO YOU REMEMBER OF GARFIELD HIGH?

Well, I suppose we all had our little cliques. Those of us in the pictures I've shown you, most of those young ladies and gentlemen, we grew up together through the years so we just stuck together. Although, I did get into trouble with them after a while. When I was a senior I was appointed, not asked if I wanted to, but appointed on the Girls' Advisory Board. So, I became a 'policeman,' so to speak, and I lost some friends. Even my best girlfriends stopped speaking to me for a while, because I was going around spying on people.

WHAT WERE YOU SUPPOSED TO LOOK FOR, SHORT SKIRTS?

Oh no, no. Nothing like that. The big thing was smoking and skipping school, those kinds of things. I have no idea what I did. All I know is Priscilla didn't like me for a while and it really hurt my feelings. I hate to say it, but I didn't particularly have fun in high school.

WHY?

I was so very shy. I just stuck with my close friends. I was pretty studious. I didn't read a whole lot but my main intent was to get good grades and make my dad proud of me. I can't say I didn't get into trouble that my parents didn't know about…I'll never tell you, though. Yeah, we had some sneaky times, my best girlfriend Priscilla and I…but that's water under the bridge.

WHAT DO YOU THINK YOUR DAD'S DREAMS WERE FOR YOU?

Well, after high school it was just to try to decide what I was going to do. I had one sister who was a nurse— she had to leave the city because they wouldn't teach Black nurses at the University of Washington at that time. She had to find another school. My other sister was married by that time and she was working for a doctor in Portland. My daddy's dream was that I had to do something in the medical field. We just had two choices. I decided I was either going be a dietitian or a pharmacist. That was his dream.

WHAT WAS YOUR DREAM?

To get out of school…and to get married. I eventually flunked, you know. I flunked the first year at university.

YOU WERE STUDYING NUTRITION?

No, for both majors. I had to study chemistry, botany…Anyway, I had to take three sciences. It was just too much for me. At the same time, I had met my husband-to-be so I was cutting classes. I didn't want to go there anyway, so I ended up going to Broadway Edison (which is now Seattle Community College). I took a clerical course, a secretarial course and finished it with flying colors. A two-year course and I finished in six months. That's how I knew I was meant to be, something along those lines.

WHERE DID YOU AND YOUR HUSBAND SETTLE?

We first lived in the Douglas Apartments. I forget what they're called now, on 24th right off Madison. We stayed there through the birth of our first child, then we started looking for a home; looking for a place to call home. One of the first places we looked was up on Beacon Hill, right off of Beacon Avenue.

WHAT YEAR WAS THIS, ROUGHLY?

This would have been…let's see…Gwennie was born in 1950. So it would have been '51, '52.

THERE WAS STILL REDLINING IN PLACE.

We didn't realize that at the time but we found out. The guy said, 'I won't sell to color,' which hurt me deeply. Then we came back to the Central Area and started looking and found a darling little house that is still there; it is still a darling little house. We stayed there through the birth of the second child. I think we were there through the birth of the third one too. Little two-bedroom cracker box, right on MLK Way and Jefferson. It's still there, little square house on the corner; I think they've added onto it.

SO, IT'S RIGHT SMACK ON THE CORNER?

Right on the corner. You can look right across to Powell Barnett Park. Back then, it was a playfield. Back in the days of the Mardi Gras (Nightclub), which we can talk about later if you want. When it was hot, they used to come over and drink out of our faucet, sit on our lawn and stuff.

'THEY' BEING KIDS?

208 Yeah, the kids in the neighborhood. There weren't that many at that time, they didn't have that big of a track team at the time. Barnett Park was part of Garfield High then; it was one of their first little tracks.

Then we decided we needed a bigger place, because we had two boys and a girl and one bedroom.

WHAT YEAR ROUGHLY?

Ronnie was born in 1952, Michael wasn't born until '58, so it would be about '58. We did what a lot of people do—a terrible decision, we sold our place before we were able to find another place. It was rush, rush, rush. We found another house, but it wasn't going to be available for another two months. I took off a month from work and started looking and found a rented house right around the corner. So we didn't have to go far; we moved in there. It was terrible, but it was temporary. We were there about two months until our home opened. It's right on Cherry Street, between 30th and 31st. It has a driveway. That was our home. We were there around eight years.

I THINK A WOMAN HAS A LITTLE BEAUTY SALON IN THE BASEMENT OF THAT HOUSE NOW.

That's what I had been telling people! I know she did, I remember when she opened that up. When we lived there the kids used to sit up on the lawn and watch the Panthers march past.

THE PANTHERS COME UP IN ALMOST EVERY INTERVIEW AND IT'S REALLY INTERESTING IN THAT EVERYBODY HAS A DIFFERENT TAKE. PEOPLE WHO KNEW THEM WERE VERY COMFORTABLE. AND OTHER PEOPLE WHO DIDN'T KNOW THEM WERE TERRIFIED.

Oh, yeah. We had different opinions. I was nervous because my daughter went to school with them; she knew them. They were her friends and when they walk by you can't wave to them because they were scary. My husband had to arrest them. He said that he was on their good side because, I forgot if it was Aaron, it might have been Aaron—Elmer's the one Gwennie went to school with—so it had to be Aaron. My husband said he brought him a candy bar once. He said that Aaron said, 'Don't mess around with Officer Lawson, he bought me a candy bar.' Walt (her husband) always told me that I would always be protected.

Now what year was it that what's-his-name (Stokely Carmichael) from the Panthers came here and spoke at Garfield?

209

I THINK THAT WAS AROUND 1968.

Whenever it was, I asked my mom if she wanted to go and she said, 'Sure.' We went to Garfield High. It just didn't bother me that they were up there on top with their guns. I just thought, 'Well, that's pretty cool.' It didn't bother me at all. We went in there and enjoyed whatever was being said. We got up and sang, *We Shall Overcome*. And my mother learned…I don't remember her saying, 'Colored' or 'Negro' after that. We were Black. That really surprised me, you know, coming from my mother who was from the old, old school.

YOUR MOTHER WOULD HAVE BEEN ABOUT HOW OLD AT THAT POINT?

She's a year older than the year, whatever it was. If it was 1967 she would have been '68.

THAT'S INTERESTING. WILLIAM LOWE TALKED ABOUT THAT A BIT TOO. BEFORE THE PANTHERS AND JAMES BROWN THE WORD 'BLACK' WAS CONSIDERED AN INSULT IN HIS FAMILY. AFTER, IT WAS A POINT OF PRIDE.

People of my mother's age and older would ask if someone said, 'I saw this lady down the street,' they would say, 'Is she one of us?' That was the way it was put. 'Was she one of them, or was she one of us?'

RIGHT. WOULD 'THEM' HAVE BEEN A LOT OF PEOPLE? DID IT INCLUDE THE JAPANESE AND THE JEWISH?

Oh no, they were 'Japanese,' or something like that. Or otherwise, 'Yes they were one of us.' Newspapers did a lot of that talking about 'them' and 'us.'

BUT DID 'THEM' MEAN ANYBODY WHO WASN'T BLACK OR DID IT MEAN ONLY WHITE?

They weren't really caring about that; they just wanted to know if they were one of us.

IT WAS A WAY OF DEFINING IF YOU WERE PART OF THE BLACK COMMUNITY?

There was another phrase that was used but I can't remember.

I had another thing that happened to me in grade school. Back in the day we had, 'I Am An American Day.' Have you heard of that? I don't know if this was before Pearl Harbor. Anyway, we had this assembly. They picked out different children from different races by colors. We were supposed to get up and say, 'I am an American.' Now, I forgot what I was. I think I was a member of the brown race. 'I am an American. I am a member of the brown race. I am American.' In my recollections, I've often wondered who was representing the Black race? Was there a yellow race? I don't remember. All I remember was what I was supposed to say. Isn't that funny? Just a little kid.

YOUR FAMILY STAYED (IN THE CENTRAL AREA). WHY WERE ALL THESE OTHER PEOPLE SO AFRAID? DID THE CRIME RATE REALLY GO UP?

Oh, I don't know about the crime rate. I think it was probably due to the Panthers. Got to love the Panthers, but, I'm sorry, it was probably them. Now, we left but not because of that. My children hate the idea that we moved so far out. We moved out to Bangor Street out there in the Rainier neighborhood. There is a bank there. I remember when I agreed to move I had to go up there and my sister went with me. That's another story. While we were in there, the bank was robbed and we didn't know it until they left.

WELL, THAT TURNED OUT WELL.

We stayed up there until Walt retired from the Seattle Police Department and started working for Law Enforcement Assistance Administration and got an offer to go with the main office back in DC. So, again we had been in the office eight years, so then we moved back East.

SO YOU DON'T REMEMBER THE 1960S AND SEVENTIES BEING A PARTICULARLY TROUBLED TIME?

No, I think as I said Walt pretty much put me at ease. The main thing that concerned me over those years was that I was raising the kids almost alone because he worked long hours. He'd work extra shifts. He worked all holidays. He was never home for Christmas morning. His reason for doing that was to get promoted—so he went from a patrolman to a sergeant to a captain. I mean, in his mind, it was all worth it. I wasn't a very good policeman's wife. Anyway, no, I wasn't really affected by what happened in the neighborhood. I never went on a demonstration march. My daughter probably did, I don't know if she would have, they didn't dislike her.

DID YOU WORK DURING ANY OF THIS TIME?

Always! Now where was I working? I'm trying to think if I was working at Boeing when we first got married. Isn't that awful? I can't remember. Yeah, I worked at Boeing for a couple of years. In fact, I often regret not accepting a position there. I was working in the print shop and my boss wanted to get me promoted and so I was promoted to replace her. I was just too scared and so shy. I'm not a boss-type person, but I could have been the first Black supervisor back in those days. I worked at Boeing for two and a half years and the kids were going to school for part of that time. That was before Michael was born. Winnie and Ronnie, the two older kids, were actually living with my parents. I would go to work and then pick them up on weekends. When Michael came along, I think he stayed with my mother-in-law. I had a babysitter who lived right next door to one of the girls I rode in the carpool with to Boeing. Then after a while, I found a job at Harborview Hospital. I became the secretary to the head of the Cardiology Department. Dr. Cobb was also a University Professor.

A couple of years after I started working for him he started Medic One with the fire chief. I worked for Dr. Cobb for about eleven years but quit because of doctor's orders. It was too much pressure, because I was taking work at home. Me, who didn't want to be in the medical field, was a medical transcriptionist at home. Walt was working nights and it was just too much. My doctor said, 'You need to quit.' I'll never forget that day I went in and I said, 'Dr. Cobb, I have to quit today.' He wouldn't speak to me for a while. Long time.

WHEN DID YOU GET INVOLVED WITH THE BLACK HISTORICAL SOCIETY?

It's the Black Heritage Society, it's alright though, even members say that, even people on the board, I've heard them say that. Let me think…Oh, I was one of the founders, that's how I became involved. Esther (Mumford) called me. My husband and I went to the first meeting over at Esther's house. I was supposed to even be on the Constitution Committee, I think. And I went to the first meeting and I went to two more, and then we moved back East. So I stayed in touch and everything.

AND THEN, YOU'RE STILL COMING IN AND WORKING ON THAT...

Yeah, I've been every position they had: president, secretary, vice president, treasurer...I got involved in the collection. I was on the collection committee with Eula Helen; she just passed away. We started the collections. Esther had been collecting things for years. The original organization had been storing things away in closets and under the beds and stuff. Eula and I went and got all those things in storage.

AND NOW ALL THOSE THINGS ARE STORED THROUGH MOHAI (MUSEUM OF HISTORY AND INDUSTRY)?

They've always been. When I first came back (in 1990), I wanted to live close to the archives and to MOHAI. I started volunteering at each place immediately. While I was working at the archives—I came here from Denver—I moved around quite a bit after my husband passed away. I'd been in Denver for about three years by then. While in Denver, I joined an organization called the Black Family Search Group. They now call it, after us, the Black Genealogy Search Group. They stole our name; I stole their name and their idea when I got back to Seattle, I started the Black Genealogy Research Group here.

SO YOU WERE DOING A PROJECT FROM THE 1930s?

The Black Heritage Society got a grant to do this Heritage Project...Oh, I remember what happened with that! I was so embarrassed. I had to go before the 4Culture board, they were all sitting on the dais up there. I got nervous and my mouth was quivering and somebody had to help me say the words because I was so excited about being able to do this and nervous about having to be in front of these strangers—who really couldn't understand anyway.

The oral histories, it was interesting reading it. I think there were only two or three of us transcribing it and reading their transcriptions. In the project in the 1940s, I was one of those interviews, one of those narrators. And we were so boring. Our life was boring, I think. I had one of the interviewers tell me that, she said, 'You guys, all you did was you went to church, you went to Sunday school, you had picnics, you had family dinners and parties with your families. Maybe you played cards. You never went out anywhere, unless your parents were with you.' You know, that was our life.

213

Acknowledgments

The project from which it sprang is a work of memories so without people sharing their lives with me, it would not exist either. I'd like to thank all the participants:

Filli Abdulkdra; Brooks Andrews; Ruby Bishop; Adam Bomb; Linda Cadwell; Douglas Chin; Dorothy Cordova; Paul Byron Crane; Paul de Barros; Lilly DeJaen; Laura Dewell; Aaron Dixon; Elmer Dixon; Mrs. Francis Dixon; Jack & Bette Dunn; Stephanie Ellis-Smith; Monad Elohim; Evan Flory-Barnes: Vince Furfaro; Knox Gardner; Marcus Garrison; Carver Gayton; Marcus Goodwin; Dee Goto; Cecile Hansen; Andrew J Harris; Dave Holden; Rev. Patrick Howell; Ike & Sumiko Ikeda; Amy Johnson; Josh Johnson; Stephanie Johnson-Toliver; Mona Lake Jones: The Honorable Richard A. Jones; Lori Kane; Jackie Lawson; Maxine Loo; Daniel Louis; William G. Lowe; Dr. Rev. Samuel McKinney; Thomas Murray; Mansa Musa; Yosh Nakagawa; John Platt; Michelle Purnell-Hepburn; Jasmmine Ramgotra; Merle Richlen; Fordie Ross; Allyn Ruth; Dan Sanchez; Bob Santos; Claudia Stelle; Mike Tagawa; Herb Tsuchiya; Tricia Turton; DeCharlene Williams; Megan Wittenberg.

My Publisher, Bruce Rutledge and Editor, Kimberly Kent, who I appreciate more than I can adequately express—Also the deeply appreciated transcription volunteers and interns: Nikki Dang Agema; Tamika Carlton; Zoe Chee; Julia Eckels; Zachary Hitchcock; Andrea Lai; Mikayla Medbery; Jessie Robinson; Melissa Takai; Bea Tan; Cecilia Weber.

Special gratitude extends for their invaluable role guiding this project: Feliks Banel; Mark K. Buckley; Brian Carter; Doug Chin; Paul de Barros; Carter Gayton; Yonnas Getahun; Dee Goto; Bill Kossen; George Laney: Michael Maine; Lorraine McConaghy; Yosh Nakagawa; Merle Richlen; Bob Santos; Herb Tsuchiya.

And heartfelt thanks to those who offered their expertise: Juan Aguilera; Paul Byron Crane; Nate Gowdy; Jodee Fenton; Miguel Guillen; Irene Gomez; Bubba Jones; George Laney; Todd Matthews; Michelle Purnell-Hepburn; Dan Sanchez.

People who contributed to this project in a variety of ways: Cliff Armstrong; Joe Bopp; Paul Gray; Artranetta Gray; Ann Bailey; Pastor Greg Banks; Black Heritage Society; Glenn Brooks; *Capitol Hill Seattle Blog*; Central Area Senior Center; Benjamin Chotzen; Dr. Edith Christensen; Juanita Clemente; Jenny Crooks; Densho; Den'ea Drake; Ian Eisenberg; Ann Ferguson; Filipino American Historical Society; Anne Fitzgerald; Jamie Ford; Ricardo Frazier; Levi Fuller; German Heritage Society; Larry Gossett; Nathan Greenstein; Daniel Guenther: Richard Humphreys; Hollow Earth Radio; International Examiner; Jan Johnson; Sue Ann Kay; Lisa Kranseler; Greg Lange; Nikki Lee; Brandi Link; Daniel Louis; Kim Louis; Madrona News; Todd Matthews; Kris McRea; Vanetta Molson; Esther Mumford; Museum of History and Industry; Bruce Nordstrom; Nordic Museum Seattle; Northwest African American Museum; Northwest Danish Association; Barbara Parker; Chieko Phillips: Traci Pichette; Rachel Popkin; Joan Rabinowitz; Ben Rankin; Helen Read; Junius Rochester; Laine Ross; Tara Roth; Wazhma Samizay; Joel Shaver: John Sheets; Garth Stein; Tom Stiles; Seattle Public Library; Dr. Quintard Taylor, Jr.; Coll Thrush; Marcellus Turner; Kwame Turner; Swedish Cultural Center; Paul VanDeCarr; Inye Wokoma; Eric Wolff; Virginia Yamada; Rev. Mark AC Zimmerly; Josh Zimmerman; Professor Wendy Winters; and to the many others who've helped over the seven years this project has developed.

And finally heartfelt thanks to those who gave invaluable tangible support: 4Culture King County; Awesome Foundation Seattle; Stephanie Crocker; Jack Straw Artist Support Program; Joe Ferguson; Jane King; Office of Arts and Culture Seattle; Tom Olsen; The Eulalie and Carlo Scandiuzzi Writers' Room; Herb Tsuchiya.

CPSIA information can be obtained
at www.ICGtesting.com
Printed in the USA
BVHW070355230320
575581BV00003B/4

9 781634 059787